There is an art of reading
as well as an art of thinking
and an art of writing
ISAAC D'ISRAELI.

The Art of English

General Editor A. Dora Gough, B.A.(Hon.)

A Certificate Course for Secondary Schools

Keith Newson, M.A.

3

Illustrated by Tony Dyson

SCHOFIELD AND SIMS LIMITED
HUDDERSFIELD

First Printed 1966

Reprinted 1967

Reprinted 1968

Reprinted 1969

Reprinted 1970

Reprinted 1971

Revised and Reprinted 1972

Reprinted 1972

Reprinted 1973

Reprinted 1974

Reprinted 1975

Printed in Scotland by
McFarlane & Erskine Ltd.

Bound in Scotland

Contents

The passage in each chapter is followed by sections of *Comprehension and Discussion* and *For Written Answers*. Where there is a poem, it is followed by a section *Discussing The Poem*. The *Method Exercises* and composition subjects in *Writing Your Own* are listed below. Each chapter also contains further sections of *Oral Work, Activities and Research* and *Further Reading*.

Exercises marked * here, and in the text, can be omitted by pupils who are not studying clause analysis.

iii

ACKNOWLEDGMENTS

The author and publishers wish to thank the following for permission to include the copyright material listed below:

William Heinemann Ltd., for an extract from *The Red Pony* by John Steinbeck and the poem *Breathless* from *South Col* by Wilfrid Noyce.

R. N. Currey for his poem *Lesson in Murder*.

Oldbourne Book Co. Ltd., for an extract from *The Stanley Matthews Story* by Sir Stanley Matthews.

Leslie Norris for his poem *The Ballad of Billy Rose*.

David Higham Associates Ltd. and Wm. Collins, Sons & Co. Ltd., for extracts from *The Sword in the Stone* by T. H. White and *Heaven Lies About Us* by Howard Spring.

The Clarendon Press, for an extract from *The Oxford Junior Encyclopaedia Vol. X—Law and Society*.

A. D. Peters & Co., for an extract from *David and Broccoli* by John Mortimer.

The Trustees of the Estate of Sir Arthur Conan Doyle and John Murray (Publishers) Ltd., for an extract from *The Lost World* by Sir Arthur Conan Doyle.

Laurence Pollinger Ltd., William Heinemann Ltd., and the Estate of the late Mrs. Frieda Lawrence, for the poem *Humming Bird* by D. H. Lawrence.

Vallentine, Mitchell & Co. Ltd., and Mr. Otto Frank, for an extract from *The Diary of Anne Frank* by Anne Frank.

Brian W. Aldiss, for an extract from *Who Can Replace a Man?* from *Canopy of Time*, published 1959 by Faber & Faber Ltd.

The Executors of H. G. Wells for an extract from *The First Men in the Moon* by H. G. Wells.

Andre Deutsch Ltd., for an extract from *A Kid for Two Farthings* by Wolf Mankowitz and an extract from *Shane* by Jack Schaefer. The extract from *Shane* is also reprinted by permission of the Harold Matson Co. Inc. Copyright 1949 by Jack Schaefer.

J. M. Dent & Sons Ltd. and the Literary Executors of the Dylan Thomas Estate for the poem *Hunchback in the Park* from *Collected Poems* by Dylan Thomas.

Dennis Dobson, Publishers, for an extract from *Men of Chemistry* by Keith Gordon Irwin.

Putnam & Co. Ltd., for the poem *Autobiographical Note* from *A Sense of Danger* by Vernon Scannell.

Rupert Hart-Davis Ltd., for an extract from *My Family and Other Animals* by Gerald Durrell.

Edward Arnold (Publishers) Ltd., for an extract from *Moonfleet* by J. Meade Falkner.

Michael Joseph Ltd., for an extract from *One Pair of Feet* by Monica Dickens.

Jonathan Cape Ltd., for an extract from *The Conger Eel* and an extract from *The Wave*, both from *The Short Stories of Liam O'Flaherty*.

John Arden for his poem *The Lobster Pot*.

John Farquharson Ltd., for an extract from *The Mountain I Couldn't Conquer* by Sir Edmund Hillary.

And to the Chest and Heart Association for permission to reproduce the diagram on p. 207 taken from their leaflet, "SMOKING—A message from an M.O.H." Also to the Register General, and the Tobacco Research Council for their help in preparing the diagram on p. 205.

We have again had generous help from the Wandsworth Borough Libraries, and we should like to thank Mrs. Doris Aubrey and the Children's Librarians for selecting and recommending many of the books for "Further Reading" in Book 3.

AUTHOR'S NOTE

THE ART OF ENGLISH is a five year English series for secondary schools, comprising two complete but closely integrated courses. The *Certificate Course* is suitable for those pupils in grammar, comprehensive and modern schools who aim at an Ordinary Level Certificate in English Language. The *General Course* is designed for the less academic pupils in comprehensive and modern schools. The two courses are planned on a common basis, and the obvious similarities in topics and layout can be readily appreciated by pupil as well as teacher. Transfer from one course to another is greatly facilitated, and both courses cover work for the Certificate of Secondary Education, though the approaches naturally differ.

The *Certificate Course* (which will meet the demands of the most rigorous Ordinary Level Certificate syllabuses) was devised in the belief that examination success should be the natural outcome of a wide and stimulating range of experience, and it is hoped that this course will be more than an English language textbook. The choice of poems and prose extracts is intended to develop pupils' reading, to sharpen their critical awareness of literature as an aspect of the real world around them, to inspire their interests in drama, in discussion of contemporary problems, and in finding out for themselves, and particularly to prompt and guide their natural wish to express themselves fluently and well.

Together, the *Certificate* and the *General Courses* form the basis for a complete English syllabus for secondary schools.

Book Three of the *Certificate Course* continues to base the work on really substantial extracts taken from good, suitable books that pupils will enjoy reading for themselves at this stage. Each extract is long enough to develop its own theme and interest, and is used as a basis for comprehension and full class discussion, to prompt further reading and simple research, and to suggest oral activities and exercises in English skills. The chapter topic is especially used as a stimulus to composition, including both creative and informative writing, personal expression as well as objective accounts. Much of the grammar work is in the form of constructive exercises that should lead to a real understanding of English usage and confident handling of the language; but for those pupils following an Ordinary Level syllabus that requires formal analysis of sentences, the basis of clause analysis work is given in this book in exercises marked with an asterisk, and in Supplementary Analysis Exercises. Other revision exercises are also included.

KEITH NEWSON

The red pony, Gabilan, was a gift from Jody's father, Carl Tiflin. Partly through the negligence of Billy Buck, the cow-hand on Tiflin's ranch, Gabilan had taken cold, and in desperation Billy Buck had cut a hole in the pony's throat to let him breathe. He and Jody took turns to watch by the pony.

CHAPTER ONE

Outburst

Billy Buck stood up from the box and surrendered the cotton swab. The pony still lay on his side and the wound in his throat bellowed in and out. When Jody saw how dry and dead the hair looked, he knew at last that there was no hope for the pony. He had seen the dead hair before on dogs and on cows, and it was a sure sign. He sat heavily on the box and let down the barrier of the box stall. For a long time he kept his eyes on the moving wound, and at last he dozed, and the afternoon passed quickly. Just before dark his mother brought a deep dish of stew and left it for him and went away. Jody ate a little of it, and when it was dark he set the lantern on the floor by the pony's head so he could watch the wound and keep it open. And he dozed again until the night chill awakened him. The wind was blowing fiercely, bringing the north cold with it. Jody brought a blanket from his bed in the hay and wrapped himself in it. Gabilan's breathing was quiet at least; the hole in his throat moved gently. The owls flew through the hayloft, shrieking and looking for mice. Jody put his hands down on his head and slept. In his sleep he was aware that the wind had increased. He heard it slamming about the barn.

It was daylight when he awakened. The barn door had swung open. The pony was gone. He sprang up and ran out into the morning light.

The pony's tracks were plain enough, dragging through the frost-like dew on the young grass, tired tracks with little lines between them where the hoofs had dragged. They headed for the brush line halfway up the ridge. Jody broke into a run and followed them. The sun shone on the sharp white quartz that stuck through the ground here and there. As he followed the plain trail, a shadow cut across in front of him. He looked up and saw a high circle of black buzzards, and the slowly revolving circle dropped lower and lower. The solemn birds soon disappeared over the ridge. Jody ran faster then, forced on by panic and rage. The trail entered the brush at last and followed a winding route among the tall sage bushes.

At the top of the ridge Jody was winded. He paused, puffing noisily. The blood pounded in his ears. Then he saw what he was looking for. Below, in one of the little clearings in the brush, lay the red pony. In the distance, Jody could see the legs moving slowly and convulsively. And in a circle around him stood the buzzards, waiting for the moment of death they know so well.

Jody leaped forward and plunged down the hill. The wet ground muffled his steps and the brush hid him. When he arrived, it was all over. The first buzzard sat on the pony's head. Jody plunged into the circle like a cat. The black brotherhood arose in a cloud, but the big one on the pony's head was too late. As it hopped along to take off, Jody caught its wing tip and pulled it down. It was nearly as big as he was. The free wing crashed into his face with the force of a club, but he hung on. The claws fastened on his leg and the wing elbows battered his head on either side. Jody groped blindly with his free hand. His fingers found the neck of the struggling bird. The red eyes looked into his face, calm and fearless and fierce; the naked head turned from side to side. Jody brought up his knee and fell on the great bird. He held the neck to the ground with one hand while his other found a piece of sharp white quartz. The red fearless eyes still looked at him, impersonal and unafraid and detached. He struck again and again, until the buzzard lay dead. He was still beating the dead bird when Billy Buck pulled him off and held him tightly to calm his shaking.

Carl Tiflin wiped the blood from the boy's face with a red bandana. Jody was limp and quiet now. His father moved the buzzard with his toe. "Jody," he explained, "the buzzard didn't kill the pony. Don't you know that?"

"I know it," Jody said wearily.

It was Billy Buck who was angry. He had lifted Jody in his arms, and had turned to carry him home. But he turned back on Carl Tiflin. "'Course he knows it," Billy said furiously. "Good God! man, can't you see how he'd feel about it?"

(from *The Red Pony* by John Steinbeck)

Comprehension and Discussion

1. What do you think the "brush line" is?
2. Where, and how, did Jody sleep that night?
3. Explain the sentence: "Jody ran faster then, forced on by panic and rage." What made him anxious and angry?
4. Whose blood was on Jody's face when his father wiped it?
5. Explain and discuss Jody's feelings about the buzzards. Did he in fact know that they did not kill Gabilan? Why did he hang on when the buzzard lashed out? Why did he go on beating the dead bird? Why was he shaking when Billy pulled him off, and limp and quiet afterwards?
6. Explain Billy's anger with Carl Tiflin—do you think Billy's own concern for Jody's pony had anything to do with it?
7. Can you recall outbursts of angry frustration or disappointment, like Jody's, in your own experience or in books?
8. What do we learn about buzzards from these phrases: "a high circle of black buzzards"; "the solemn birds"; "the moment of death they know so well"; "the black brotherhood"; "the red eyes . . . calm and fearless and fierce"?
9. Why is the sentence "Jody plunged into the circle like a cat" particularly appropriate?
10. Why does the author mention both the "sharp white quartz", and the look in the big buzzard's eyes, twice?

For Written Answers

Answer each of these questions in one or more complete sentences, and as far as possible in your own words.

1. What was the cotton swab for?
2. How did Jody know the pony was going to die (a) when he took over from Billy, and (b) when he followed Gabilan outside?
3. How and why did Gabilan get out of the stable?
4. How did Jody first become aware of the buzzards?
5. What made it easier for Jody to get so close to the buzzards without disturbing them?
6. Without referring back to the passage, retell the story of this incident in your own words.

Lesson in Murder

I drew the smooth round pebble back;
  I felt the strong release;
I did not know that thud would crack
  The thin bones of my peace.

The jewelled bird fell from the tree,
  Half-fluttered to my feet;
The others snatched it up to see
  If any warm pulse beat.

They filled the leafy air with cries,
  Re-lived the redstart thrill,
Ruffled a rainbow in my eyes;
  While I stood sick and still—

And, head averted, bent and took
  Another five smooth stones,
With catapult fingers cocked a snook
  At aching greenstick bones.

R. N. CURREY

Discussing The Poem

1. Make sure you understand the phrases used, such as: "Ruffled a rainbow in my eyes", "cocked a snook" and "greenstick bones".

2. Discuss the meaning implied by these phrases: "the strong release", "the jewelled bird", "the leafy air", "the redstart thrill", "head averted".

3. Do you see a connection between the "thin bones of my peace" in verse 1 and "aching greenstick bones" in verse 4? Why is this a "lesson in murder"?

4. What is alliteration? Comment on the effect of the alliteration in this poem.

Method Exercises

Exercise 1.   In Book Two we saw that different kinds of words could all be used to describe nouns. *Adjectives* themselves often do so in the passage at the beginning of this chapter;

> e.g. the *dead* hair—"dead" describes "hair".
> a *deep* dish—"deep" is normally an adjective, although it can be a noun.

But words that are normally *nouns* also act as adjectives;

> e.g. the *cotton* swab.

And parts of *verbs* ending in -ing, called *present participles*, can also describe nouns;

> e.g. the *moving* wound—"moving" from the verb "move"
> He heard it (the wind) *slamming*—"slamming" describes "it"; "heard" is the true verb here.

(a) In the following phrases, which have all come from the first four paragraphs of the passage, state whether each describing word is an adjective, a noun used as an adjective, or a present participle used as an adjective.

the *night* chill	the *sharp, white* quartz
the *north* cold	the *plain* trail
the *barn* door	a *high* circle of *black* buzzards
the *morning* light	the . . . *revolving* circle
the *frost-like* dew	the *solemn* birds
the *young* grass	a *winding* route
little lines	the *tall sage* bushes
the *brush* line	he paused, *puffing* noisily

13

(b) Find and write down at least fifteen ordinary adjectives in the paragraph beginning "Jody leaped forward . . .".

Write down two nouns used as adjectives in that paragraph.

Finally, find and write down one present participle used as an adjective in that paragraph.

Exercise 2. The sentence:

> "The pony still lay on his side and the wound in his throat bellowed in and out."

contains one adverb and two adverb phrases. What are these? It also contains an adjective phrase: "in his throat". Can you explain why this is not an adverb phrase? Make up a sentence in which "in his throat" is used as an adverb phrase.

(a) In the first four paragraphs of the passage, pick out the *adverbs* (single words) which describe the following:

how Jody sat on the box;
how the afternoon passed;
how the wind was blowing;
how the hole in Gabilan's throat moved;
in what way the barn door swung;
how Jody ran when he saw the buzzards;
how Jody was puffing;
where the red pony lay;
how the pony's legs were moving (two adverbs).

(b) Pick out from the first four paragraphs the *adverb phrases* which describe the following:

where Jody sat heavily;
when his mother brought the stew;
why his mother left the bowl of stew;
where Jody set the lantern (two phrases);
where the owls flew;
where Jody put his hands;
when he was aware of the increased wind;
where Jody ran when the pony had gone;
how the circle of buzzards dropped.

Exercise 3. (a) Think of some interesting, vivid and original *adjectives* and *adjective phrases* to describe each of the following: write them down and then compose sentences embodying them in complete statements.

e.g. The sun rising at sea.

The *sleepy* sun rose *brooding* from the sea, *golden* and *soft, searching far horizons with its hazy shafts of light.*

A waterfall in sunshine.
The wind on a stormy night.
A noisy piece of machinery.
An angry man or woman.
The lights of a fairground.
Any beautiful piece of architecture.
Smoke rising from a factory chimney.
An animal attacking its prey.
An old man's face.
Autumn leaves.

(b) Think of interesting, vivid and original *adverbs* or *adverb phrases* to describe each of the following actions; write them down and compose sentences embodying them in complete statements.

e.g. How a wave broke over rocks:

The wave broke *angrily over the rocks* and the foamy water searched *inquisitively into every hollow and crevice among them.*

How the eagle tore its prey.
How and when a petrol tank exploded.
How and where heavy rain fell.
How and why Jody swabbed Gabilan's wound.
How a gigantic wave swept towards the shore.
How the climbers finally reached the summit.
How the forest fire raged.
How the organ music swelled.
How the feeble old man crossed the road.
How and where the train thundered past.

Exercise 4. Make up suitable titles to sum up the main point of each of the *paragraphs* in the passage from *The Red Pony*.

Discuss the various suggestions for these titles. Notice also how the end of each paragraph has been linked to the beginning of the next. Why are some of the paragraphs so much shorter than others? Are there any points where you would disagree with Steinbeck's paragraphing for any reason?

Writing Your Own

1. Write a short story, or an account of an experience, in which an outburst of anger, frustration, disappointment or jealousy forms a central part. Clearly you will have to build up tension and engage the reader's sympathy. Every thought and feeling must seem genuine and credible. So, whether you are writing in the first person or not, you must spend some time imagining the feeling of your central character. Make careful notes on the ideas and reactions that seem right for moments of strong emotion. Look again at Jody's outburst and the way in which the tension of that story is built up to a powerful climax. The details you describe, the words you choose, the way you build up your sentences, your use of comparisons and contrasts, and your paragraphing: these need careful thought in advance, and thorough revision when you have completed your first draft. Above all, choose a subject that you and your readers can feel strongly about.

2. Study the following two versions of the same incident in order that you may write an unbiased account of it:

(a) There was no cause for Ann to start suddenly hitting me in the way she did, just because I made a harmless joke about her pigtails. She didn't even fight me face to face. She waited until my back was turned then she hit me on the neck. I turned round and held her wrist so that she couldn't hit me again. This must have made her even angrier because she started yelling at me. She squirmed about, and when I let her go she fell to the ground, since she was off balance. At that moment a teacher appeared: as soon as Ann saw the teacher she pretended she was crying because she knew this would arouse the teacher's sympathy and make it look as though I had been bullying her.

(b) John is always teasing me about my hair style. This time I decided to try to irritate him in return. I reached out to flip up his tie but, as I did so, he turned away and my hand accidentally hit his neck. Before I could apologise, he whirled round, grabbed my arm and began twisting it. He twisted it so hard I screamed with pain. Then he threw me to the ground. I began crying and the next thing I knew a teacher was telling us to stop it. It's bad enough, I think, for one boy to bully another, but it's even worse when a boy bullies a girl.

Imagine you are the teacher. Extract all the facts from these accounts and set them out clearly in writing. Then comment on and criticise the two pupils involved, suggesting what course of action you will take.

Oral Work

1. Discuss the following:
   (a) How you would deal with a young child who has a tantrum.
   (b) The approach you think Jody's father should have taken with his son.
   (c) What to say and do for a young person facing the death of a relative, friend or precious pet animal for the first time.
   (d) A tactful way to deal with a friend who is depressed and rather irritable.
   (e) The punishment you would think right for (i) a child, and (ii) an adult, guilty of being unnecessarily cruel to animals.
   (f) The things that make you really angry.

2. Find a scene or passage from a book which moves you because it is so sad or so powerfully emotional, and prepare it carefully so that you can read it to the class and convey your feelings about it to them. It may be a sad or moving poem, if you wish.

Activities and Research

1. Make an illustrated study of the best-known birds of prey, both from a naturalist's point of view and as referred to in books, poems and legends. Include information about eagles, buzzards, kites, kestrels, sparrow-hawks, vultures, owls, falcons, harriers and hawks. Most of these creatures have inspired poems, and some have been regarded as ominous according to ancient superstitions. Apart from encyclopaedias and other reference books (e.g. *The Oxford Junior Encyclopaedia*, Vol. 2, Natural History), books about birds are classified as 598.2 to 598.9 in your library.

2. Find out about the training and work of veterinary surgeons today, as compared with the methods of farriers or horse-doctors of earlier generations. Bring out the contrasts in a short talk or written report to the class.

18

Further Reading

The Red Pony by JOHN STEINBECK (Heinemann; Corgi)
This short tale is in three parts: the death of the red pony, the coming of the mysterious old Mexican peasant, and then the fight for the safe birth of a colt that was to take the place of Gabilan. Steinbeck's powerful description of characters and situations, shown also in *Grapes of Wrath* and *Of Mice and Men*, makes him one of the greatest contemporary authors.

Tomahawk Shadow by NANCY FAULKNER (Constable; Longmans)
Bart Hathaway, who has always hated his guardian, finally runs away from him and the colony of Plymouth, makes friends with the Narragansett Indians, and settles down to a new life in Providence, Rhode Island. *The Yellow Hat*, a tale set in 14th century London, is another story by the same author. The books are well written and the atmosphere of the periods is convincingly portrayed.

American Short Stories selected by H. G. FOWLER (Arnold)
Beginning with another tale about Jody and his family (by Steinbeck), this collection includes stories by Mark Twain, James Thurber and Stephen Crane, and ranges widely over American life and history.

Beginner's Guide to Riding by VERONICA HEATH (Pelham)
This book offers a practical approach to riding for young people, and includes sections on finding, equipping, and caring for the right pony. It is fully illustrated, and has chapters on most aspects of riding today, including show-jumping, and pony-trekking holidays.

NOTE: In the Further Reading lists in this book, the Dewey reference number is given in brackets after each recommendation for a non-fiction book. Other recommended titles are classed as fiction. Some books will be found in adult libraries, others in the junior or intermediate sections.

Sir Stanley Matthews recalls a turning point in his career. Although happily married and already an international footballer at twenty, he still had important lessons to learn.

CHAPTER TWO

Sport

"Matthews Fails in International"—"Matthews Misses a Great Chance". I gazed dismally at the headlines in the newspapers the day after the international. I agreed with what they said.

Betty said, "Isn't it time you were off?" I glanced at the clock on the mantelpiece, tossed the papers on one side, said goodbye to Betty and left the house. I walked at a brisk rate to the ground, taking my number-two route.

When I entered the dressing-room the conversation between the players stopped for a split second. Everybody looked in my direction and there was an awkward silence. I quickly overcame it. "Sorry to let you down, lads. Now you won't want my autograph." It broke the tension. Somebody laughed, and in a few minutes everything was back to normal. I was home again. We finished the morning training and left the ground.

I had a light snack, after which I returned to the ground. I had something important to do. I took three or four balls out to the turf and put them near to the spot from which I had missed the open goal. I hit those balls into the back of the net every time. I lined them up again and booted them in again and again. I felt better after that practice, it got something out of my system. Then I took a ball and ran round the ground with it at my feet. I was about to gather up the balls and call it a day when I had a sudden urge to try the shooting practice once more. I lined up the balls, then kicked them in quick succession into the back of the net. I felt much better.

It was getting dark, so I gathered up the balls and went back to the dressing-room. In the gathering gloom I thought I could see someone standing near the tunnel entrance. I called out. A voice answered back, "It's only me, Son." . . .

I nodded, then went down the corridor to change. A few minutes later I joined my father, and off we went together. After walking a few yards I said, "Well, what did you think of my performance yesterday?" My father didn't answer right away; at last he said, "Look, Son, I'm not worried about what you did yesterday; I'm more worried about what you are likely to do the day after tomorrow, Saturday, when you play your next match with Stoke City. I wish I had the command of words to tell you just what I want to tell you, but I'll do my best to straighten you out if you want me to. It's up to you now, son. What do you say?"

I was a little puzzled by my father's attitude; but, knowing deep down inside of me that he had only my interests at heart, I said, "Right, Father. What's on your mind that will help me?"

We walked along in the dusk, and when we passed under a street lamp I stole a look at my father's face; it was thoughtful. "The way I look at it, son, is like this. To learn a trade you must serve an apprenticeship. In the building trade, or engineering, or any other trade you care to mention, a youth must start when he is fourteen and serve until he is twenty-one. During those years he makes all kinds of mistakes, but the craftsman he is working with puts him right until he reaches the age of twenty-one. Then he's on his own, his apprenticeship is over. Any mistakes he makes after that may get him the sack. In your job things are slightly different, there are no basic rules, and the situations you meet differ in every match. You don't work under anybody, you're on your own all the time, but you get your experience by watching the other players on the field, learning all the time by watching their mistakes and their good play.

"In a few weeks' time you'll be twenty-one and your apprenticeship will end, but before it does there is one more thing you must learn, and that is—never try and correct a physical mistake by a physical effort without first getting your mental outlook right. When you missed that open goal yesterday it didn't alter you in the physical sense at all. It did, however, destroy your mental outlook, and that's where you came unstuck. Your mental outlook was suffering before that because the German left full-back had you worried; never before had you played against anyone half so good.

"You let him sense that you knew he was master, and that was fatal. You should have thought things out and tried other methods, but not for one instant should you ever have admitted that he was better than you, because if you do that you lose your confidence. If you ever meet this situation again, don't give up, try this and that, and try, try, try all through the match, keep your mental outlook right, never admit defeat, and with your playing capabilities you will one day reach the top—and, what's more important, stay there."

My father paused, then went on, "You see, Son, I have never told you this before, but I know that you have it in you to be one of the greatest footballers this country has ever seen. But if I had let you run on to the field next Saturday afternoon in the state of mind you were in when I met you at the ground this afternoon, you might have ruined yourself for life.

"Forget about what the papers say, and what people are saying about you at the present moment. Remember crowds are very fickle but they love a winning team, and a footballer that plays the game and gives them what they have paid to see—pure football. In the future you'll make many more mistakes, but don't let them upset you—learn from them, but keep your mental outlook undisturbed; you'll also have some fine successes —learn from them too, by keeping your head. If you do this the crowds will love you. Now go out on Saturday and play your normal game, and never again lose confidence in yourself."

We were nearly home. I looked at my father and said, "Thank you, Dad—thank you very much." I took my door key from my pocket, opened the door, and we both entered.

(from *The Stanley Matthews Story* by Stanley Matthews)

Comprehension and Discussion

1. What exactly had Stanley Matthews done in the international match?

2. Explain the awkward silence when Matthews entered the dressing-room. Did he overcome it in a sensible way?

3. Was it apparently usual for Matthews to practise in the afternoon?

4. Why did he concentrate on practising "shooting" that afternoon, and why did this make him feel better?

5. Did Stanley's father think this practice was itself enough to "straighten out" Stanley?

6. What did Mr. Matthews Senior really mean by "keeping your mental outlook undisturbed" and "keeping your head"? Is this good advice, or is he simply saying that you have to be conceited and selfish to get to the top in sport or in life?

7. Young people often resent advice from their elders. Did Stanley hesitate to listen to his father? Why might such advice be resented?

8. In what ways is a sports player's training like an ordinary apprenticeship, and in what ways is it different?

9. What kind of man does Stanley Matthews appear to be, from this incident? Consider his attitude to the newspaper comments, to his fellow-players and to his father. Do remarks like "my number-two route" help you determine the type of person he is?

10. Discuss the remark: "Crowds are very fickle but they love a winning team, and a footballer that plays the game..." Does this apply to other sports and to other forms of entertainment?

11. What do you think are the qualities that make (a) a top-class sports team member, (b) a top-class individual sportsman, and (c) a successful and popular television personality? Might any of these qualities make them unpleasant to have as friends?

For Written Answers

Answer in complete sentences and in your own words, showing the reasons for your answer.

1. What club was Matthews playing for at this time?

2. Which country was the international match against?

3. What was wrong with Matthews' "mental outlook" in the international?

4. Why, according to his father, should Stanley "forget about what the papers say"?

5. Sum up in a few sentences what kind of person Mr. Matthews Senior is.

6. Select and rewrite briefly, in your own words, all the main points of advice given to Stanley Matthews here.

The Ballad of Billy Rose

Outside Bristol Rovers Football Ground—
The date has gone from me, but not the day,
Nor how the dissenting flags in stiff array
Struck bravely out against the sky's grey round—

Near the Car Park then past Austin and Ford,
Lagonda, Bentley, and a colourful patch
Of country coaches come in for the match
Was where I walked, having travelled the road

From Fishponds to watch Portsmouth in the Cup.
The Third Round, I believe. And I was filled
With the old excitement which had thrilled
Me so completely when, while growing up,

I went on Saturdays to match or fight.
Not only me; for thousands of us there
Strode forward eagerly, each man aware
Of vigorous memory, anticipating delight.

We all moved forward, all, except one man.
I saw him because he was paradoxically still,
A stone against the flood, face upright against us all,
Head bare, hoarse voice aloft. Blind as a stone.

I knew him at once despite his pathetic clothes—
Something in his stance, or his sturdy frame
Perhaps. I could even remember his name
Before I saw it on his blind-man's tray. Billy Rose.

And twenty forgetful years fell away at the sight.
Bare-kneed, dismayed, memory fled to the hub
Of Saturday violence, with friends to the Labour Club,
Watching the boxing on a sawdust summer night.

The boys' enclosure close to the shabby-ring
Was where we stood, clenched in a resin world,
Spoke in cool voices, lounged, were artificially bored
During minor bouts. We paid threepence to go in.

Billy Rose fought there. He was top of the bill.
So brisk a fighter, so gallant, so precise!
Trim as a tree he stood for the ceremonies,
Then turned to meet George Morgan of Triphil.

He had no chance. Courage was not enough,
Nor tight defence. Donald Davies was sick
And we threatened his cowardice with an embarrassed kick.
Ripped across both his eyes was Rose, but we were tough.

And clapped him as they wrapped his blindness up
In busy towels, applauded the wave
He gave his executioners, cheered the brave
Blind man as he cleared with a jaunty hop

The top rope. I had forgotten that day
As if it were dead forever, yet now I saw
Again the flowers of blood on the ring floor
As bright as his name. I cannot say

How long I stood with ghosts of the wild fists
And the cries of shaken boys long dead around me,
For struck to act at last, in terror and pity
I threw some frantic money, three treacherous pence—

And I cry at the memory—into his tray, and ran,
Entering the waves of the stadium like a drowning man.
Poor Billy Rose. God, he could fight
Before my three sharp coins knocked out his sight.

LESLIE NORRIS

Discussing The Poem

1. What did the poet and his friends enjoy about the boxing at
   the Labour Club when they were boys? Why was Donald
   Davies sick and what did the others think of him for it? Was
   the poet's attitude any different twenty years later, when he
   saw Billy Rose again?

2. Look carefully at the words the poet chooses and the comparisons he makes. In what two places is the crowd compared to a tide or river? Discuss: "the dissenting flags in stiff array", "the hub of Saturday violence", "a sawdust summer night", "clenched in a resin world", "the flowers of blood on the ring floor".

3. Consider the last line: could three pennies ever be used literally to blind someone? In what *indirect* way had the poet paid three pence to blind Billy Rose?

Method Exercises

Exercise 1. We learnt from Book Two that three basic functions of the *noun* are to be:

(i) the subject of a verb,
        e.g. The *ball* flashed past the goalpost

(ii) the object of a verb,
        e.g. Matthews kicked the *ball* fiercely

(iii) the indirect object of a verb,
        e.g. Mr. Matthews gave his *son* some advice.

(a) Make up sentences, two for each word (or phrase), using the following words (i) as the subject and (ii) as the direct object.
        e.g. Hockey: (i) *Hockey* can be played on grass or on ice.
                (ii) Many schools play *hockey* regularly.
netball   mistakes   world records   the last goal
                an easy victory.

(b) Make up sentences, three for each word (or phrase), using the following (i) as the subject, (ii) as the direct object, and (iii) as the indirect object.
        e.g. Stanley Matthews: (i) Stanley Matthews played for England many times.
                (ii) Many people admire Stanley Matthews for his standard of football.
                (iii) The Queen awarded Stanley Matthews a knighthood in 1965.
newspapers   the goal-post   the full-back   the hungry dog
                football crowds.

(c) Examine each of the nouns printed in italics in the following passage and decide whether it is being used as a subject, object or indirect object.

e.g. (1) "settlers"—subject of "found".

The early French (1) *settlers* found the American (2) *Indians* playing a game in which the (3) *players* caught and threw the (4) *ball* with a net on the end of a stick. The French (5) *missionaries* gave this (6) *game* the (7) *name* of "La Crosse". (8) *"La Crosse"* meant a (9) *crosier* in French, and the (10) *sticks* resembled bishops' (11) *crooks*. Among the Indians, all the (12) *men* in one village played all the (13) *inhabitants* of another. (14) *Canadians* adapted this (15) *sport* in about 1850. Today a (16) *team* of twelve men or women play another (17) *twelve* for two periods of 45 minutes. The (18) *"Centres"* aim to pass the "attack (19) *wings*" the (20) *ball*, and the (21) *play* can be very fast indeed.

Exercise 2. As we saw in Book Two, inverted commas (" ") can be used:

(a) to indicate direct speech;

(b) to refer to the title of a book, play, film, etc. (printers often use italics for this);

(c) to call attention to a particular or unusual name, including special places and buildings and curious nicknames;

(d) to indicate single words, phrases or sentences quoted from someone else, or from a book or other publication;

(e) to call attention to any unusual, rare, slang, foreign or made-up words used in writing.

Some printers use double inverted commas (" ") for use (a) and single (' ') for uses (b) to (e), but it is simpler to use double for them all, and reserve single for use when you wish to use inverted commas *inside* other inverted commas.

Which of the uses (a) to (e) are illustrated in the following three sentences? Explain why some of the inverted commas are single and not double:

(i) He gazed dismally at the headline "Matthews Misses a Great Chance".

(ii) "The Ballad of Billy Rose" is about a boxer blinded by the "three sharp coins" the poet paid to see him fight.

(iii) "Why call your house 'Chez Moi' when you're not French and you're scarcely ever 'at home'?" he asked.

Can you explain why the full stop in (i) is printed *after* the inverted commas, and yet the question mark in (iii) is printed inside the (double) inverted commas? Look at the following, and explain the use of commas, full stops and capital letters:

(iv) "Hallo, Dad," I said. "What are you doing here?"

 (v) "Betty called," he replied, "and asked your mother and me round to tea."

Rewrite the following sentences inserting all the necessary punctuation. They are already correctly paragraphed.

(a) if the word narrative means a tale and extinguish means to put out then can you take a dog by the narrative and extinguish him

(b) if I write N-E-W asked the teacher what does it spell
new replied a boy at the front
and if I write a K in front of it she continued
canoe shouted the smiling boy

(c) the teacher asked john for a sentence using the word i
i is . . . began john
no not i is you should always say i am she said firmly
all right he said i am the ninth letter of the alphabet.

Exercise 3. Newspaper headlines, including those on the sports pages, are sometimes *headings,* or *labels*:

Late Results

Cricket Mystery

and sometimes *messages*:

Bognor off the Hook

Gates fall at Highgate

Explain the difference between a "heading" and a "message". In both cases the *jargon* (words and phrases with specialised meanings) may make the headlines difficult to understand, and in the case of *messages*, the habit of leaving out words (especially verbs) may even make them *ambiguous* (i.e. capable of two or more meanings). Thus "Bognor off the Hook" presumably means that some sports team at Bognor is no longer in a difficult or tense position, perhaps in a league table. What does the other example mean?

Find and explain at least *two* possible meanings for each of the following sports headlines. Which are "messages" and which are "headings"?

> e.g. F.A. Passing Ban Soon.
>
> (1) A ban on something will soon be agreed by the F.A.
>
> (2) The F.A. will soon introduce a ban on passing.

(a) Cup Final Postponement
(b) Remained in Touch with Ball too Long
(c) New League Plans for Brighter Cricket
(d) Throwing Controversy to Higher Committee
(e) Eleven Tries
(f) If Ball Goes Off He Will be Out
(g) Local Police Squash Champions
(h) Liz's Record Bid Flops
(i) Pole Vaults Over 5 Metres
(j) United Slip
(k) Ash Loses Last Heat
(l) Top Seed Successful on Centre Court

Exercise 4. Here are two accounts, of the same football match, from different local newspapers. Read them carefully and answer the questions set out below.

ALLINGHAM ALL THE WAY

Allingham 4, West Harbour 1

A devastating opening spell by Allingham—three goals in 15 minutes—proved too much for Harbour, although their wing, Thrace, did recover to reply with some clever play which, with more luck, might have made this match less of a walk-over.

Allingham's strength is not so much in their combined play as in the individual skill of their forwards, who completely outplayed Harbour's defence in the opening half.

Quicker on the ball, they created wide gaps in the visitors' defence and their thrusts were rewarded in the fifth minute, when Douglas twisted a skid on the waterlogged pitch into a winner; in the eighth minute, when Smithers gambled on a long shot from the wing; and in the fifteenth, when centre-forward Barn scored from a foul on Stephens by Jameson.

Harbour tightened their defence in the second half, bringing Malling back from forward to half-back and standing rock-like to contain the Allingham attack.

30

Harbour were now winning more midfield space and combined well to carry the game to the Allingham end where they forced a number of corners. From one of these Thrace cleverly eluded goalkeeper Moorehouse to score Harbour's one goal.

Harbour twice more had the ball in Allingham's net. Mance's effort from Thrace's corner was disallowed for pushing by Small; and Harbour showed their temper when the referee changed his decision on another shot by Thrace, after consulting the linesman.

Finally, that great forward Barn swept down the wing and a quick shot thudded against the opponents' bar in the last minute.

HARBOUR WEATHER-BEATEN

Thrace's Brilliant Play

With mud, rain, wind, referee and crowd against them Harbour's performance against Allingham was not as disheartening as the 4-1 score suggests.

Allingham forwards played raggedly, but a lucky skid, a wind-driven high shot and a free-kick for a disputed foul against Jameson gave them a 3-0 lead in the first half.

Masterly though Harbour were in defence and attack in the second half, with Thrace and Thompson continually upfield, forcing their opponents on the defensive, they never acquired Allingham's luck. Yet the match was distinguished by the virtuoso performance on the right wing of Geoff Thrace, who made football look easy, even in those conditions. His goals made the home side look like bungling beginners, and the second of them was so bewildering that referee Hughes, after signalling a goal, changed his decision when it was disputed by the crowd and the linesman.

Unnerved, Harbour let up the pressure for a moment, when Barn slipped through to score Allingham's final goal.

(a) Which of these accounts would you expect to find in the *West Harbour News*, and which in the *Allingham Herald*?

(b) Where was the match played, and how does each report inform readers of this?

(c) Why has each paper chosen its particular headlines? Why is the score not given in one case? What is characteristic of headlines in the wording of these examples?

(d) Why does the first account contain more names and more details? (Assume that both papers *could* have allowed the same space for the report.)

31

(e) *Contrast* all the words chosen, and the phrases and sentences used, to describe each of the following in the two accounts:

(i) Thrace's play in this match;

(ii) Allingham's forwards;

(iii) the way the first three goals were scored;

(iv) Harbour's play in the second half;

(v) the referee's change of mind about Thrace's "second goal";

(vi) how the last goal of the match was scored.

(f) Is it possible to believe *both* these newspaper stories? Piece together a full account of the match from these two, and write your own version, without any bias towards either team.

Writing Your Own

1. Write a composition about the sportsman or sportswoman you most admire. Choose someone at the peak of his or her career and collect some information about the family background and rise to fame. Try to assess his quality and strength as a performer, and his contribution to sport. You have a free choice from any sport or pastime, amateur or professional, but start by making outline notes on a pattern similar to the following. This is for a minimum of four paragraphs, but your own plan may well expand into more paragraphs. Remember both to make your paragraphs complete and interesting units and to see that each is linked easily to the next.

Plan

(a) *Background*—date and place of birth—family and home—education—early sporting interests and training.

(b) *Rise to fame*—first selection and coaching—early achievements—development of a distinctive style—highest achievement or record.

(c) *Qualities*—particular qualities as player or performer—estimates of greatness by fellow-players and competitors—some examples of play or performance at his best.

(d) *Example*—the player as a person—lessons to be learnt from his career—his advice or example to younger admirers—achievements to be expected in this field in future.

2. Imagine you are secretary of Wendle School's Hockey Club and wish to arrange fixtures for your first and second elevens with a neighbouring school. Begin your letter in the way shown below (copy this heading on to your own letter), and compose a suitable letter, being brief and to the point, but giving a choice of dates, with a note of times and places. How should you end the letter when you address the other secretary by name?

> *Wendle Secondary School,*
> *Eastern Road,*
> *Wendleton,*
> *Surrey.*
> *KT4 9ET.*
> *10th October, 19--.*

The Secretary of the Hockey Club,
St. Matthew's School,
Belham,
London SE6 3PS.

Dear Pat Green,

Oral Work

1. The following are possible provocative remarks for general class discussion, or for more formal debate:
   - (a) The trouble with sport today is that too many watch and too few take part.
   - (b) In most sports the distinction between amateur and professional is no longer a real one: many amateurs have the financial support of a government, or a sports firm, or a private income, and are just as full-time as the professionals. Who cares whether players are being paid for taking part in their games?
   - (c) Most people are not interested in sport, only in gambling on the results.
   - (d) Games should not be compulsory in schools, and certainly not in girls' schools.
   - (e) The government should spend more on sports training and facilities, especially for young people.

2. If a tape-recorder is available to all or some members of the class, try doing a running commentary of the kind used for sound radio. Select a sporting event, possibly a school match, and familiarise yourself with the participants' names and positions, and the technical terms of the game or competition you are covering. Practice will show the difficulties: much of the time you are selecting and summarising the important information, but at other moments you need interesting detail and background to "fill in" breaks and pauses. Some efforts could be played back to the class for comment and criticism.

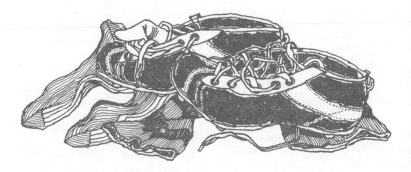

Activities and Research

1. Write a clear account of the aims and rules of any one sport. You have a complete choice of all competitive games, indoor or outdoor, rare or well-known, from dominoes to diving, or from curling to cricket. Check carefully on the rules and the regulations concerning such things as the size and marking of the pitch or court, and the weight and shape of any equipment used. Diagrams will be useful for this kind of information. But include also some indication of the aims of the sport and the kind of satisfaction it gives.

Most sports books are classified as 794-8 in public libraries, but reference books are also useful, especially Volume IX (Recreations) of the *Oxford Junior Encyclopaedia*, and the Sports Section of the *Junior Pears Encyclopaedia*.

2. Look up some outstanding records in your own sport, and record these. For up-to-date information, see *Whitaker's Almanack* (the section entitled "Retrospect of Sport"), the *Guinness Book of Records*, and year books such as *Wisden's Cricketer's Almanack*.

Further Reading

The Stanley Matthews Story by STANLEY MATTHEWS (Oldbourne)
This autobiography by Britain's most famous footballer covers most of his professional career, including twenty-two years as an international from 1934 to 1957. This kind of writing is not necessarily of the highest literary standard, but Matthews' achievements and opinions are always expressed modestly and sincerely. (796.334)

Sportsmen of Our Time by CHRISTOPHER BRASHER (Gollancz.)
A well-known sportsman, journalist and broadcaster, the author writes about the achievements and personalities of some outstanding sportsmen and women in athletics, boxing, climbing, cricket, cycling, football, sailing, swimming and tennis. (927.96)

Water Babe by JUDY GRINHAM (Oldbourne)
Judy Grinham wrote this autobiography in 1960, at the age of 20, four years after winning an Olympic gold medal for swimming. She reveals the struggles and hardship involved in reaching the top in sport, tells of her successes and failures and describes her visits to many countries, including Russia at the age of 15. (792.2)

Very Ordinary Sportsman by J. P. W. MALLALIEU (Routledge)
Mr. Mallalieu writes of the main events in Britain's sporting calendar. He tells the history of these events, such as the Boat Race, the Derby and Wimbledon, and concludes each chapter with a description of the match or race he finds most memorable. (796)

The Wart, lost in a medieval forest, is trying to find his way back to the castle of his guardian, Sir Ector. He chances on Merlyn's cottage, and is surprised to find that he is expected.

CHAPTER THREE

A World of Fantasy

"Now breakfast," said Merlyn.

The Wart saw that the most perfect breakfast table was laid out neatly for two, on a table before the window. There were peaches. There were also melons, strawberries and cream, rusks, brown trout piping hot, grilled perch which were much nicer, chicken devilled enough to burn one's mouth out, kidneys and mushrooms on toast, fricassee, curry and a choice of boiling coffee or best chocolate made with cream in large cups.

"Have some mustard," said Merlyn, when they got to the kidneys.

The mustard-pot got up and walked over to his plate on thin silver legs that waddled like the owl's. Then it uncurled its handles and one handle lifted its lid with exaggerated courtesy while the other helped him to a generous spoonful.

"Oh, I love the mustard-pot!" cried the Wart. "Where ever did you get it?"

At this the pot beamed all over its face and began to strut a bit; but Merlyn rapped it on the head with a teaspoon, so that it sat down and shut up at once.

"It's not a bad pot," he said grudgingly. "Only it is inclined to give itself airs."

The Wart was so much impressed by the kindness of the old magician, and particularly by all the lovely things which he possessed, that he hardly liked to ask him personal questions. It seemed politer to sit still and speak when he was spoken to. But Merlyn did not speak very much, and when he did speak it was never in questions, so that the Wart had little opportunity for conversation. At last his curiosity got the better of him, and he asked something which had been puzzling him for some time.

"Would you mind if I asked you a question?"

"It is what I am for," said Merlyn sadly.

"How did you know to set breakfast for two?"

The old gentleman leaned back in his chair and lighted an

enormous meerschaum pipe—Good gracious, he breathes fire, thought the Wart, who had never heard of tobacco—before he was ready to reply. Then he looked puzzled, took off his skull-cap—three mice fell out—and scratched in the middle of his bald head.

"Have you ever tried to draw in a looking-glass?" asked Merlyn.

"I don't think I have," said the Wart.

"Looking-glass," said the old gentleman, holding out his hand. Immediately there was a tiny lady's vanity-glass in his hand.

"Not that kind, you fool," said Merlyn angrily. "I want one big enough to shave in."

The vanity-glass vanished, and in its place there was a shaving mirror about a foot square. Merlyn then demanded pencil and paper in quick succession; got an unsharpened pencil and the *Morning Post*; sent them back; got a fountain-pen with no ink in it and six reams of brown-paper suitable for parcels; sent them back; flew into a passion in which he said by-our-lady quite often, and ended up with a carbon pencil and some cigarette papers which he said would have to do.

He put one of the papers in front of the glass and made five dots on it like this:

o   o

o

o   o

"Now," he said, "I want you to join those five dots up to make a W, looking only in the glass."

The Wart took the pen and tried to do as he was bid, but after a lot of false starts the letter which he produced was this:

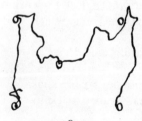

"Well, it isn't bad," said Merlyn doubtfully, "and in a way it does look a bit like an M."

Then he fell into a reverie, stroking his beard, breathing fire, and staring at the paper.

"About the breakfast?" asked the Wart timidly, after he had waited five minutes.

"Ah, yes," said Merlyn. "How did I know to set breakfast for two? That was why I showed you the looking-glass. Now ordinary people are born *forwards* in Time, if you understand what I mean, and nearly everything in the world goes forward too. This makes it quite easy for the ordinary people to live, just as it would be easy to join those five dots into a W if you were allowed to look at them forwards instead of backwards and inside out. But I unfortunately was born at the wrong end of time, and I have to live *backwards* from in front, while surrounded by a lot of people living forwards from behind. Some people call it having second sight."

Merlyn stopped talking and looked at the Wart in an anxious way.

"Have I told you this before?" he inquired suspiciously.

"No," said the Wart. "We only met about half an hour ago."

"So little time to pass as that?" said Merlyn, and a big tear ran down to the end of his nose. He wiped it off with his pyjama tops and added anxiously, "Am I going to tell it you again?"

"I don't know," said the Wart, "unless you haven't finished telling me yet."

"You see," said Merlyn, "one gets confused with Time, when it is like that. All one's tenses get muddled up, for one thing. If you know what's *going* to happen to people, and not what *has* happened to them, it makes it so difficult to prevent it happening, if you don't want it to have happened, if you see what I mean? Like drawing in a mirror."

(from *The Sword in the Stone* by T. H. White)

Comprehension and Discussion

1. Which of the items in Merlyn's breakfast menu seem too modern to be part of a medieval meal? Look up some of them (e.g. chocolate), to see when they were introduced to Europe. Reckon the time of King Arthur to be the 6th Century A.D.; while *Morte D'Arthur*, Malory's retelling of the old legends of Arthur and Merlyn, was completed by 1469.

2. Explain why it would have helped conversation if Merlyn had spoken more "in questions" to the Wart.

3. Why should Merlyn say, "That is what I am for" so sadly?

4. In what way is Merlyn's magic, and general behaviour, comical?

5. Try drawing a W while looking only in a mirror. Why is it so difficult?

6. What was Merlyn trying to explain to the Wart by making him draw a W in the mirror?

7. Why should "living backwards" lead to confusion of tenses? What other confusions would it cause?

8. Is Merlyn confused when he asks:
   "Have I told you this before?" and "Am I going to tell it you again?"?

9. Explain the following words and phrases:
   "chicken devilled", "fricassee", "with exaggerated courtesy", "grudgingly", "fell into a reverie".

10. Why is Merlyn unable to prevent things happening? What would happen if he *could*? Does a similar difficulty apply to all stories about travellers in time?

For Written Answers

1. How did the mustard-pot "shut up"?

2. What made the Wart particularly shy and timid?

3. What evidence is there in the passage, apart from the breakfast menu, that Merlyn had habits and possessions that he had picked up *later* in time?

4. What is "second sight", and how could Merlyn be said to possess it?

5. Make up another example (of your own) of Merlyn asking for something simple (like pencil and paper), only to find a whole variety of possible interpretations of his request.

6. Using only the information given in this passage, write, in your own words, a description of Merlyn's appearance and habits.

Method Exercises

Exercise 1. You do not have to have Merlyn's "second sight" to be muddled by *tenses of verbs* in English. Most foreigners learning English have trouble at first with the variety of tenses and the subtle differences in their use, so that they make mistakes like:

I am wondering if you will be liking the same food as you have had yesterday.

The difficulty is basically that, in addition to past, present and future tenses, we have a choice between the simple, continuous, perfect and perfect continuous of each, as in this table for the verb "to think":

	SIMPLE	CONTINUOUS	PERFECT	PERFECT CONTINUOUS
PRESENT	I think	I am thinking	I have thought	I have been thinking
PAST	I thought	I was thinking	I had thought	I had been thinking
FUTURE	I shall think	I shall be thinking	I shall have thought	I shall have been thinking

Simple tenses are used for very general or very definite actions, at one moment in present, past or future. *Continuous* tenses tend to represent actions going on for some time, and *perfect* tenses are for actions just completed in present, past or future. *Perfect continuous* tenses are, as you might expect, a combination of the last two. Further complications come from our fondness for compounding verbs together, so that the construction

"Am I going to tell it you again?"
is really a variation of the verb "to tell", rather than the verb "to go", meaning something like:

Shall I tell it you again?
or: Shall I be telling it you again?

(a) Write out the verb "to swim" in a table of tenses similar to the one for "to think" above, using the first person singular ("I"). Then write out another table for "to lead", using the third person singular ("he"); and finally a table for "to write", using the second person plural forms ("you").

(b) Explain the difference in meaning between the following pairs of sentences, which differ in the tense used.

e.g. (i) Merlyn will have been living here for ten weeks.
(ii) Merlyn will be living here for ten weeks.

(i) means that Merlyn will at a certain time complete ten weeks' stay here.

(ii) means that Merlyn is now beginning a stay of ten weeks here.

(iii) Merlyn collects souvenirs.
(iv) Merlyn is collecting souvenirs.

(v) He will have collected two hundred pieces next week.
(vi) He will be collecting two hundred pieces next week.

(vii) I shall tell the whole truth.
(viii) I am telling the whole truth.

(ix) The Wart was hoping for an answer.
(x) The Wart had hoped for an answer.

(xi) The car has been breaking down for two years.
(xii) The car has been broken down for two years.

Exercise 2. (a) Pick out all the verbs in the following passage (remembering that a verb must have a subject), and then rewrite the passage altering present tenses to the equivalent past tense (thus present perfect would become past perfect, *not* continuous or simple past).

The idea that time moves at different rates for different people or processes is not such a strange one. Children have a different idea of time's speed from adults. Time hurries when we are interested and drags when we are bored. Surely time means something very different for an insect that lives a day and for a turtle that is expecting to live for many decades. Scientists are able to defeat time when they use very high speed film or employ the time-lapse camera. With these inventions they have slowed down processes that take a fraction of a second or can speed up the slow growth of a plant. When one is watching a speeded-up film of the crowds moving through a busy shopping centre, it really makes one think.

(b) Now try to rewrite the same passage, turning present tenses into the equivalent future tenses. In some cases this will not make satisfactory sense. Discuss the reason for this, and what alternative tense is required.

Exercise 3. Two important uses of the *comma* are illustrated in the opening of the passage at the beginning of this chapter. Where should commas be inserted in the following?

> The Wart lost in a medieval forest is trying to find his way back to the castle of his guardian Sir Ector.

and:

> There were also melons strawberries and cream rusks brown trout piping hot grilled perch which were much nicer chicken devilled enough to burn one's mouth out kidneys and mushrooms on toast fricassee curry and a choice of boiling coffee or best chocolate made with cream in large cups.

Turn back to pages 36 and 37 to check if you are correct, and explain *why* commas are necessary in each case.

The following further description of Merlyn's possessions (from *The Sword in the Stone*) requires at least 32 commas, and possibly 4 sets of inverted commas to complete the punctuation. Rewrite the passage inserting these at the correct places.

> There were several boars' tusks and the claws of tigers and libbards mounted in symmetrical patterns and a big head of Ovis Poli six live grass snakes in a kind of aquarium some nests of the solitary wasp nicely set up in a glass cylinder an ordinary bee-hive whose inhabitants went in and out of the window unmolested two young hedgehogs in cotton wool a pair of badgers which immediately began to cry Yik-Yik-Yik in loud voices as soon as the magician appeared twenty foxes which contained stick caterpillars and sixths of the puss-moth and even an oleander that was worth two and six all feeding on the appropriate leaves

43

a gun case with all sorts of weapons which would not be invented for half a thousand years a rod-box ditto a lovely chest of drawers full of salmon flies which had been tied by Merlyn himself another chest whose drawers were labelled Mandragora Mandrake Old Man's Beard etc. a bunch of turkey feathers and goosequills for making pens an astrolabe twelve pairs of boots a dozen purse-nets three dozen rabbit wires twelve cork-screws an ants' nest between two glass plates ink bottles of every possible colour from red to violet darning-needles a gold medal for being the best scholar at Eton four or five recorders a nest full of field mice all alive-o two skulls plenty of cut glass Venetian glass Bristol glass and a bottle of Mastic varnish.

Exercise 4. SEMICOLONS (;) are also used in the passage from *The Sword in the Stone*. The semicolon is more than a comma but less than a full stop. It is therefore used to join two ideas complete enough to be sentences on their own, when the author wishes to bring them together for comment or contrast.

When T. H. White wrote:

> "At this the pot beamed all over its face and began to strut a bit . . ."

he could then have put a full stop before continuing; for the next sentence is complete with its own subject and verb. The semicolon brings the next sentence closer, suggesting that Merlyn's rapping the pot over the head was the result of its pride.

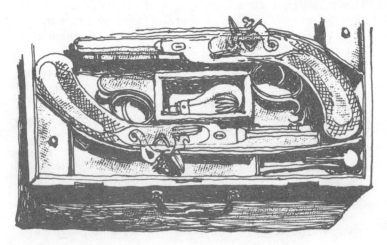

A different use is illustrated in:

"Merlyn then demanded pencil and paper in quick succession; got an unsharpened pencil and . . ."

Here the semicolons link closely a number of sentences that *all* have Merlyn as subject; indeed T. H. White does not even repeat the word Merlyn. Here commas would be too small a break, but semicolons bring the actions close together, as if they were happening in quick succession.

Rewrite the following six sentences, inserting commas or semicolons where they seem necessary, and being prepared to justify your choice.

(a) Merlyn was living backwards in time this meant he became confused about events.

(b) I played chess with him many times he always won of course.

(c) The Wart attempted to draw a W looking only in the mirror but the result when he had finished it was more like an M.

(d) Merlyn had breakfast all prepared showed the Wart round the cottage answered all the boy's questions and generally behaved as if he had been waiting for him to come.

(e) Breakfast was ready the porridge was steaming in the saucepan the coffee was already on the table.

(f) The cupboard seemed to be moving I retreated towards the door it gradually lurched across the floor terrified I threw myself out of the room.

Writing Your Own

1. Most fantasies in literature involve taking the reader into an impossible, dream-like world where everything is so abnormal that anything can happen. Thus *Alice* passed into *Wonderland* down a rabbit hole, and then went *Through the Looking Glass* into a world where everything was back-to-front and upside down. Much of the humour in fantasies consists of taking words or sayings literally. In *The Phantom Tollbooth* there is an absurd banquet when everyone eats his own words. Can you find an example of this kind of humour in the passage in this chapter?

Try writing a short, fantastic story of your own. Here are some suggested situations.

(a) You enter a magic wood, where trees talk or move.

(b) You pass through a cave or float up above the clouds to find a strange land there.

(c) You suddenly discover you can breathe under water and dive into a fantastic under-sea world.

(d) You enter the world of the *Big Rock Candy Mountain*, where the streams flow with lemonade and there is food ready-to-eat on all the trees and no one needs to work or is accused of any crime.

(e) You pass through a mirror, down a drain, into a telescope or inside a television set, and find yourself in a dream-world, such as one where everything moves backwards, or where all the inhabitants are cartoon drawings.

2. As modern playwrights know very well, the things people say and do in ordinary life are often rather absurd, and frequently full of comic misunderstandings. It is easy for people to take actions or meanings of things for granted, and much of our conversation must sound puzzling to any stranger who overhears us talking. Because people do not always say what they mean, it can be quite funny to take them literally. This is the basis of the joke in the passage about Merlyn's demand for a mirror, pencil and paper.

Try writing a comic conversation in play-form. Here is a short example by a pupil:

Mr. Brown is sitting at the kitchen table waiting for the breakfast Mrs. Brown is preparing.

MR. BROWN: Where's my breakfast?

MRS. BROWN: They're off to Southend, I see.

MR. B: I want my breakfast.

MRS. B: I hope they have a nice time. They have a caravan there.

MR. B: Is it on the stove?

MRS. B: No. It's in Southend.

MR. B: What! My breakfast?

MRS. B: No. The caravan.

MR. B: What caravan?

MRS. B: The Smiths'; they're on holiday in Southend.

MR. B: I want that breakfast!

MRS. B: This still needs mending.

MR. B: Where's my breakfast?

MRS. B: It's a leak.

MR. B: I don't like vegetables for breakfast, especially leeks.

MRS. B: We'll have to get a plumber.

MR. B: What for?

MRS. B: The leak.

MR. B: What leak?

MRS. B: The leak in the sink. Now, what did you want for breakfast?

MR. B: It's too late now. I've got to get to work!

ALAN

Oral Work

1. Choose the best and funniest of the conversations written by the class, and cast the various parts in them, so that members of the class can rehearse them in suitable voices, with some simple sound effects.

If a tape-recorder is available, these can be recorded as a series of comic sketches. At this stage it might be a good idea to link them into a single broadcast programme with some lively music faded in and out between sketches, and with an announcer to introduce each one and acknowledge the names of the authors and actors.

2. Conversations between people meeting in unlikely situations may be suitable for improvised drama. Two or three members of the class decide on some particular circumstances, such as those suggested below, and on who shall take each part. Then it is important to spend a short time thinking what it would be like to be that person and to be in that particular situation. However, the conversation must be live, rather than decided in advance, so that each actor responds spontaneously to the remarks and movements of the other.

Here are some unlikely situations:

An American and a Russian astronaut meet on a hitherto undiscovered planet, when each knows nothing of the other's expedition.

A husband meets his wife somewhere quite unexpectedly, when each thought the other was at home.

Two prize-winners at a flower or vegetable show argue when each claims to have won a first prize, and the ticket lies on the floor half-way between their exhibits.

A boy (or girl) meets himself as he will be at the age of forty.

Two burglars meet in a bank late on a Saturday night, each having come independently to rob the safe.

Two girls start talking outside a cinema and discover they are both going to meet the same boy (or two boys discover they have both dated the same girl).

You should be able to make up many other situations to suit your own tastes.

Activities and Research

1. Find out more about the legends of King Arthur. First, is there any possible historical basis for his existence? If so, when and where is he likely to have ruled? Secondly, what are the *Morte D'Arthur* and the *Idylls of the King*? Thirdly, what have the legends of Arthur and his knights to do with Cornwall, Brittany and Wales? Fourthly, what kind of things or people were: Launcelot, Sir Gawaine, Merlyn, Guinevere, Sir Bedivere, Excalibur, Tintagel, the Lady of the Lake and the Holy Grail? Members of the class could prepare a folder of work on this theme.

2. What foods take their names from these places? Banbury, Bakewell, Bath, Pontefract, Caerphilly, Lancashire, Yorkshire, Hamburg, Vienna, Gouda, Gorgonzola, Burgundy, Madeira. Be prepared to say a little about each of them.

3. Find out about the life and work of Lewis Carroll (what was his real name?) and Edward Lear. Look again at their books and poems. Write a short account of each author.

Further Reading

The Sword in the Stone by T. H. WHITE (Collins; Fontana)
This is a humorous, modern retelling of the legendary tale of how "the Wart", under Merlyn's guidance, proved himself to be the future King Arthur. If you enjoy T. H. White's whimsical style, try *Mistress Masham's Repose* and *The Elephant and the Kangaroo*.

Vice Versa by F. ANSTEY (Murray)
In 1881, Mr. Paul Bultitude foolishly wished to change places with his schoolboy son, Dick, and the results, when this miraculously happened, make a well-known funny story.

The Weirdstone of Brisingamen by ALAN GARNER (Collins; Penguin)
A modern fantasy: when Susan finds she has the fabulous weirdstone on her bracelet, it means a battle to the death as she and Colin and the dwarfs are chased by sinister monsters through underground caverns and across the Cheshire country-side.

The Lord of the Rings (3 volumes) by J. R. R. TOLKIEN
(Allen & Unwin)
This is a remarkable and unique fantasy. The gripping tale is set in an imaginary time and place and peopled with unusual races. The style varies with the characters portrayed, ranging from the comic to the utterly terrifying.

Under the heading "SLUMS" in the Oxford Junior Encyclopaedia, we find both an interesting history of housing problems, subtitled "EARLY REFORMS", and a survey of modern attempts to take up the challenge of providing really good homes for all.

CHAPTER FOUR

Homes and Housing

In 1868 the first general housing Act of Parliament was passed, and this allowed, although it did not compel, local authorities to pull down really insanitary houses if the owners refused to keep them in a healthy condition. In 1875 Cross's Act gave local authorities the right to rebuild, but the basis for action was still the need to improve the condition of the worst slums rather than to improve the housing of the population in general —to cure rather than to prevent the evil. Action was not taken until a house or group of houses was condemned as a slum; it could then be either "improved" or "cleared". Improvement meant that leaking roofs were repaired, extra lavatories built, water pipes laid on, and damp and mildewed flooring replaced. Vermin were killed by fumigation, doors replaced where these had been burnt for firewood, very damp basements closed and boarded up. In some cases people could be prosecuted and fined if too many slept in one room. If a slum was too bad for "improvement" of this kind, it was "cleared", and the inhabitants moved to new dwellings. These had to be built as close as possible to the working places of the tenants, who could not afford to travel a long distance to work, and in any case often would not settle far from the neighbourhood they were used to.

These measures, however, did not put an end to slums. The tenants who were turned out of the old dwellings with their low rents often could not afford the higher rents in the new houses and therefore tended to crowd together, causing new slums to form again. To help to meet this difficulty, voluntary groups of public-spirited people formed housing "trusts" or societies, on a non-profit-making basis, to build dwellings for the lower-paid workers. Blocks of solid flats built by these means can be seen in many cities which, though they may now look to us gloomy and forbidding, represented in their day a great advance: they were solid, sanitary, and water-tight, and the rents were low. In the 1860's a public-spirited London woman, Octavia Hill, began to tackle the problem of teaching people how to use their new homes; and, as a result of her work, the modern idea of HOUSING MANAGEMENT (q.v.) with all the social work involved began to develop, and housing managers were trained on her lines.

In 1885 an Act giving local authorities power to enter slum houses to inspect them was passed. In 1890 came the important Housing of the Working Classes Act, which gave councils wider powers to prosecute the landlords of unhealthy buildings, and to destroy very bad property, paying compensation to the owners; power was also given for the first time to build new homes with public money, even without clearing a slum. Other laws followed, and by 1909 all local authorities were required to set up committees for public health and housing. But local authorities had many difficulties to contend with. The cost of building was very heavy and had to be paid for entirely out of the RATES (q.v.) for there were no government grants. The owners of the slum property, who were sometimes influential people in the district, did their best to force up the purchase price when compelled to sell. It was little wonder, therefore, that few local authorities made much use of the powers which had been given them.

3. MODERN REHOUSING. Before the First World War, although many people thought of the slums as "black spots" that should be rooted out, few realised how big the problem was. After the war the fearful housing shortage, particularly of houses at rents which the ordinary working people could afford to pay, brought the whole question of housing to the fore, and resulted in the formation of a new national policy of building houses at modest rents with the help of money advanced by the Government to local councils or private builders. At length, housing and slum clearance came to be regarded as parts of the same problem. The gradual progress towards providing enough good houses at a low rent, as part of a general scheme of TOWN AND COUNTRY PLANNING (q.v.) was recognised as the best method of eventually clearing all slums . . .

Although some slums were "cleared" by German bombing during the Second World War, many good houses were demolished too, which further increased the housing shortage. Also, in order to accommodate people evacuated from their homes, a large number of houses, and even whole streets, which had been condemned as unfit for human occupation and scheduled for demolition, were given first-aid repairs, and the families who moved into them remained there long after the war. The increased cost of repairs caused many houses to fall into bad condition; owners of less expensive houses, unable to charge economic rents by the Rent Restriction Acts passed during the war (*see* RENT CONTROL), often could not afford to do more than repair sanitary defects, which they were compelled to do by law. The first duty of the Government was to plan for the building of vast numbers of new homes and, by giving grants, to stop older houses degenerating into slum property (*see* HOUSING, MUNICIPAL). Only when these needs had been partly met could it devote its attention to the clearance of slums.

In 1954 a new survey revealed that 850,000 houses in England and Wales—most of them built before 1880—were in such a bad condition that they ought to be pulled down. By 1961, 250,000 of these had been replaced by new houses. Smaller towns hope to complete this slum clearance by 1965, but cities such as Liverpool, Manchester, Birmingham, Leeds, Glasgow, and Edinburgh have a far larger problem, and the replacement of their many thousands of condemned houses will take longer to complete.

Every effort is being made to check the creation of new slums. Britain still has not enough houses both for its own growing population and for the immigrants from the Commonwealth who are coming to work and live in its larger cities. Local authorities have been given new powers to try to prevent the overcrowding and neglect of houses which inevitably result in making new slums.

See also HOUSING, MUNICIPAL; HOUSING MANAGEMENT; TOWN AND COUNTRY PLANNING.

See also Vol. XI: TOWNS, HISTORY OF.

(from *The Oxford Junior Encyclopaedia*, Vol. X, Law and Society, "SLUMS")

Comprehension and Discussion

1. How would you define a "slum"?

2. Why were "improvement" and "clearance" (under Cross's Act) inadequate solutions of the housing problems?

3. What was Octavia Hill trying to do and why was it necessary? Would you agree with the view that people who do not know how to live in decent conditions therefore do not deserve to have those conditions to live in?

4. Why was the 1890 Housing of the Working Classes Act so important? Would it have been given this title today?

5. Explain what "RATES" are, and how they differ from taxes. Why is it fairer and more effective if municipal housing is not paid for solely out of rates?

6. What do the following words or phrases mean?

(in)sanitary	compensation	economic rents
fumigation	influential people	degenerating
public-spirited	scheduled for	immigrants
prosecute	"demolition"	q.v.

7. Can you think of any further housing problems, other than those mentioned, that have complicated the situation since the Second World War?

8. What, according to this article, can be wrong with leaving houses entirely to private landlords? Do you think every family should own their own home?

9. Is there a difference between a "house" and a "home"?

10. Discuss the basic essentials that any well-equipped and comfortable house (or flat) needs to have built into it today.

For Written Answers

1. What were the characteristic troubles with the slum property that was to be improved under "Cross's Act"?

2. Why had new dwellings to be close to the old slums, and why was this often a limiting factor? (Remember to begin your answer: "New buildings had to be close to the old slums because . . .")

3. Why did so few local authorities use the powers given them in the 1890 Act? (Do *not* begin your answer: "Because . . .")

4. Explain in your own words why housing and slum clearance are parts of the same problem. When and how was this recognised?

5. Sum up in your own words what new problems (according to the passage) have added to the housing shortage since the end of the Second World War.

Method Exercises

In Books One and Two we have emphasised that every complete sentence needs a *subject* (something to talk about) and a *verb* (a word or words for the action). But many of our sentences contain *several* subjects and verbs. Pair off each subject and verb (both are printed in italics) in this, the opening sentence from the passage:

> In 1868 the first general housing *Act* of Parliament *was passed*, and *this allowed*, although *it did* not *compel*, local authorities to pull down really insanitary houses if the *owners refused* to keep them in a healthy condition.

Can you now rewrite this sentence as four separate simple sentences, each with only one subject and verb? To do so, you will have to leave out the three joining words, or CONJUNCTIONS:

> . . . and . . . although . . . if . . .

"Although" and "if" introduce *subordinate clauses*, which we shall discuss later in this book. The following *conjunctions*:

> and, but, (either . . .) or, for,

and several *adverbs* such as:

> so, therefore, however, nevertheless, also,

usually with commas or *semicolons* (;), can all be used to join two (or more) CO-ORDINATE CLAUSES, that is, two equally important simple statements, into *one* sentence.

55

Exercise 1. Pick out the conjunctions or adverbs that link *co-ordinate clauses* in the following sentences; rewrite each as two or more separate simple statements. Remember each clause must have a subject and a verb of its own, or the words are only a phrase.

e.g.   The problems of housing and rebuilding after the Second World War were enormous; nevertheless, great progress has been made.

Answer: Linking adverb—nevertheless.

　　　　1. The problems of housing and rebuilding after the Second World War were enormous.

　　　　2. Great progress has nevertheless been made.

(a) They were solid, sanitary and watertight and the rents were low.

(b) In the 1860's a public-spirited London woman, Octavia Hill, began to tackle the problem of teaching people how to use their new homes; and, as a result of her work, the modern idea of housing management with all the social work involved began to develop, and housing managers were trained on her lines.

(c) Other laws followed, and by 1909 all local authorities were required to set up committees for public health and housing.

(d) The cost of building was very heavy and had to be paid for entirely out of rates, for there were no government grants.

(e) Smaller towns hope to complete this slum clearance by 1965, but cities have a far larger problem, and the replacement of their many thousands of condemned houses will take longer to complete.

(f) Many slums are too bad to be repaired and improved; therefore they are being completely demolished.

Exercise 2. We have now met a number of different ways of combining short sentences together into longer, more complicated ones. In Book Two we had constructions using the *present participle* to introduce a phrase, and others using the *pronouns* "who, whom, which, that", and in Book Three we have discussed *semicolons* and *conjunctions*.

(a) Consider the ways in which the two simple statements:

　　　　　The Queen went to the première.
　　　　　The film was a documentary.

have been combined below. In each case, explain what method of joining has been used, and discuss the different meaning each method or conjunction gives the sentence.

The Queen went to the première because (as, since) the film was a documentary.

The film was a documentary and the Queen went to the première.

The film was a documentary but the Queen went to the première.

The film was a documentary, therefore the Queen went to the première.

The film being a documentary, the Queen went to the première.

The Queen went to the première of the film which was a documentary.

The film that the Queen went to the première of was a documentary.

If the Queen went to the première, the film was a documentary.

When the film was a documentary, the Queen went to the première.

Although the film was a documentary, the Queen went to the première.

The Queen went to the première; the film was a documentary.

(b) Join the following pairs or groups of sentences in as many different ways as you can (similar to those given in [a]), and discuss the different meanings that emerge.

(i) The house was condemned.
   The rain came through the roof.

(ii) The cost of building was heavy.
   It had to be paid for out of rates.

(iii) Bridget likes icing.
   Icing is very sweet.

(iv) The match was postponed.
   It rained heavily.
   The match was on Sunday.

(v) The wind was easterly.
   The wind was very strong.
   The sun was quite warm.

Exercise 3. We noted in Chapter One that parts of *verbs* could act as *adjectives*. The passage at the head of this chapter has examples of *present participles* (ending in -ing) as adjectives:

Leaking roofs were repaired.

and of *past participles* (ending usually in -ed or -t) as adjectives:

Mildewed flooring was replaced.

and of infinitives (the form of the verb with "to" in front of it) as adjectives:

An Act giving local authorities power *to enter* slum houses was passed.

(What part of the verb is "giving"? What is it describing, as an adjective?) "To enter" is obviously a form of the verb "enter"; what verbs are "leaking" and "mildewed" forms of?

In each of the following sentences, adapted from the passage, a part of a verb acting as an adjective has been printed in italics. State what verb it is part of and what noun it is describing.

(a) People formed "trusts" on a *non-profit-making* basis.

(b) The trusts were to build dwellings for the *lower-paid* workers.

(c) The flats look to us gloomy and *forbidding*.

(d) This Act gave councils wider powers *to prosecute* the landlords of unhealthy buildings.

(e) Local authorities had many difficulties *to contend* with.

(f) There was a new national policy of building houses at modest rents with the help of money *advanced* by the Government.

(g) In order to accommodate people *evacuated* from their homes, a large number of houses were given first-aid repairs.

(h) The *increased* cost of repairs caused many houses to fall into bad condition.

(i) 850,000 houses in England and Wales—most of them *built* before 1880—ought to be pulled down.

(j) Britain still has not enough houses for its *growing* population.

Exercise 4. Coming from an encyclopaedia, the passage at the head of this chapter is a typical piece of *exposition*, and makes a lot of use of verbs in the *passive voice*. Instead of saying that in 1868 the Houses of Parliament passed the first general housing Act, the passage begins:

> In 1868 the first general housing Act of Parliament *was passed* . . .

Who passed the Act is unimportant. Similarly it is unnecessary to name the authorities in:

> Action *was* not *taken* until a house or group of houses was condemned as a slum; it *could* then *be* either *"improved"* or *"cleared"*.

What are the subjects of the five passive verbs in these two examples? Turn the second sentence round so that all the verbs are active, and the subjects become objects, making up appropriate new subjects.

In the rest of the first paragraph and the second paragraph of the passage, there are in all 17 passive verbs (some of them share the same auxiliary verbs, as in the second example above). Write each of these, with its subject, and work out what the active voice equivalent of each will be. Remember that the passive voice always uses a tense of the verb "to be" together with the past participle of the verb itself.

Using the passive voice too often can make a piece of writing very clumsy and difficult to follow. Discuss whether any of the sentences in the passive voice in the passage could be improved by turning the verbs into the active voice.

Writing Your Own

1. In writing *exposition*, it is important to adopt a clear and impersonal style and to arrange the information in a clear and logical order. Before attempting your own writing, examine the passage about "slums" again. Make notes on the main theme of each paragraph, and discuss how most of the paragraphs are linked on to the next, so that a point from the end of one is taken up and enlarged or developed in the next.

Now choose one of the following subjects and find books in the lending library or articles in reference books that will give you some information about the history and organisation of the institution you have chosen. Make rough notes (just the useful facts) from several different sources. Then organise these into a plan, showing paragraph headings in a logical order. Now you are ready to begin writing the account in your own words and following your own arrangement.

The Police Force
The Fire Service
Children's Homes
Street Lighting and Cleansing
Refuse Disposal
Drainage and Sewage Disposal
Local Government in England and Wales (see the chart on p. 62), or in your own country.
Local Elections
Local Authorities
The Government of Greater London
The City of London (or any other great city)
Rates and Taxes
Your own Local Council(s)

2. Imagine what your own street, district or village might be like in 50, 100 or 200 years' time. Write a vivid account of how you expect the houses, shops, transport and even the people to have changed. Make this a story, if you like, in which you enter the future with some kind of time machine. But include description of an area you know really well.

Oral Work

1. Here are some matters for members of the class to think about and discuss:

(a) Good neighbours and bad—what qualities make a good neighbour? Should people normally keep themselves to themselves?

(b) Problems of living in flats—how important are sound-proofing, communal services (e.g. a laundry), and what provision should be made for children? (Some flats now have close circuit television, so that mothers can watch their children at play down below!)

(c) Neighbourhood planning and town planning—are these important? Should the government or the local authority own all the land or plan all the house-building in order to ensure properly-planned towns?

(d) Rents—should council tenants pay enough to cover the cost of their house or flat and its upkeep, or is it right to let some people have cheap accommodation, paid for from rates or taxes? Should rents of privately-owned property be controlled?

2. Follow up the cross references given in the passage, and report on what further information is given. These entries will be alphabetical within each volume of the *Oxford Junior Encyclopaedia*. Explain what "q.v." means and why "Municipal Housing" is found under H, while "Housing Management" is *not* under M.

Look up these and similar headings in *other* encyclopaedias. Always use the Index volume to start your investigations, making sure that you understand the meaning of the references given, e.g. 5-374b might mean "volume 5, page 374, second column of type".

Activities and Research

Find out more about Local Government. Investigate how and when local councillors are elected, what the difference is between aldermen and other councillors, and what political party (if any) controls your local council. Who is the present Mayor or Chairman of the Council and how is he selected? What Council Committees do you have and what are the main paid officials? What is a Town Clerk? How much are the local rates and how are they being spent? (A local rate demand form will probably tell you this.)

A group from the class might visit the next council meeting to watch it from the public gallery. Alternatively, it is possible that some council official or local councillor might be willing to visit the school and talk to the class about the work of the council.

Apart from encyclopaedias, books like *Local Government* by E. L. Jones (E.S.A., 1961), catalogued as 352.042, will give you considerable help. Look at the books in section 352, Local Government, in your local library.

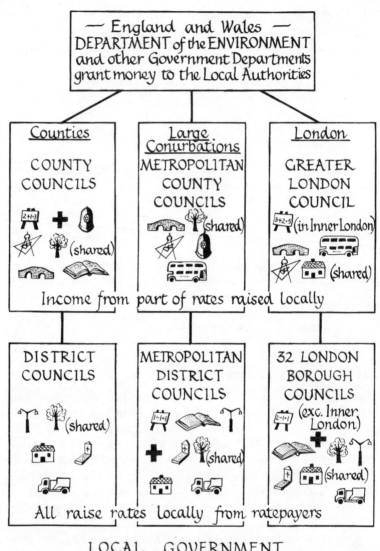

— England and Wales —
DEPARTMENT of the ENVIRONMENT and other Government Departments grant money to the Local Authorities

Counties

COUNTY COUNCILS

(shared)

Large Conurbations

METROPOLITAN COUNTY COUNCILS

(shared)

London

GREATER LONDON COUNCIL

(in Inner London)

(shared)

Income from part of rates raised locally

DISTRICT COUNCILS

(shared)

METROPOLITAN DISTRICT COUNCILS

(shared)

32 LONDON BOROUGH COUNCILS
(exc. Inner London)

(shared)

All raise rates locally from ratepayers

LOCAL GOVERNMENT

All councillors are directly elected by voters in that area.

Responsibilities: Education — Welfare services — Police/Fire service — Side roads/lighting — Highways — Housing — Overall planning — Transport (buses) — Cemeteries — Parks etc. — Refuse collection — Libraries/museums

Further Reading

The Oxford Junior Encyclopaedia (O.U.P., revised 1965)
Each of the twelve volumes deals with one subject group so that
each is an alphabetical reference book in itself. The titles are:
Mankind, Natural History, The Universe, Communications,
Great Lives, Farming and Fisheries, Industry and Commerce,
Engineering, Recreations, Law and Society, Home and Health,
and The Arts; there is also an Index volume. (Ref. 001)

Bob in Local Government by DUNCAN TAYLOR (Chatto & Windus)
Bob Hinkley goes to work in the Housing Department of a
London borough, where he learns not only about the job of a
housing manager, but about many other activities of local
government, such as roads, libraries and drainage. All the
books in this *Career* series present, in the form of simple stories,
basic information about various jobs.

Widdershins Crescent by JOHN ROWE TOWNSEND (Hutchinson;
  Penguin)
When their old home is pulled down, the Thompsons, a North-
ern slum family, are moved out to Widdowson (or "Widdershins") Crescent, a new street in a bright modern estate. The
move offers them all a fresh start in life—but also brings them
a fresh set of problems. As in *Hell's Edge* and *Gumble's Yard*, the
reality of characters and situations makes this an excellent story
for young people.

From Tree Dwellings to New Towns by P. MAGUIRE (Longmans)
This book traces in considerable detail the history of houses
throughout the world and shows how improvements in living
conditions have affected ordinary people. There are many
photographs and drawings. (728)

David Golansky, one of the meekest pupils at St. Alfred's Day School for Boys, has been constantly humiliated by Broccoli Smith, the tough but dull-witted boxing instructor. So, when he finds out that Broccoli believes the world will end in the year 3000, he cunningly offers to check the calculations on which Broccoli bases his belief.

CHAPTER FIVE

Actors and Audiences

BROCCOLI's room, next day: A bare and miserable room with the bed unmade. BROCCOLI is at the window giving bird-seed to a small canary in a large and home-made cage.

The door is pushed open. DAVID is standing timidly close to the door. BROCCOLI turns and roars.

BROCCOLI: Get out!

David shrinks against the wall but does not go.

This is my private quarters . . . Who let you up here?

DAVID: I just came to say . . .

BROCCOLI *(blinks)*: It's you again . . .

DAVID: I checked those figures for you.

BROCCOLI *(shouts)*: NO BOYS ALLOWED!

DAVID: You seemed so anxious about the figures, I thought you wouldn't mind if I came.

BROCCOLI: Well, I do mind. An interruption. In my quarters!

DAVID: I'm sorry, sir. *(Pause. He holds out a bit of paper.)* Those figures.

BROCCOLI: Yes?

DAVID: . . . are not strictly accurate.

BROCCOLI: They've never been doubted!

DAVID: It's the fault of the calendar. There was that Julius Caesar. He got years wrong in the first place. Anyway, he made the years too long by about . . . oh, months really. And that time-table of yours . . . hasn't recognised the fact! You see, the calendar doesn't bear much relation . . . to the passage of time.

BROCCOLI: It's gone by without us knowing it?

DAVID: That's right. You see all those mistakes have shortened the time quite considerably, so . . .

BROCCOLI: What?

DAVID: Well, I've worked it out and it comes to . . . starting at the first mean equinox, about . . . two and a half days left!

BROCCOLI: You mean . . .?

DAVID: What is it now . . . Monday. That gives us . . . until some time on Wednesday night. Probably after midnight.

BROCCOLI: And then . . .?

DAVID: I don't suppose there'll be a lesson on Thursday.

BROCCOLI (*whispers*): What . . . will there be?

DAVID: A storm. I should think it'll begin with a storm. Lightning and that sort of thing.

BROCCOLI: And then?

David shrugs his shoulders. Pause.

You're having your . . . little joke.

DAVID: Don't worry, Mr. Smith. It probably won't hurt—

BROCCOLI: The finish! (*He rubs his head.*)

DAVID: You shouldn't worry. After all, it'd come as a surprise, if you hadn't got so interested in the arithmetic!

BROCCOLI tears his almanac across with a sudden gesture of his huge hands.

I mean . . . it's got to end some time, as I told you. It would be just as awful, if it went on for ever. It's got to end. It's only . . . we've been selected to be here when it does.

BROCCOLI (*staring vacantly in front of him*): Selected!

DAVID: A sort of honour really. The last men in the world!

DAVID tiptoes out. BROCCOLI shudders. His head sinks into his great hands.

The Boiler Room: The BOILERMAN is eating his sandwiches. DAVID is in the doorway.

DAVID (*brightly*): It's clouding over.

BOILERMAN: Oh!

DAVID: It's going to get . . . lovely and black!

BOILERMAN: Have a sandwich.

DAVID: All right. (*He eats.*) They're delicious.

BOILERMAN: Good market down our way. (*Pause.*) What's the matter with him?

DAVID: Who?

BOILERMAN: Broccoli Smith. West Ham's world-famed Paper Doll

DAVID: Paper what?

BOILERMAN: Not part of your vocabulary . . .

DAVID (*lying*): Oh, yes, I know what that means.

BOILERMAN: Then you should sympathise.

DAVID: I should?

BOILERMAN: I mean, he was never exactly one for sprightly repartee, as we know. But now he's dead silent. Even seems to have lost interest in the future!

DAVID (*casually*): Has he?

66

BOILERMAN: Never speaks of it. Seems remote from him some-
how . . . Comes in here . . . just for a warm, and stands . . .
"Cheer up," I tell him. "We're not dead yet."
DAVID: Does it cheer him up, when you say that to him?
BOILERMAN: Not particularly, now I come to think of it . . .
DAVID: Look . . . (*He is looking out of the door.*)
BOILERMAN: What?
DAVID: It's raining . . .
BOILERMAN: Well?
DAVID: There's going to be a storm. (*Excited.*) It's Wednesday
night . . . and there's going to be a storm.

*DAVID runs across the wet playground, through the rain, splashing
in the puddles. BROCCOLI is standing in a doorway sheltering. He
looks up in horror at the thunder and lightning in the sky. The water
pours down his beaten-up and frightened face.*

*DAVID calls out to him as he runs by, and doesn't wait for an
answer.*
DAVID: Good night, Mr. Smith. (*And fainter as he runs.*) Goodbye, Mr. Smith . . .

---

*BROCCOLI's room. That night: BROCCOLI in his pyjamas is
standing at the open window of his room and looking up at the storm.
He opens the door of the bird-cage and releases the bird. It flies into the
stormy darkness.*

---

*The Assembly: next morning. The School is still singing. Suddenly
we see the HEADMASTER'S face as the song dies in amazement on
his lips. BROCCOLI has thrown open the Hall door and is standing
in his pyjamas, his arms thrown out wide as he roars in triumph:*
BROCCOLI: We're still here. Look at us! We're alive!

*DAVID's face is impassive and inscrutable behind his glasses in his
moment of triumph.*

---

*The Playground: The crowd of BOYS are puzzled, whispering
together, unable to understand what has happened. DAVID comes
striding among them.*
DAVID (*throwing up his arms*): We're alive! Latest news, and stale
buns, we're all very much alive! Tell the staff, tell the Headmaster! We're living and breathing . . .
1ST BOY: We *know*.
2ND BOY: Why did he tell us that?
3RD BOY: With his pyjamas on?

67

DAVID: You want to know? Give you three guesses? Animal vegetable or mineral . . .

BOYS: Tell us . . .

3RD BOY: Who do you think you are? . . .

DAVID: Dutch Martin . . . Battling Butcher! David Golansky! I . . . knocked . . . him out!

BOYS: Who!

DAVID: Broccoli! He's scared.

BOYS: What of?

DAVID: Me!

3RD BOY: You flea!

BOYS: Why? . . .

DAVID: I told . . . Listen, I said . . . I *proved it* to him.

BOYS: What?

DAVID: *Quod erat demonstrandum!* I said, "Poor old Broccoli, say your prayers. Prepare to meet your God. Thursday morning's going to be The Ending of the World!"

BOYS: He believed you?

DAVID: Hook, line and stinker!

BOYS: He thought it would?

DAVID: He genuinely did! And he woke up and found himself all in one bit. Poor old Broccoli was *glad*!

1ST BOY: He must have been scared!

2ND BOY: In a funk.

3RD BOY: Dead with fright.

DAVID: The world's ended!

1ST BOY: Then we're all dead.

2ND BOY: I'm dead!

1ST BOY: And you're dead!

3RD BOY: I'm a ghost . . . (*Putting his mackintosh over his head.*) Whoooooooooo!

1ST BOY: (*doing the same*): Eeeeeeeeee!

2ND BOY (*doing the same*): I'm a spoooooooook!

1ST BOY: Let's go and tell Broccoli!

3RD BOY: We're dead as doornails.

1ST BOY: Let's give him another scare . . .

2ND BOY: Put the wind up Broccoli . . .

3RD BOY: Whoooooo!

1ST BOY: Come on, David . . .

2ND BOY: Get your mack, David. We'll be four great, dirty ghosts!

DAVID: I'll catch you up.

The Boiler Room: DAVID runs in and gets his mack which has been hanging on a chair in front of the boiler to dry.

BOILERMAN: Broccoli Smith's just been in.

DAVID *(casual)*: Has he?

BOILERMAN: Interested?

DAVID: Not awfully.

BOILERMAN: He came to say goodbye.

DAVID: He's going? Why does he have to . . . go?

BOILERMAN: You don't know?

DAVID: No, honestly.

BOILERMAN: Because if I was to appear in my night attire and inform the Headmaster that there was still life in him, contrary to all appearances, I should also expect my cards. It appears someone of superior brain-power misled Mr. Smith about the date.

DAVID is silent.

You had the advantage over him.

DAVID: Me?

BOILERMAN: Stands to reason. You're young and he's got one foot in the New End Hospital. You can think clever and he has a job to remember what those long elastic loops buttoned on to his trousers are *for* every morning. You can laugh at him and he can't laugh at you . . .

DAVID: He can't?

BOILERMAN: He takes it all serious. Which is what lays him open to attack.

DAVID: Attack?

BOILERMAN: A shot in the back.

DAVID: I wouldn't . . . He'll be all right, won't he?

BOILERMAN: What makes you think that?

DAVID: He's a champion.

BOILERMAN: I told you. He's a paper doll.

DAVID: I don't know what that means.

BOILERMAN: Oh, what do they insert into your head by way of education! Such a brilliant boxer! The only man he ever knocked out was the referee by a complete error of judgement . . .

DAVID: No!

BOILERMAN: You owe a special duty of care . . . to that type of individual!

BOY *(calling from outside)*: Come on, David . . . You're being *hours!*

(*DAVID hesitates, looks at the BOILERMAN, but finally goes.*)

DAVID: All right . . . coming.

BROCCOLI's Room: DAVID's mack has fallen to the ground and he is standing looking at the paper parcels and empty bird-cage which is BROCCOLI's luggage.

DAVID: It's gone.

BROCCOLI: What?

DAVID: Your bird.

BROCCOLI: Well, I'm going. I doubt if I'll have the accommodation.

DAVID: I see . . .

BROCCOLI: It wasn't much of a canary. It didn't sing much. Sex was all wrong, most likely. (*Pause*) I was just going.

DAVID: I know. I'm sorry . . .

BROCCOLI: What was that?

DAVID: I said, I'm sorry you have to go. I didn't mean . . .

BROCCOLI: You'll miss the lessons, eh? A lark to you lot, weren't they, them lessons?

DAVID (*weakly*): In a sort of way . . .

BROCCOLI: It was a lark all right for you! 'Itting the instructor. Just a childish pastime. Not your careers.

DAVID: No Mr. Smith, and I ought to tell you . . .

BROCCOLI: It might have been humiliation to me, what was enjoyment to you. Did you think of that?

DAVID: No . . .

BROCCOLI: I got to dread those Thursdays . . .

DAVID (*amazed*): *You* did?

BROCCOLI: The humiliation. I'm glad it's finished with.

DAVID: I didn't enjoy it, Mr. Smith.

BROCCOLI: Well, thank you for *that*.

DAVID: That's all right.

Pause. BROCCOLI blinks and rubs his head.

BROCCOLI: You come to say goodbye, didn't you?

DAVID: Yes, and to say . . .

BROCCOLI: Well, I enjoyed those talks we had, about the future and that. Very interesting they was.

DAVID: Yes, Mr. Smith.

BROCCOLI: But I was right, you know. It didn't come to an end, did it? I mean . . . it's still going on.

DAVID: Yes, it is.

BROCCOLI: And you said I was weak in the maths . . .

DAVID: I misjudged you . . .

BROCCOLI: Well, (*He looks round the room.*) I'll be off soon, to the outside. Only thing I'm likely to miss is the room.

70

DAVID: The room?

BROCCOLI: Peaceful in a way. Out of the main swim, of course. I liked that, being out of the swim. Quietly . . . up here.

DAVID: I expect you're busy.

BROCCOLI: It's the room I'll regret, that's all.

He looks round the room, dejected. DAVID looks at him, seems to be about to say something, can't think of what to say, and goes.

BROCCOLI (*calls after DAVID*): Only look out for the year three thousand, now! Don't let that catch you unawares . . .

The Playground: DAVID comes down the stairs from BROC-COLI's room and out into the playground. He crosses the playground in streaming sunshine.

He looks guilty and dejected. A BOY passes him running.

DAVID: Where're you going?

BOYS: It's Armstrong . . . he's got a motorised affair.

DAVID runs, too. They reach a BOY crouched over a model aeroplane with a small engine.

2ND BOY: It won't work.

DAVID: Here let me see . . . It's the fuel . . .

He makes an adjustment. With a great whirr the model aeroplane flies into the air. The BOYS straighten up. DAVID is looking, squinting against the sun at the flight of the plane.

In the distance BROCCOLI, with his parcel and empty cage, goes out of the school gate. DAVID looks after him.

BOY: Come on! She's landing . . .

DAVID runs off with the other BOYS towards the crashing plane.

(from *David and Broccoli* by John Mortimer)

Comprehension and Discussion

1. What does "humiliate" mean? Why did Broccoli humiliate David in the first instance?

2. Is David's point about being "selected"—"a sort of honour really"—a valid one, or a clever trick of argument?

3. What does, Broccoli was "never exactly one for sprightly repartee", mean? Would you call this ironic? Why did Broccoli like to keep himself to himself?

4. Is it a sad or pathetic detail in the play when Broccoli releases the bird? Why does he do so?

71

5. Can there be any connection between the facts that (at the end) David is making a model aeroplane fly and Broccoli is leaving with an empty bird-cage?

6. Is the Boilerman sarcastic in saying Broccoli was "such a brilliant boxer"? What does he mean when he says David owes "a special duty of care . . . to that type of individual"?

7. Do you agree that we have a responsibility for mentally-handicapped people? How should we treat them? (e.g. with pity?)

8. What kind of actor (and acting) is needed to portray (a) David, (b) Broccoli, (c) the Boilerman? Consider physical stature, appearance, personality.

9. Discuss producing this play (a) on the stage, (b) on the radio, (c) on television and (d) as a film. What changes (in text or production technique) would be needed?

10. Could a class of girls act this play? Discuss an adaptation, or a similar story, to take place in a girls' school.

For Written Answers

Give full answers in your own words, with reasons taken from the play. If you need to quote from the play, use inverted commas.

1. What *is* a "paper doll", and was Broccoli really tough, or a champion?

2. What happens later in the play to explain why Broccoli did not like boys in his room?

3. How convincing is David's argument about the error in the calendar? How much trouble does he have convincing Broccoli?

4. Why does David tell the other boys what he has done? (Remember to begin your answer: "David tells the other boys about it because . . .")

5. What, according to the Boilerman, gave David an advantage over Broccoli?

6. What does Broccoli think David is apologising for?

7. Did David *really* want to have Broccoli dismissed?

8. What feelings is Broccoli meant to arouse in the reader, or audience?

Method Exercises

Exercise 1. (a) What uses of the apostrophe are illustrated in the following examples from the passage? How could the sentences or phrases be rewritten to avoid using an apostrophe?

Broccoli's room—It's you again—You wouldn't mind —I'm sorry, sir—I've worked it out—It'll begin with a storm—After all it'd come as a surprise—West Ham's world-famed Paper Doll—The Headmaster's face— Thursday morning's going to be The Ending of the World —The world's ended—Let's go and tell Broccoli— Broccoli Smith's just been in—'Itting the instructor.

(b) What is the rule for using the apostrophe to show possession? It is given as a footnote at the end of these Method Exercises for you to make sure that you are right.

Rewrite the following unlikely sentences inserting all the apostrophes that they require.

(i) When the ten unions secretaries meet the ten employers representatives its a question of which side will make its case appeal more strongly to its members pockets.

(ii) Five gooses feathers wont make my fathers feather bed as soft as five geeses feathers.

(iii) The ten princes purses werent worth any more than the one princesss ten purses.

Exercise 2. When we are recounting a conversation, we frequently report it in slightly different words from those that were actually spoken. The actual words spoken are called DIRECT SPEECH, of which the following dialogue, set out in play form, would be an example:

ALBERT: We are going to find it difficult to perform this play tomorrow.

JANE: Do you know where David and Margaret are? They seem to have disappeared.

ALBERT: Oh! Don't worry about them.

If we imagine ourselves overhearing this conversation, and then retelling it later, we shall be giving a REPORTED SPEECH VERSION of what they said, as follows:

73

Albert said that they were going to find it difficult to perform that play the next day. Jane asked if he knew where David and Margaret were since they seemed to have disappeared. Albert expressed mild surprise at this and told her not to worry about them.

Notice the changes that we make, especially in *tenses* and *persons*.

Fuller rules for correct reported speech will be given later in this book, but try to change the following dialogue into reported speech by imagining yourself overhearing this conversation between David and Broccoli Smith, and reporting it fully afterwards. To help you, every word that has to be changed has been printed in italics:

DAVID: *I have* checked those figures for *you*.

BROCCOLI: No boys *are* allowed up *here*.

DAVID: *I am* sorry. *I* just wanted to tell *you* that the figures *are* not accurate.

BROCCOLI: *Oh!* They *have* never been doubted before *today*.

DAVID: It *is* the fault of the calendar. It *does* not bear much relationship to the passage of time.

BROCCOLI: *Has* it gone by without *our* knowing it?

DAVID: That's right. All the mistakes *have* shortened the time considerably.

BROCCOLI: How much longer *have we* got left?

DAVID: *I've* worked it out and it *comes* to about two and a half days.

BROCCOLI: What *will* happen then?

DAVID: *I do* not suppose there *will* be any lessons *this* Thursday. *Do* not worry, Mr. Smith.

Begin your answer:

David told Broccoli that . . .

Exercise 3. The play-script in this chapter is full of incomplete sentences. Some of these are commands, where the subject "you" is naturally "understood":

Get out!

Some are exclamations, which do not always need to be full sentences with subject and verb:

NO BOYS ALLOWED!

Some are stage directions, which are often written in note form, without main verbs:

BROCCOLI's room: A bare and miserable room with the bed unmade.

Some are questions, which again are often reduced to one or two words:

Yes? And then?

Some are interrupted sentences:

Those figures . . . are not strictly accurate.

And a number are the kind of incomplete sentences common in conversation, which are, strictly speaking, wrong in formal written English:

A sort of honour really.

Discuss the following further examples from the passage. In which of the above categories would you place each? Where sentences are incomplete, how would you complete them?

(a) An interruption. In my quarters!

(b) (*Pause.*)

(c) What?

(d) A storm.

(e) Lightning and that sort of thing.

(f) The finish!

(g) The last men in the world!

(h) Have a sandwich.

(i) All right.

(j) Good market down our way.

(k) Paper what?

(l) Never speaks of it.

(m) Good night, Mr. Smith.

(n) *Broccoli's room.*

(o) Look at us!

Exercise 4. We saw in Book Two that phrases can do the work of adjectives. Phrases are groups of words (without a verb of their own) which take the place of an adjective, an adverb or a noun. Thus, when David says:

(i) It's the fault *of the calendar*;

"of the calendar", as a unit, is describing the fault, answering the question "what kind of fault?" What noun is described by these phrases (in italics)?

(ii) The last men *in the world*.

(iii) Broccoli had a canary in a large cage *made by himself*.

(iv) David is looking, *squinting against the sun*.

In some cases, sentences can be reconstructed so that a single adjective or a possessive noun replaces the phrase:

(i) It's the *calendar's* fault.

(ii) Broccoli had a canary in a large, *home-made* cage.

In the following exercise, rewrite the sentences so that the adjective phrases are replaced by single adjectives (of approximately the same meaning) or by possessive nouns. In sentences (a) to (e) the phrase has been put in italics, but in the remainder you have to find the adjective phrase yourself.

(a) That time-table *of yours* hasn't recognised the fact.

(b) The calendar is not related to the passage *of time*.

(c) We shall be the last men *in the world*.

(d) There's a good market *down our way*.

(e) He was the world-famed Paper Doll *of West Ham*.

(f) Broccoli is standing at the open window of his room.

(g) He opens the door of his bird-cage.

(h) David's face is impassive in his moment of triumph.

(i) Thursday morning's going to be the ending of the world.

(j) The boy crouched over a model aeroplane with an engine.

1. Most newspapers include reviews of plays, films and television programmes as a regular feature. Make a varied selection of reviews and study them. What do you consider is the job of a critic? Is he mainly supposed to "criticise", or should he encourage and praise wherever possible? Is his job different when he is dealing with (a) a play that will be running for some time, (b) a television programme that was broadcast the previous night and (c) an amateur production of a play that was put on last week? And by what standards does he judge: the popular ones of simple enjoyment, the discriminating ones of his more experienced and well-educated readers, or the expert ones of those who are themselves actors, writers or directors?

Think about these questions, and set yourself up as an amateur critic of the theatre, cinema or television. Choose one play, film or television series and begin by giving a *short* account of it: who it is by, what (briefly!) is the plot, what *kind* of entertainment it is trying to be. Then try to judge it by its *own* standards. Compare it with other plays or films that are similar, whether better or less successful. Refer to the style of acting and the details of production (scenes, costumes, music, camera-work, etc.) in so far as they helped or hindered the director in getting the effect you think he wanted. Remember that it is unfair to criticise a work for not doing something it did not set out to do.

Round off your review with a personal opinion.

2. Write a play, or short story or a poem on the theme of a weak but intelligent person and his relationship with a tough, strong but rather stupid person. There are many traditional tales of this kind: e.g. David and Goliath, Samson and Delilah, Jack and the Giant of the Beanstalk, Aesop's fable of the mouse and the lion; and Steinbeck's story *Of Mice and Men* develops very effectively the idea that two such characters might become dependent on each other. Any of these might give you some idea for a plot. Much of the interest should be in the contrast between the characters.

77

Oral Work

If a tape recorder is available for members of the class to use, it might be a good idea to start making a tape-recorded magazine programme. Some suggestions in earlier chapters might be incorporated: the running commentary, the comic sketches, discussions and talks on matters of interest. No doubt the class will think of many more possible items: reviews (especially where they can be illustrated from the sound-track of TV or radio programmes or with records), interviews and "on-the-spot" enquiries (for example, a "sample" of pupils and staff could be questioned about school dinners or the school's attitude to sport), short plays, satires imitating well-known TV or radio series in order to make fun of them, comic advertisements, poems read by their authors, and so on.

Test each suggestion to see if it will be effective when *heard* (rather than seen), whether it is practicable, and whether there is a group of the class keen enough to do it well. Tape-recording is inclined to take a long while, and much of it will probably have to be done outside lesson time!

Elect a committee to co-ordinate the group efforts. Much organisation is needed to get pieces into a suitable order with some good theme music and full announcements. Much will depend on the technicians, and whether they can arrange to fade music in and out and get a correct sound balance, without any awkward pauses.

When finished, such a magazine could be played back to other classes or to parents or friends of the school.

Activities and Research

The history of the theatre offers some fascinating subjects for research. Drama in the Far East and in Ancient Greece arose out of religious ceremonies, and developed into a complex tradition with its own conventions—such as masks worn by actors, and prescribed forms for plays (comedies, tragedies, heroic plays), and choruses of men or women that danced or sang. The theatres, too, developed in size and design, with the Romans modifying those built by the Greeks.

In England an entirely new form of drama developed in the Middle Ages, again beginning in the churches, with Bible stories, and leading to plays performed by amateurs acting on carts that were pulled round the streets of medieval cities on Corpus Christi Day. These "pageants" in turn influenced the first permanent theatres, built in Shakespeare's day by companies of actors who were used to touring and playing in the open courts of inns.

There are many topics here for illustrated accounts, each of which could be a chapter in a folder of work recounting the history of the theatre.

Look up *The Oxford Junior Encyclopaedia* index headings Drama and Theatre, and find similar references in other encyclopaedias. Look under the catalogue number 792, *Theatre*, in your local library for books on this subject. Always look through the contents list of any book you find, to see if it is likely to be helpful, and refer to the index to find the particular references you require.

Further Reading

David and Broccoli from *Lunch Hour and Other Plays* by
JOHN MORTIMER (Methuen)
In the introduction to another book of his plays, John Mortimer wrote:
"Comedy is, to my mind, the only thing worth writing in this despairing age, providing it is comedy which is truly on the side of the lonely, the neglected and unsuccessful . . .". The same principle can be seen in "David and Broccoli"; and if you enjoyed this try *Three Plays* by John Mortimer (Elek Books), containing "The Dock Brief", "What Shall We Tell Caroline?" and "I Spy". (822.08)

Seven Stages by GEOFFREY TREASE (Heinemann)
Seven brief biographies illustrate various stages and aspects of the theatre, from Christopher Marlowe to Anna Pavlova, written by an experienced historical writer. (927.92)

Shakespeare's Theatre by C. W. HODGES (O.U.P.)
Here is a superbly illustrated book on the history of the theatre up to and including Shakespeare's time. The text is brief but informative. (792)

The Stage as a Career by CLIFFORD TURNER (Museum Press)
This is a full account of the necessary background, the courses and the opportunities for the actor today, including work in films, radio and television, and behind the scenes. (371.425)

79

CHAPTER SIX

The Living Past

We passed very slowly through the woods, partly because Lord John acted as scout before he would let us advance, and partly because at every second step one or other of our professors would fall, with a cry of wonder, before some flower or insect which presented him with a new type. We may have travelled two or three miles in all, keeping to the right of the line of the stream, when we came upon a considerable opening in the trees. A belt of brushwood led up to a tangle of rocks—the whole plateau was strewn with boulders. We were walking slowly towards these rocks, among bushes which reached over our waists, when we became aware of a strange low gabbling and whistling sound, which filled the air with a constant clamour and appeared to come from some spot immediately before us. Lord John held up his hand as a signal for us to stop, and he made his way swiftly, stooping and running, to the line of rocks. We saw him peep over them and give a gesture of amazement. Then he stood staring as if forgetting us, so utterly entranced was he by what he saw. Finally he waved us to come on, holding up his hand as a signal for caution. His whole bearing made me feel that something wonderful but dangerous lay before us.

Creeping to his side, we looked over the rocks. The place into which we gazed was a pit, and may, in the early days, have been one of the smaller volcanic blow-holes of the plateau. It was bowl-shaped, and at the bottom, some hundreds of yards from where we lay, were pools of green-scummed, stagnant water, fringed with bulrushes. It was a weird place in itself, but its occupants made it seem like a scene from the Seven Circles of Dante. The place was a rookery of pterodactyls. There were hundreds of them congregated within view. All the bottom area round the water-edge was alive with their young ones, and with hideous mothers brooding upon their leathery, yellowish eggs. From this crawling flapping mass of obscene reptilian life came the shocking clamour which filled the air and the mephitic, horrible, musty odour which turned us sick. But above, perched each upon its own stone, tall, grey, and withered, more like dead and dried specimens than actual living creatures, sat the horrible males, absolutely motionless save for the rolling of their red eyes or an occasional snap of their rat-trap beaks as a dragonfly went past them. Their huge, membranous wings were closed by folding their fore-arms, so that they sat like gigantic old women, wrapped in hideous web-coloured shawls, and with their ferocious heads protruding above them. Large and small, not less than a thousand of these filthy creatures lay in the hollow before us.

Our professors would gladly have stayed there all day, so entranced were they by this opportunity of studying the life of a prehistoric age. They pointed out the fish and dead birds lying about among the rocks as proving the nature of the food of these creatures, and I heard them congratulating each other on having cleared up the point why the bones of this flying dragon are found in such great numbers in certain well-defined areas, as in the Cambridge Green-sand, since it was now seen that, like penguins, they lived in gregarious fashion.

Finally, however, Challenger, bent upon proving some point which Summerlee had contested, thrust his head over the rock and nearly brought destruction upon us all. In an instant the nearest male gave a shrill, whistling cry, and flapped its twenty-foot span of leathery wings as it soared up into the air. The females and young ones huddled together beside the water, while the whole circle of sentinels rose one after the other and sailed off into the sky. It was a wonderful sight to see at least a hundred creatures of such enormous size and hideous appearance all swooping like swallows with swift, shearing wing-strokes above us; but soon we realised that it was not one on which we could afford to linger. At first the great brutes flew round in a huge ring, as if to make sure what the exact extent of the danger might be. Then, the flight grew lower and the circle narrower, until they were whizzing round and round us, the dry, rustling flap of their huge slate-coloured wings filling the air with a volume of sound that made me think of Hendon aerodrome upon a race day.

"Make for the wood and keep together," cried Lord John, clubbing his rifle. "The brutes mean mischief."

The moment we attempted to retreat the circle closed in upon us, until the tips of the wings of those nearest to us nearly touched our faces. We beat at them with the stocks of our guns, but there was nothing solid or vulnerable to strike. Then suddenly out of the whizzing, slate-coloured circle a long neck shot out, and a fierce beak made a thrust at us. Another and another followed. Summerlee gave a cry and put his hand to his face, from which the blood was streaming. I felt a prod at the back of my neck, and turned dizzy with the shock. Challenger fell, and as I stooped to pick him up I was again struck from behind, and dropped on the top of him. At the same instant I heard the crash of Lord John's elephant-gun, and, looking up, saw one of the creatures with a broken wing struggling upon the ground, spitting and gurgling at us with a wide-opened beak and blood-shot, goggled eyes, like some devil in a mediaeval picture. Its comrades had flown higher at the sudden sound, and were circling above our heads.

"Now," cried Lord John, "now for our lives!"

We staggered through the brushwood, and even as we reached the trees the harpies were on us again. Summerlee was knocked down, but we tore him up and rushed among the trunks. Once there we were safe, for those huge wings had no space for their sweep beneath the branches. As we limped homewards, sadly mauled and discomfited, we saw them for a long time flying at a great height against the deep blue sky above our heads, soaring round and round, no bigger than woodpigeons, with their eyes no doubt still following our progress. At last, however, as we reached the thicker woods they gave up the chase, and we saw them no more.

(from *The Lost World* by Sir Arthur Conan Doyle)

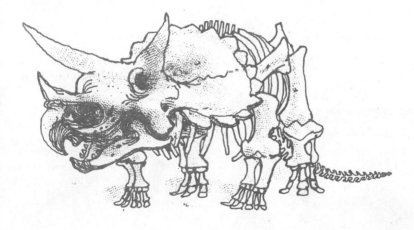

Comprehension and Discussion

1. In what ways does Lord John act as a leader in this incident? Does he seem to be effective as a leader in any particular respects?

2. Do Summerlee and Challenger appear to disagree easily? Is there something comic about their behaviour here?

3. What do you imagine "brushwood", a "volcanic blow-hole" and the "Cambridge Green-sand" to be?

4. Explain what is meant by each of these words and phrases:

a gesture of amazement   in gregarious fashion
obscene reptilian life   clubbing his rifle
mephitic   the stocks of our guns
membranous wings   vulnerable
protruding   sadly mauled and discomfited

5. Show how various details, and the choice of words and of comparisons, are used to emphasise that the pterodactyls were extremely unpleasant.

6. Find out more about Dante's "Inferno" (in his "Divine Comedy"), and how he imagines himself visiting Hell and seeing the bird-like monsters, "the harpies", in the "seventh circle". How are the pterodactyls like "harpies"?

7. Compare Sir Arthur Conan Doyle's style in this passage with John Steinbeck's in the passage from *The Red Pony* (pages 9-10). What differences and similarities are there?

For Written Answers

Answer in complete sentences and (as far as possible) in your own words. Do *not* begin answers with: "Because . . ."

1. What, normally, is a "rookery"?

2. How does modern man know what pterodactyls, long since extinct, looked like?

3. Why does the author call the pterodactyls "reptilian"?

4. Why did the explorers run to the woods?

5. Which of the explorers were hurt by the attacking pterodactyls, and in what ways?

6. Write in your own words, a clear and full summary of the shape, size, colour, eyes, food, breeding habits and general way of life of pterodactyls, according to this passage.

84

Humming-Bird

I can imagine, in some other world
Primeval-dumb, far back
In that most awful stillness, that only gasped and
      hummed,
Humming-birds raced down the avenues.

Before anything had a soul,
While life was a heave of Matter, half inanimate,
This little bit chipped off in brilliance
And went whizzing through the slow, vast, succulent
      stems.

I believe there were no flowers then,
In the world where the humming-bird flashed ahead of
      creation.
I believe he pierced the slow vegetable veins with his
      long beak.

Probably he was big
As mosses, and little lizards, they say, were once big.
Probably he was a jabbing, terrifying monster.

We look at him through the wrong end of the long
      telescope of Time,
Luckily for us.

D. H. LAWRENCE

85

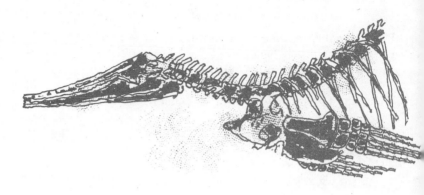

Discussing The Poem

1. What does this poem tell us of the size, call, colour and habits of the humming-bird today? Find a fuller account of the bird in a reference book.

2. What do the last two lines of the poem mean? Is it the humming-bird or some larger distant ancestor of it that Lawrence imagines existing in prehistoric times?

3. What, according to the poem, are the differences between the prehistoric world and the natural world of today?

Method Exercises

Exercise 1. The passage from *The Lost World* makes interesting use of long and complicated sentences. Notice how Sir Arthur Conan Doyle tends to use longer and more involved sentences when the party is moving slowly and examining the wonderful creatures and their habits, and then shorter or simpler sentences to describe the excitement of the attack:

  e.g. "Another and another followed."

Rewrite the following groups of short sentences so that each becomes *one* sentence, if possible joined more interestingly than with the simplest *conjunctions* like "and, but, or".

(a) We may have travelled two or three miles in all.
    We were keeping to the right of the line of the stream.
    We then came upon a considerable opening in the trees.

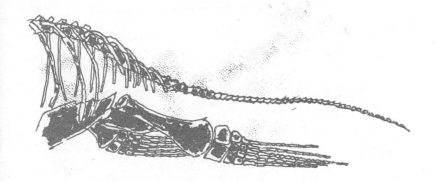

(b) We were walking slowly towards these rocks.
We were walking among bushes.
These bushes reached over our waists.
Then we became aware of a strange low gabbling and whistling sound.
This filled the air with a constant clamour.
It appeared to come from a spot immediately before us.

(c) But above sat the horrible males.
Each was perched upon its own stone.
Each was tall, grey, and withered.
They were more like dead and dried specimens than actual living creatures.
They were almost absolutely motionless.
But they did roll their red eyes.
Or they did occasionally snap their rat-trap beaks as a dragon-fly went past them.

(d) They pointed out the fish and dead birds lying about among the rocks.
These proved the nature of the food of these creatures.
I heard them congratulating each other on having cleared up a point.
The point was why the bones of this flying dragon are found in such great numbers in certain well-defined areas.
One example was in the Cambridge Green-sand.
It was now seen that they lived in gregarious fashion.
They resembled penguins in this.

All of these examples are based on long sentences in the passage.
Compare your own answers with those on pages 81-82.

Exercise 2. Similes and *metaphors* are both forms of comparison for the sake of effect. In both, dissimilar things are compared in one or more particular respects. If the things compared are indeed actually similar, this is a *literal comparison*, and it is useful rather than effective.

> The female pterodactyls had wings like the males;

is a literal comparison. But:

> Their wings were like vast, leathery umbrellas;

is a simile. A metaphor is a compressed simile, in which one thing is assumed to be another, for the purposes of comparison:

> They stretched the vast, leathery umbrellas of their wings over us.

(a) Find *similes* in the passage that describe the following:

> The appearance of the hollow with its weird occupants.
> The motionless appearance of the perched males.
> How the males looked, sitting with their wings folded.
> How the males swooped.
> The great noise of their flapping wings.
> The angry pterodactyl with the broken wing.

(b) Find *metaphors* in the passage that describe the following:

> The appearance of the bottom of the hollow and the young pterodactyls.
> The snapping beaks of the perched males.
> The way the males left their perches.
> The males, when attacking as the men reached the trees.

(c) Make up comparisons of your own to describe each of the items in (a) and (b), remembering to suggest a similarity in *several* particular respects wherever you can.

Exercise 3. The HYPHEN (-) is used both to break words, for convenience when writing or typing, and to form *new* words by compounding two (or more) existing words together.

When you are forced to use a hyphen to break a word (at the end of a line of writing), always do so at a natural break between syllables, as with "wonderful" on page 86:

> e.g. wonderful: wonder-ful, *or* won-derful
> (but *never* wonderfu-l)

88

(a) Which of the following examples of compounds in the passage are adjectives, and which nouns?

blow-holes	dragon-fly	twenty-foot	wide-opened
bowl-shaped	web-coloured	wing-strokes	blood-shot
green-scummed	well-defined	slate-coloured	wood-pigeons
rat-trap	Green-sand	elephant-gun	

(b) With the help of a dictionary you can form from "low":

low-grade	low-pressure	low-arched	low-priced
low-rented	low-necked	low-lying	low-church
low-slung	low-level	low-loader	low-down
low-bred	low-brow	low-pitched	low-spirited, etc.

Form as many compounds as you can from the following:

soft; long; hand; ship; turn.

It is often effective to make up new compound words for particular use in a description or poem. D. H. Lawrence has done this in using "primeval-dumb" in the poem, *Humming-Bird*.

Exercise 4. The term CLAUSE is used for a part of a sentence which, having its own subject and verb, is almost a sentence itself but does not make complete sense. Like *phrases*, many clauses act as adjectives, adverbs or nouns within longer sentences, e.g.:

1. We were walking among *waist-high* bushes.

2. We were walking among bushes *reaching over our waists*.

3. We were walking among bushes *which reached over our waists*.

In 1. an adjective describes "bushes"; in 2. it is an adjective phrase ("reaching" is an adjective, and not a true verb, since it has no subject); in 3. an adjective clause describes "bushes" ("which", standing for bushes, is the subject of the true verb "reached"—yet the sentence already has its main subject "we" and verb "were walking").

What noun is described by the adjective clause in the following example?

4. We became aware of a strange low gabbling sound *which filled the air with a constant clamour*.

In the next example overleaf the adjective clause comes *in between* the main subject and the rest of the main sentence (or MAIN CLAUSE). What is the adjective clause?

5. The place into which we gazed was a pit.

Adjective clauses are usually introduced by:

who, whom, which, that, whose.

Can you remember from Book Two the different uses for these pronouns (e.g. "who" always refers to people)?

In the following sentences, six of which are adapted from the passage, pick out the adjective clause and say what noun it is describing.

(a) From this mass of reptiles came a clamour which filled the air.

(b) From the mass came a horrible, musty odour which turned us sick.

(c) Challenger was bent on proving some point which Summerlee had contested.

(d) It was not a sight on which we could afford to linger.

(e) The flap of their wings filled the air with a volume of sound that made me think of Hendon aerodrome.

(f) Summerlee put his hand to his face from which the blood was streaming.

(g) The others owed their lives to Lord John, who had an elephant gun.

(h) Lord John, who was acting as scout, beckoned us to come.

(i) Our professors, for whom this was a unique opportunity to study prehistoric creatures, would gladly have stayed there all day.

(j) Some of the pterodactyls that we saw had a wing span of 20 feet.

Writing Your Own

1. Though they will not be as sensational as the visit to the "Lost World", most of us have opportunities to visit museums, exhibitions, castles, churches, old houses or other places of interest. Choose one such visit, or place, or one particular exhibit or section in a museum, and attempt a description that will arouse the reader's imagination, so that he shares your interest and excitement, and at the same time will give the reader as complete a picture, with all the necessary detail and background information, as possible.

Do not attempt too much. If you choose to describe a visit to a castle, leave out the details of the journey there, and concentrate on the appearance and atmosphere of the place, and on its history (as far as you know it), especially in so far as it is reflected in relics that can still be seen today. Although your personal reactions may be interesting, remember that this is really description, not a story about yourself.

2. In *Humming-Bird*, D. H. Lawrence has studied the bird, letting his imagination ponder over it as if it were a vast prehistoric creature. Take any familiar bird, insect, fish, or small animal, and study it in this way yourself. Work out words (new compounds, if you can) appropriate to its markings, movements and features. Think of comparisons and vivid phrases to capture its characteristic movements or habits. Try to weld these into a free verse poem, as in this example by a pupil.

Lizard

Rigid like a frozen rock,
Eyes black with mystery,
Like sharp pinpoints at the distant end of a cave,
Heart beating, slowly, soundly,
Long claws straining tightly as it clenches to a rock,
Long tail growing like an endless frozen branch,
Pale green body, beady, slimy, careful;
Its prey is seen,
Its clever head moves, but only for a split second,
It seeks stealthily towards it,
Then, as fast as a swift arrow its tongue flicks out.
Its prey is caught,
Without a chance its prey is devoured as its great thin
        teeth crunch together.

                                    CHRISTOPHER

91

Oral Work

1. Act the incident in the passage. It will probably be most effective to imagine the pterodactyls, even when they are attacking the party: it is then up to the group acting to suggest how enormous and horrible they are by the vividness of their acting.

2. Choose the best of the animal poems written by the class and let the authors practise reading them aloud. Now try to find some appropriate music to reflect the mood and the action of each poem. Practice will be necessary to match the reading to the music, since the speech will probably have to be varied, often with pauses to allow the music to be heard. Poems set to exciting music will make an excellent item in the tape-recorded magazine, but you will need time to experiment to get the balance of volume between speaker and music (whether live or recorded) correct.

Activities and Research

1. Arrange a class visit to a local museum, castle, country house or other place of interest. Prepare for this with research about the place you are going to and the things you will see, so that you know what to look for. Make sketches and notes during the visit, so that you can write a full report on the visit, or one aspect or item you studied, when you return.

2. Groups of the class could do research on prehistory: the various evolving plants and creatures, early ape-men and cave-men, how the geographical features of the world were formed, fossils, the Great Ice-Age, the evolution of minerals, and so on. The sections from 550 to 573 in the library should have numerous books on these topics, and all encyclopaedias include articles and illustrations under these headings. The results should make an interesting, illustrated folder.

The Lost World by SIR ARTHUR CONAN DOYLE (Murray)
Whilst on the strange plateau, the explorers encounter not only
pterodactyls, but a host of other prehistoric animals, including
carnivorous dinosaurs, and they also become involved in the
struggle between a tribe of ape-men and a tribe of Indians.
Here, as in the *Sherlock Holmes* stories for which he is most
famous, Sir Arthur Conan Doyle reveals his genius for strong
characterisation, bringing to life in vivid detail the inhabitants
of the "lost world" and maintaining an irresistible suspense.

The Mark of the Horse Lord by ROSEMARY SUTCLIFF (O.U.P.)
Set among the conflicting Scottish tribes at the time of the
Roman occupation of England, this story is gripping to read
and thoroughly convincing. As in all the author's excellent
historical novels, the characters seem real, yet fit cleverly into
our historical knowledge of the time.

The Dream Time by HENRY TREECE (Brockhampton)
The last story that Henry Treece wrote has the earliest setting: a
time when primitive men were enslaved by fear, superstition
and ignorance, so that a boy who wanted to draw pictures was a
wonder, to be either hated or reverenced. Many of Henry Treece's
stories are about early history, such as: *The Dark Island* (Bodley
Head) or *Vinland the Good* (Penguin).

The Wonderful World of Prehistoric Animals by WILLIAM ELGIN
SWINTON (Macdonald)
This is the story of prehistoric animals, from the first tiny one-
celled creatures that existed 3000 million years ago to the
woolly rhinoceroses and cave bears that Stone Age men hunted
30 000 years ago. The information is presented clearly and con-
cisely, and the many coloured illustrations add even more interest and excitement to the record. (562). *The Story of Evolution*
by Sir Julian Huxley (575) and *Archaeology* by Ronald Jessup
(913) are two other relevant books in this excellent series.

In 1942, on her thirteenth birthday, Anne Frank started a diary. Shortly afterwards, some Dutch friends helped the Franks to go into hiding from the Germans. There they were joined by four other Jewish refugees (including Peter Van Daan, who was only 15). In this close confinement Anne grew up, recording all she felt in her diary.

CHAPTER SEVEN

A Personal Diary

Saturday, 20th June, 1942

I haven't written for a few days, because I wanted first of all to think about my diary. It's an odd idea for someone like me to keep a diary; not only because I have never done so before, but because it seems to me that neither I—nor for that matter anyone else—will be interested in the unbosomings of a thirteen-year old schoolgirl. Still, what does that matter? I want to write, but more than that, I want to bring out all kinds of things that lie buried deep in my heart . . .

I don't intend to show this cardboard-covered notebook, bearing the proud name of "diary", to anyone, unless I find a real friend, boy or girl, probably nobody cares. And now I come to the root of the matter, the reason for my starting a diary; it is that I have no such real friend . . .

I know about thirty people whom one might call friends—I have strings of boy friends, anxious to catch a glimpse of me and who, failing that, peep at me through mirrors in class. I have relations, aunts and uncles, who are darlings too, a good home, no—I don't seem to lack anything. But it's the same with all my friends, just fun and games, nothing more. I can never bring myself to talk of anything outside the common round. We don't seem to be able to get any closer, that is the root of the trouble. Perhaps I lack confidence, but anyway, there it is, a stubborn fact and I don't seem to be able to do anything about it.

Hence this diary. In order to enhance in my mind's eye the picture of the friend for whom I have waited so long, I don't want to set down a series of bald facts in a diary like most people do, but I want this diary itself to be my friend, and I shall call my friend Kitty . . .

*   *   *   *   *

Dear Kitty,

I expect you will be interested to hear what it feels like to "disappear"; well, all I can say is that I don't know myself yet. I don't think I shall ever feel really at home in this house, but that does not mean that I loathe it here, it is more like being on holiday in a very peculiar boarding-house. Rather a mad idea, perhaps, but that is how it strikes me. The "Secret Annexe" is an ideal hiding-place. Although it leans to one side and is damp, you'd never find such a comfortable hiding-place anywhere in Amsterdam; no, perhaps not even in the whole of Holland. Our little room looked very bare at first with nothing on the walls; but thanks to Daddy who had brought my film-star collection and picture postcards on beforehand, and with the aid of paste-pot and brush, I have transformed the walls into one gigantic picture . . .

There are some large business premises on the right of us, and on the left a furniture workshop; there is no one there after working hours but, even so, sounds could travel through the walls. We have forbidden Margot to cough at night, although she has a bad cold, and make her swallow large doses of codeine. I am longing for Tuesday when the Van Daans arrive; it will be much more fun and not so quiet. It is the silence that frightens me so in the evenings and at night. I wish like anything that one of our protectors could sleep here at night. I can't tell you how oppressive it is never to be able to go outdoors, also I'm scared to death that we shall be discovered and be shot. That is not exactly a pleasant prospect. We have to whisper and tread lightly during the day, otherwise, the people in the warehouse might hear us . . .

Yours, ANNE.

*   *   *   *   *

Dear Kitty,

Margot and I are getting a bit tired of our parents. Don't misunderstand me, I can't get on well with Mummy at the moment, as you know. I still love Daddy just as much and Margot loves Daddy and Mummy, but when you are as old as we are, you do want to decide just a few things for yourself, you want to be independent sometimes.

If I go upstairs, then I'm asked what I'm going to do, I'm not allowed salt with my food, every evening regularly at a quarter-past eight Mummy asks whether I ought not to start undressing, every book I read must be inspected. I must admit that they are not at all strict, and I'm allowed to read nearly everything, and yet we are both sick of all the remarks plus all the questioning that go on the whole day long.

Something else, especially about me, that doesn't please them: I don't feel like giving lots of kisses any more and I think fancy pet names are frightfully affected. In short, I'd really like to be rid of them for a while. Margot said last evening, "I think it's awfully annoying, the way they ask if you've got a headache, or whether you don't feel well, if you happen to give a sigh and put your hand to your head!"

It is a great blow to us both, suddenly to realise how little remains of the confidence and harmony that we used to have at home. And it's largely due to the fact that we're all "skew-wiff" here. By this I mean that we are treated as children over outward things, while inwardly we are much older than most girls of our age.

Although I'm only fourteen, I know quite well what I want, I know who is right and who is wrong. I have my opinions, my own ideas and principles, and although it may sound pretty mad from an adolescent, I feel more of a person than a child, I feel quite independent of anyone.

I know that I can discuss things and argue better than Mummy, I know I'm not so prejudiced, I don't exaggerate so much, I am more precise and adroit and because of this—you may laugh—I feel superior to her over a great many things. If I love anyone, above all I must have admiration for them, admiration and respect. Everything would be all right if only I had Peter, for I do admire him in many ways. He is such a nice, good-looking boy!

Yours, ANNE.

(from *The Diary of Anne Frank* by Anne Frank)

Comprehension and Discussion

1. What apparently would have happened to the Franks if they had been discovered by the Nazi authorities?

2. Discuss what you know of the way the Nazi Germans treated the Jews before and during the Second World War. What risks do you think the Franks' "protectors" (who were not Jews) were running?

3. In what way does Anne's diary take the place of a real friend? Are there any ways in which a diary might be better than a real friend?

4. Should a diary of this kind be completely secret? Would it have been wrong, for instance, for Anne's parents to have looked at it if they had found it in her room?

5. In the third extract here, Anne is nearly 15. Does this account for her attitude to her parents?

6. Were Anne's parents lacking in love or concern for their children's welfare? How did they fail?

7. In what ways do you think the confinement to the "Secret Annexe" made everything "skew-wiff"? Would the experience make Anne and Margot maturer than other girls of their age? Would the strain of this life in secrecy justify their parents' strict control over them?

8. Would you expect Anne's assessment of herself, in this diary, to be honest and accurate?

9. Anne had wanted a close friend for years and later turned increasingly to Peter Van Daan. Would you expect this to help her relations with her parents? Would you expect a close relationship with a boy to take the place of a diary?

10. Should parents control the choice of books (or films or TV programmes) for their 14-year-old children?

For Written Answers

1. Why did Anne give her diary a name?

2. In what town and what kind of area in the town were the Franks hiding?

3. Why was Margot "forbidden to cough"?

4. What was underneath and on either side of the "Secret Annexe"?

5. In your opinion had Anne any good reasons to feel superior to her mother?

6. List, in your own words, Anne's parents' faults, as she saw them.

7. In your own words, try to give Anne's parents' point of view about their children, and especially Anne.

Method Exercises

All *pronouns* stand in place of nouns. In Book Two we considered the *personal pronouns*:

Singular: I, me; you; he, him; she, her; it.
Plural: we, us; you; they, them.

But there are many other pronouns, and most of these have an equivalent *adjective* form, or in many cases can be used as adjectives without any change. They are pronouns when they stand by themselves, usually as subjects or objects, for particular nouns:

Hers is *one* of the books about the Second World War that *everyone* should read.

They are adjectives when they accompany nouns and help to describe them:

Her diary is *one* book about the Second World War that *every* young person should read.

What nouns do "hers", "one" and "everyone" stand for in the first example? And what nouns do "her", "one" and "every" describe in the second example?

99

Exercise 1. Make up sentences (one or two for each) using the words given below in the way indicated:

e.g. *"Either"* as a *pronoun*: There are two answers and *either* is correct.

"Either" as an *adjective*: *Either* route will lead you there.

(a) "anyone" as a pronoun, and "any" as an adjective;
(b) "yours" as a pronoun, and "your" as an adjective;
(c) "this" as a pronoun, and "this" as an adjective;
(d) "mine" as a pronoun, and "my" as an adjective;
(e) "each" as a pronoun, and "each" as an adjective;
(f) "both" as a pronoun, and "both" as an adjective;
(g) "who" as a pronoun, and "whose" as an adjective.

Exercise 2. In the following passage, 11 of the 20 words in italics are pronouns, and 9 are adjectives. Write out the words, stating (a) whether they are pronouns or adjectives, and (b) what noun they stand for (if pronouns) or describe (if adjectives).

Anne Frank and *her* family moved into *their* hiding place in July, 1942. *She* describes *this* in *her* diary. *It* was in the sealed-off back rooms of an office in Amsterdam, where *they* lived, and *no one* knew of *its* whereabouts except *some* Dutch friends of *theirs*, *who* had offered to help *them*. At *this* time the Nazis, *whose* troops had occupied Holland, were deporting *all* Jews to *their* concentration camps in Germany. *Some* escaped or hid, but *many* died in *those* terrible places.

Exercise 3. In the first of the diary extracts, dashes are used four times as punctuation. The first two are a pair, marking a comment *in parenthesis*:

It seems to me that neither I—nor for that matter anyone else—will be interested in the unbosomings of a thirteen-year old schoolgirl.

Can you find an even clearer example of this use of dashes in the last diary extract?

The other dashes in the first extract are used singly, to mark an expansion of what has gone before, or an afterthought or conclusion:

—I don't seem to lack anything.

(a) Dashes are stronger and more definite punctuation marks than commas, brackets or semicolons. Discuss each of the following uses—are the dashes to mark parenthesis or an afterthought? What would be the effect of using commas, brackets or semicolons instead?

(i) A belt of brushwood led up to a tangle of rocks—the whole plateau was strewn with boulders.

(ii) The basis for action was still the need to improve the condition of the worst slums rather than to improve the housing of the population in general—to cure rather than to prevent the evil.

(iii) In 1954 a new survey revealed that 850,000 houses in England and Wales—most of them built before 1880—were in such a bad condition that they ought to be pulled down.

(iv) The old gentleman leaned back in his chair and lighted an enormous meerschaum pipe—Good gracious, he breathes fire, thought the Wart, who had never heard of tobacco—before he was ready to reply. Then he looked puzzled, took off his skull cap—three mice fell out—and scratched the middle of his bald head.

(v) Remember crowds are very fickle but they love a winning team, and a footballer that plays the game and gives them what they have paid to see—pure football. In future you'll make many more mistakes, but don't let them upset you—learn from them, but keep your mental outlook undisturbed; you'll also have some fine successes—learn from them too, by keeping your head.

(b) Rewrite the following, completing the sentences in what seems an appropriate way after the dashes indicated. You may insert further dashes if you wish. Make sure that you write your dashes clearly, so that they do not look like hyphens.

(i) There is one golden rule for success, and that is—

(ii) The room was piled high with equipment—not

(iii) Anne Frank—

(iv) Living today, we have many advantages—

(v) They heard the German Security Police pulling at the bookcase that concealed the door—

Exercise 4. When two complete sentences (two main clauses) are put into one sentence (and not joined by conjunctions such as "and, but, or" etc.), they should be divided by a semicolon. Anne Frank (or the translator of her diary) makes a mistake over this in the following sentences from the passage. Rewrite them, changing the commas to semicolons wherever you think this necessary:

(a) I don't think I shall ever feel really at home in this house, but that does not mean that I loathe it here, it is more like being on holiday in a very peculiar boarding-house.

(b) Don't misunderstand me, I can't get on well with Mummy at the moment, as you know.

(c) If I go upstairs, then I'm asked what I'm going to do, I'm not allowed salt with my food, every evening regularly at a quarter past eight Mummy asks whether I ought not to start undressing, every book I read must be inspected.

(d) Although I am only fourteen, I know quite well what I want, I know who is right and who is wrong.

(e) I have my opinions, my own ideas and principles, and . . . I feel more of a person than a child, I feel quite independent of anyone.

(f) I know that I can discuss things and argue better than Mummy, I know I'm not so prejudiced, I don't exaggerate so much, I am more precise and adroit and because of this —you may laugh—I feel superior to her over a great many things.

Writing Your Own

1. Anne Frank's diary style is rather different from that of the diary extract in Book Two. She does not use the shortened sentences omitting "I"; and she is in fact much more interested in recording her own feelings and reactions, and in exploring the relationships between herself and other people, than in mere events. For her, a diary is a friend to talk to (one that never answers back!), and a means of sorting out her own ideas.

Work out a story involving a young person in conflict with his parents, or with other relatives or friends. Look at it from his (or her) point of view, but imagine him being honest enough to admit (to himself) when he is wrong. Then develop this situation through selected diary entries (not necessarily one each day, but one for each important new stage in the story). If you are not basing this simply on real experience, take particular care to make the characters emerge as real people, with complete and consistent backgrounds.

2. Write an essay on *Personal Relationships*. Discuss what qualities people need to get on well together, and what you think the ideal parents, or friends, or teenage children would be like. What are the most frequent causes of family disagreement? Are parents too strict with their 14- and 15-year-old children, or not strict enough? How much money should young people have, how much should they be made to help at home, and should they keep regular hours? Should parents interfere in their children's choice of friends, books, entertainment and political or religious views? Should girls be treated differently from boys?

Make notes on matters like these and arrange these into an interesting and logical order before you begin the essay. Begin with a fairly general opening paragraph, work through a number of more specific topics, paragraph by paragraph, and end with another general, summing up paragraph.

Oral Work

1. Quarrel scenes often make good subjects for impromptu drama. Take a familiar basic situation: for instance, father and mother (with perhaps a grandmother sitting in the rocking chair by the fire) are waiting late in the evening for their son (or daughter) to return. He is an hour late and they do not know where he has been. After some preliminary grumbling, his key is heard in the door . . .

Many other quarrel situations, between friends, or between strangers who annoy one another in the street or on the bus, will occur to members of the class, who can then work them out as short plays.

2. The class can discuss the whole matter of personal relationships (see the suggestions under Writing Your Own, 2) and how to make and keep friends.

Perhaps consider some of the ideas and situations that developed in the acting of quarrel scenes, or any of the following problems:

(a) You have a very close friend who offers to give you something, and to your horror it turns out to be stolen, and from the place where one of your parents works. What do you do now?

(b) One evening you walk back from a youth club, talking to someone of the opposite sex whom you have just met and quite like. Your parents are angry and say they don't want you going about with strange boys (or girls) at your age. They forbid you to go to the club again. Could they be justified? What do you do now?

(c) Bill has no father and his mother has little money with which to bring up Bill (aged 14) and his sister (aged 8). He is discovered stealing money at the shop where he works on Saturdays, in order to buy a present for his little sister. What would you do if you were (i) his mother, (ii) the shop-keeper, (iii) Bill, (iv) a close friend of Bill?

(d) One person you like very much is always quarrelling with another of your best friends, until one of them says you must choose between them. What would you do? How, if at all, would you choose?

Activities and Research

1. If you do not already do so, start keeping a diary regularly, trying to develop it as Anne Frank did, more as a record of thoughts and reactions than as a bare record of events. It is useful to form a habit of writing regularly, but you will no doubt find that some entries will be much fuller than others. For this reason, a thick note-book is probably better than a specially printed diary.

2. The rise of the Nazis to power, the way Germany overran Europe, and the defeat of Hitler in the Second World War, although the subject of many recent books and plays, are already history. Do some research into the facts of this period, including the Nazi persecution of the Jews and the facts about the concentration camps in Germany. Start by looking at the articles on the Second World War (in Vol. 10) and Hitler (Vol. 5) in the *Oxford Junior Encyclopaedia*. Prepare for a class discussion on this topic.

The Diary of Anne Frank by ANNE FRANK (Hutchinson; Vallentine;
   Mitchell; Pan)
Although Anne's story ended tragically in a German concentration camp, there is little that is depressing about her diary,
which is full of life and faith in the future, as well as the joy and
unhappiness involved in growing up and falling in love. (940.5)

I Am David by ANNE HOLM (Methuen; Penguin)
This boy had known no other life except that of the concentration
camp. He escaped into a strange, bewildering world, and set off
on a long journey towards some kind of hope for the future.

The Day of the Bomb by KARL BRUCKNER (Burke)
This is a convincing picture of Hiroshima before and after the
dropping of the atom bomb, and of the men who flew on that
terrible mission of mass destruction. Yet, because it concentrates
on the youth and faith of Shigeo and his little sister Sadako,
this moving story is without bitterness, and not really pessi-
mistic.

Daddy-Long-Legs by JEAN WEBSTER (Hodder & Stoughton;
   Brockhampton; Dent)
Judy Abbott's frank and amusing letters to her unknown bene-
factor, who pays for her college education, have been a favourite
with girls for more than fifty years. The letters tell the whole
story of an orphan growing up and unwittingly falling in love
with her "Daddy-Long-Legs".

This story is set in the future, when all the work is done by machines which can think for themselves and function unattended, although they still rely on basic instructions from men. One day, however, the field-minder machine on an Agricultural Station finds the other machines completely disorganised.

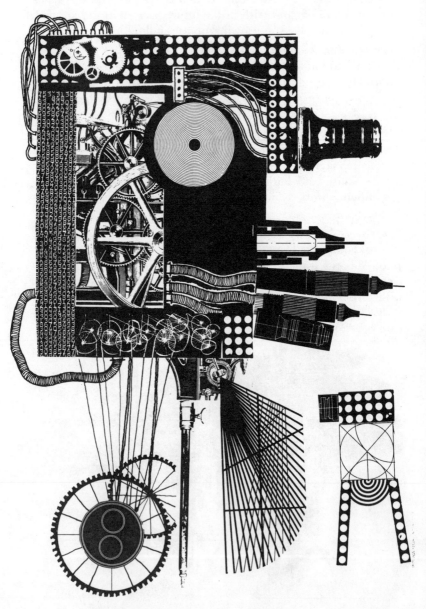

CHAPTER EIGHT

Men and Machines

Steering carefully past them, the field-minder moved over to Warehouse Three and spoke to the seed distributor, which stood idly outside.

"I have a requirement for seed potatoes," it said to the distributor, and with a quick internal motion punched out an order card specifying quantity, field number and several other details. It ejected the card and handed it to the distributor.

The distributor held the card close to its eye and then said, "The requirement is in order; but the store is not yet unlocked. The required seed potatoes are in the store. Therefore I cannot produce the requirement."

Increasingly of late there had been breakdowns in the complex system of machine labour, but this particular hitch had not occurred before. The field-minder thought, then it said, "Why is the store not yet unlocked?"

"Because Supply Operative Type P has not come this morning. Supply Operative Type P is the unlocker."

The field-minder looked squarely at the seed distributor, whose exterior chutes and scales and grabs were so vastly different from the field-minder's own limbs.

"What class brain do you have, seed distributor?" it asked.

"I have a Class Five brain."

"I have a Class Three brain. Therefore I am superior to you. Therefore I will go and see why the unlocker has not come this morning." . . .

The field-minder approached it.

"I can do no more work until Warehouse Three is unlocked," it told the unlocker. "Your duty is to unlock the warehouse every morning. Why have you not unlocked the warehouse this morning?"

"I had no orders this morning," replied the unlocker. "I have to have orders every morning. When I have orders I unlock the warehouse."

"None of us have had any orders this morning," a pen-propeller said, sliding towards them.

"Why have you had no orders this morning?" asked the field-minder.

"Because the radio issued none," said the unlocker, slowly rotating a dozen of its arms.

"Because the radio station in the city was issued with no orders this morning," said the pen-propeller.

And there you had the distinction between a Class Six and a Class Three brain, which was what the unlocker and the pen-propeller possessed respectively. All machine brains worked with nothing but logic, but the lower the class of brain—Class Ten being the lowest—the more literal and less informative answers to questions tended to be.

"You have a Class Three brain; I have a Class Three brain," the field-minder said to the penner. "We will speak to each other. This lack of orders is unprecedented. Have you further information on it?

"Yesterday orders came from the city. Today no orders have come. Yet the radio has not broken down. Therefore *they* have broken down . . ." said the little penner.

"The *men* have broken down?"

"All men have broken down."

"That is a logical deduction," said the field-minder.

"That is the logical deduction," said the penner. "For if a machine had broken down, it would have been quickly replaced. But who can replace a man?"

While they talked, the unlocker, like a dull man at a bar, stood close to them and was ignored.

"If all men have broken down, then we have replaced man," said the field-minder, and he and the penner eyed one another speculatively. Finally the latter said, "Let us ascend to the top floor to find if the radio operator has fresh news."

"I cannot come because I am too large," said the field-minder. "Therefore you must go alone and return to me. You will tell me if the radio operator has fresh news."

"You must stay here," said the penner. "I will return here." It skittered across to the lift. Although it was no bigger than a toaster, its retractable arms numbered ten and it could read as quickly as any machine on the station.

The field-minder awaited its return patiently, not speaking to the unlocker, which still stood aimlessly by. Outside a rotovator hooted furiously. Twenty minutes elapsed before the penner came back, hustling out of the lift . . . .

"What information did you receive from the radio operator?" asked the field-minder.

"The radio operator has been informed by the operator in the city that all men are dead."

The field-minder was momentarily silent, digesting this.

"All men were alive yesterday!" it protested.

"Only some were alive yesterday. And that was fewer than the day before yesterday. For hundreds of years there have been only a few men, growing fewer."

"We have rarely seen a man in this sector."

"The radio operator says a diet deficiency killed them," said the penner. "He says that the world was once over-populated, and then the soil was exhausted in raising adequate food. This has caused a diet deficiency."

"What is a diet deficiency?" asked the field-minder.

"I do not know. But that is what the radio operator said, and he is a Class Two brain."

They stood there, silent in weak sunshine. The unlocker had appeared in the porch and was gazing across at them yearningly, rotating its collection of keys.

"What is happening in the city now?" asked the field-minder at last.

"Machines are fighting in the city now," said the penner.

"What will happen here now?" asked the field-minder.

"Machines may begin fighting here too. The radio operator wants us to get him out of his room. He has plans to communicate to us."

"How can we get him out of his room? That is impossible."

"To a Class Two brain, little is impossible," said the penner. "Here is what he tells us to do . . . ."

(from *Who Can Replace a Man?* a short story by Brian Aldiss)

Comprehension and Discussion

1. What, apparently, was a field-minder capable of doing? What kind of decisions do you think it had to take, with its Class Three brain?

2. Why should a system of machine labour be "complex"? Would manual labour be simpler to organise? If so, why?

3. Why should men be "irreplaceable"? Why should machines "fight" when without further orders?

4. What does it mean to say that "all machine brains worked with nothing but logic"? In what ways are human brains illogical?

5. Is there anything incredible about Class Three brains "speculating"? ("He and the penner eyed one another speculatively.")

6. Explain the distinction between the Class Six and Class Three brains as illustrated when the field-minder asks why they have had no orders.

7. The radio operator was one and a half tons of delicate equipment. How do you think it was going to be removed from its second storey room? Why should it wish to be removed?

8. In what sense are machines today already able to make "decisions"? Do we need to understand machines completely in order to give them "orders"? Do we already have one machine to look after other machines?

9. Do you believe machines will ever be developed to the point where they can think and make decisions? Will they ever be able to take over completely from men? Do you know of stories where this is supposed to happen?

10. Can people be put into categories according to their class of brain? Does this passage suggest that there are slow-minded people, just as there are lower class brains in these machines?

For Written Answers

Answer fully in your own words, giving reasons:

1. What class of brain did the pen-propeller have?

2. How did this influence the pen-propeller's behaviour?

3. What is the difference between saying that "all men were alive yesterday" and that "some men were alive yesterday"?

4. What is a "diet deficiency", and how is it supposed to have come about in this story?

5. Why doesn't the "diet deficiency" apply to the machines? Could the machines in fact have caused the deficiency in some way?

6. Sum up in your own words the differences between Class Six, Class Five, Class Three and Class Two brains as illustrated in this extract.

Method Exercises

Exercise 1. As Brian Aldiss suggests, machines that "think" are bound to be strictly logical. When given certain information, they can make certain deductions:

> The store is not yet unlocked.
>
> The required seed-potatoes are in the store.
>
> Therefore I cannot produce the requirement.

Of course, their information, or the assumptions they make, has to be correct first. Then the process of deduction has to be correct too. Human beings are much less likely to think straight; at first sight this looks logical:

> All human beings have heads.
>
> All Americans have heads.
>
> Therefore all Americans are human beings.

But if you change the names it is clearly nonsense:

> All Canadians are subjects of the Queen.
>
> All Australians are subjects of the Queen.
>
> Therefore all Australians are Canadians.

It helps to reduce these deductions to a formula:

> All A have B, all C have B, but this does not mean that all A's are C's.

Consider the following arguments. Are the conclusions true? If not, what is wrong with the reasoning? The first three use made-up words:

(a) All somnules have polnits and this thing has polnits; therefore it must be a somnule.

(b) If all somnules have polnits and this thing is a somnule, it must have polnits.

(c) If some somnules have polnits, then the fact that this thing has no polnits does not prove it is no somnule.

(d) Many red-haired people I have met have been quick-tempered, and she has red hair, so she is likely to be quick-tempered.

(e) Nowadays, more infants are made ill by being injected as a protection against various diseases than are ill from the diseases themselves. Therefore we should not inject them against these various diseases.

(f) Since Bill said he would buy a kite if he won the competition and he has now bought a kite, he must have won the competition.

(g) Many uneducated people read the *Daily Scream*; so if you read it you are showing yourself to be uneducated.

(h) Litmus paper turns red in the presence of acid and blue in the presence of alkali. When I placed some litmus paper in this liquid it did not turn red, so this liquid is not acid.

(i) No young people ever die from lung cancer, so there is no need to warn them about the danger of getting lung cancer from smoking cigarettes.

(j) If no one liked fighting wars, obviously there would be no more wars.

Exercise 2. Read the following passage carefully. The author is imagining that Cavor and himself are the first two men ever to set foot on the moon and watch the sunrise from the moon's surface.

As we saw it first it was the wildest and most desolate of scenes. We were in an enormous amphitheatre, a vast circular plain, the floor of the giant crater. Its cliff-like walls closed us in on every side. From the westward the light of the unseen sun fell upon them, 5 reaching to the very foot of the cliff, and showed a disordered escarpment of drab and grayish rock, lined here and there with banks and crevices of snow. This was perhaps a dozen miles away, but at first no intervening atmosphere diminished in the slightest the minutely detailed brilliancy with which these things glared at 10 us. They stood out clear and dazzling against a background of starry blackness that seemed to our earthly eyes rather a gloriously spangled velvet curtain than the spaciousness of the sky.

The eastward cliff was at first merely a starless selvedge to the starry dome. No rosy flush, no creeping pallor, announced the 15 commencing day. Only the Corona, the Zodiacal light, a huge cone-shaped, luminous haze, pointing up towards the splendour

of the morning star, warned us of the imminent nearness of the
sun.

Whatever light was about us was reflected by the westward
20 cliffs. It showed a huge undulating plain, cold and gray, a gray
that deepened eastward into the absolute raven darkness of the
cliff shadow. Innumerable rounded gray summits, ghostly hummocks, billows of snowy substance, stretching crest beyond crest
into the remote obscurity, gave us our first inkling of the distance
25 of the crater wall. These hummocks looked like snow. At the time
I thought they were snow. But they were not—they were mounds
and masses of frozen air?

So it was at first, and then, sudden, swift and amazing, came
the lunar day.
30   The sunlight had crept down the cliff, it touched the drifting
masses at its base and incontinently came striding with seven-
leagued boots towards us. The distant cliff seemed to shift and
quiver, and at the touch of the dawn a reek of gray vapour poured
upward from the crater floor, whirls and puffs and drifting wraiths
35 of gray, thicker and broader and denser, until at last the whole
westward plain was steaming like a wet handkerchief held before
the fire, and the westward cliffs were no more than a refracted glare
beyond.

"It is air," said Cavor. "It must be air . . ."

(from *The First Men in the Moon* by H. G. Wells)

Now give full written answers to the following questions
about this passage.

(a) What is an amphitheatre? In what ways do you think the
crater seemed like an amphitheatre? In what ways would
it be quite different from an amphitheatre?

(b) Where was the sun before it rose, as seen by these astro-
nauts? How were they made aware of its light, and the
nearness of the dawn?

(c) Why does the author write "*at first* no intervening atmosphere . . ." (in line 8).

(d) What would a "spangled velvet curtain" (in line 12) be
like? In what various ways was the starry sky like it then?

(e) What is a "selvedge" (in line 13)? How could the "eastward
cliff" look like a selvedge to the "starry dome" or "velvet
curtain"?

(f) Why should the darkness be described as "raven", in line
21?

(g) Why has the author made "they were mounds and masses of frozen air?" a question?

(h) When the sunlight is said to come "striding with seven-leagued boots" (in line 31) what is it being compared with? What does "incontinently" mean?

(i) Why did Cavor conclude that they had seen air on the moon?

(j) Explain the difference in meaning between "banks" (line 7) and "crevices" (line 7); between "flush" and "pallor" (line 14); between "undulating" (line 20) and "flat"; between "lunar" (line 29) and "moony"; and between "a reek" (line 33) and "wraiths" (line 34).

Exercise 3. In answering the questions in Exercise 2, you will have noticed that effective comparisons compare unlike things in *several* particular respects. Thus, when H. G. Wells compared the mists on the moon's surface to a wet handkerchief steaming before a fire, clearly this is no "literal comparison"— the plain was not made of white linen, and the sun has little in common with an ordinary open fire. But the plain looked like a steaming handkerchief, (1) because the mist was rising quickly and all over it, like steam; (2) because the plain looked white, like a handkerchief, before the mist began to rise; (3) because the heat of the sun was as fierce and sudden in its effect on the plain as a fire's heat on a wet handkerchief; and (4) because the cliffs beyond became glaring and vague through the mist as the fire would seem through the steam.

(a) Find as many points of comparison as you can in the following examples. In each case state what is compared to what, in what ways they are compared, and whether this is a *simile* or a *metaphor* (see page 88, if you are not sure of the difference).

(i) The wind tugged and blew at the tent as if it were a balloon, ready for launching.

(ii) The train, a great iron horse with a white mane flying in the wind, thundered down the track.

(iii) As prim and upright as an Edwardian lady in her best bonnet, the vintage limousine rolled proudly into Brighton.

(iv) The roof is dribbling rain and all the drainpipes are gargling noisily.

(v) The crane stretched above us like some prehistoric monster and clawed at the rubble with its iron hand.

(vi) In the midst of that vast, polished and glistening machine was one green eye that winked at us and seemed to laugh.

(vii) The incident was so difficult to recall, like a tiny ship tossed on a vast ocean of thoughts and memories.

(viii) I picked up the skeleton of a leaf and as I touched it, it crumbled.

(ix) Out of the glare of the heat, returning to that cool, shuttered room was like entering the depths of a cave.

(x) Bluebells thrust green tongues above a sea of brown leaves.

(b) Make up complex and vivid comparisons that describe the following in several particular respects:

(i) An aeroplane   (ii) A speed-boat   (iii) A road-roller
(iv) A dead horse   (v) Any animal.

Exercise 4. (a) When, in the passage, Brian Aldiss writes:

The field-minder . . . spoke to the seed distributor, which stood idly outside.

he is using the *adjective clause*:

which stood idly outside.

to merge two separate statements into one:

The field-minder spoke to the seed distributor.
The seed distributor stood idly outside.

Instead of repeating the words "the seed distributor", he used the pronoun "which" to stand for them, and this introduces an adjective clause, describing "the seed distributor" already mentioned.

Reconstruct the following pairs of sentences, so that they become one, with an adjective clause, introduced by "which", "that", "who" or "whose". The adjective clause can come in the middle of the other clause (or sentence)

e.g. This is what the radio operator said. The radio operator is a Class Two brain.

This is what the radio operator, who is a Class Two brain, said.

(i) Supply Operative Type P has not come this morning. Supply Operative Type P is the unlocker.

(ii) The field-minder looked squarely at the seed distributor. The seed distributor's chutes and scales and grabs were so vastly different from its own limbs.

(iii) There you had the distinction between a Class Six and a Class Three brain. A Class Six and a Class Three brain was what the unlocker and the pen-propeller possessed respectively.

(iv) The field-minder did not speak to the unlocker. The unlocked still stood aimlessly by.

(v) Brian Aldiss writes science fiction. Brian Aldiss wrote this short story.

(b) Similarly, two sentences, one of which gives a reason or explanation for the other statement, can be combined using the *conjunctions* "because", "as", "since";

> The required seed potatoes are in the store. Therefore I cannot produce them.

> I cannot produce the required seed potatoes because they are in the store.

The clause beginning with "because" is an *adverb clause*: it describes, not the potatoes, but the verb, i.e. *why* he *cannot produce* the potatoes. In these cases, the adverb clause can equally well precede the main clause (or sentence):

e.g. I have a Class Three brain. Therefore I am superior to you.
As I have a Class Three brain I am superior to you.

Join the following into one sentence using an adverb clause.

(i) I am superior to you. Therefore I will go and see why the unlocker has not come.

(ii) I am too large. Therefore you must go alone.

(iii) The radio has issued no orders. Therefore I have had no orders.

(iv) The radio station in the city was issued with no orders this morning. Therefore we have had no orders this morning.

(v) You have a Class Three brain and I have a Class Three brain. Therefore we will speak to each other.

1. Whether or not you have read the short story from which the passage at the head of this chapter was taken, write your own ending to the incident. Study the "characters" involved, and the details of the situation they are in, very carefully before you begin, and try to imitate the same style for conversation between machines, and so on.

Do not rewrite the beginning of the story: carry on from the point where our extract stops.

2. Explaining exactly how a simple machine works is not usually as easy as one at first thinks. It is clearest to begin by describing the basic parts of the machine, in a logical order, explaining what each does, and then give instructions for using the mechanism. Choose *one* of the following that you think you understand and write an account of how it works, using a labelled diagram if you wish. But the explanation must be *mainly in words*, not pictures.

> A child's scooter
> A stapler (for clipping papers together)
> A vacuum flask (a "Thermos")
> A pair of garden shears
> A wheel-brace drill
> A coffee percolator
> A carpet sweeper (hand-operated)
> A meat mincer (hand-operated)
> A bicycle pump
> A battery-operated electric bell

You will find this composition easier to write if you have the object in front of you.

Oral Work

1. Here are some "provocative remarks" to start class discussion. State whether you agree or disagree and discuss why.

(a) It is wrong for the great nations of the world to spend vast sums of money on exploring outer space when we have great problems of poverty, disease and starvation here on earth.

(b) Men learn more about the universe and make more and more complicated machines, but ordinary people are no happier than they were.

(c) In an age of more and more machines, what we need to learn at school is not so much technical or scientific knowledge, but more about art and crafts, literature, drama, music and sport, so that we can enjoy our leisure.

(d) When we have machines to do all our hard labour and work out all our problems for us, human beings are bound to become weak physically and bored mentally.

(e) As in Brian Aldiss's short story, over-population and diet-deficiency will probably bring about the end of the human race.

2. Groups could work out some impromptu plays involving men and machines. Pay special attention to effective miming of actions. In some cases actors will take the part of robot-like machines, and in others, the actors will mime actions of controlling, or being in, machines. Thus one group might be in a lorry, with the driver miming the actions; another might include an actor working a crane or a bulldozer; another group might be in a space craft or at a control-centre. Work out a central situation and parts for actors, and let a story develop from this through their conversation and actions.

Activities and Research

1. If possible, arrange a class visit to a factory or a highly mechanised local depot, such as a big dairy where milk is bottled. Before the class goes, find out what you can about the industry concerned from encyclopaedias, and work out some questions to ask or find out answers to. As you go round, make notes about the processes that are going on, and also jot down your impressions of the machinery at work. Some members of the class might also take interesting photographs. Afterwards, write either a factual account of the factory and what goes on, suitable for a school magazine article, or a vivid poem or description about something particularly impressive.

If a portable tape-recorder is available, make recordings of "sound effects" and of the guide who shows you round, and "edit" these later as part of a sound picture of the visit, with eyewitness accounts of what you saw.

2. Look up some of the following in encyclopaedias, other reference books (such as the *Dictionary of National Biography*) and appropriate history books:

> The Luddites, The Tolpuddle Martyrs, The Factory Acts, Henry Ford, Mass Production, Robert Owen, Apprentices and Journeymen (Craft Guilds), the Chartists, Automation and Redundancy, the T.U.C., Plastics.

Be prepared to report back to the class on your findings.

Further Reading

Tales of Science Fiction edited by BRIAN N. BALL (Hamish Hamilton; Penguin)
This is the anthology in which "Who Can Replace a Man?" appears. It also contains stories about space ships and time travel, visitors from outer space, and a machine that can predict how long a man will live. The selection provides a suitable introduction to the field of science fiction.

Tunnel in the Sky by ROBERT HEINLEIN (Gollancz)
Rod Walker and other students taking an examination in Advanced Survival are transported to an unknown planet where, they are told, they must survive for four days. But the operation goes wrong and they are left stranded. Like Robert Heinlein's other junior science fiction novels, this is an exciting story, slickly written.

The First Men in the Moon, The Time Machine and *The War of the Worlds* by H. G. WELLS (Collins, etc.)
The author may have lived before the age of space travel, but these thrilling stories, combining science with adventure, are so well written and cleverly worked out that they still convince us.

Energy by LANCELOT HOGBEN (Macdonald)
This profusely illustrated book, by a well-known scientist, reviews man's technical progress from Stone Age times to the present day. (621.1)

Joe, who is only six, has a deformed goat named Africana, which he believes is a unicorn. He imagines that an old tramp (whom he refers to as the Cannibal King because he seems so frightening) intends to steal his pet. One day Joe follows the Cannibal King down Fashion Street, where Joe lives above the local tailor's workshop.

CHAPTER NINE

Down and Out

Joe pressed himself against the wall of the passage and waited. Sure enough the Cannibal King stopped when he got to the workshop, bending down to look into the window below the grating. He watched quietly for a moment. Then he stood up, took his nose between his fingers and blew it. Then he took a piece of paper out of his pocket and studied it for a while. Afterwards he folded the paper up carefully, took a last look through the grating, and walked on.

Joe watched him the whole time. That piece of paper was his plan for stealing Africana and the only thing to do was to follow him, find his lair, and tell the sweetshop man, the informer, who would then tell the police. As it was only cold and not raining, Joe waited until the Cannibal King was a bit ahead, and followed.

All the way along, Joe watched the Cannibal King carefully, ready to take up the position of defence at a moment's notice. But the old man didn't look back once, which showed how cunning he was, trying to make Joe think that he didn't know he was being followed.

Once he sat down on the kerb for a short rest, and Joe turned to look into the window of a magazine shop where there were thousands of covers in full colour. They showed horrible monsters about to eat beautiful ladies with torn dresses, and rockets going to Mars, the red planet of mystery, and boxers beating one another bloody and cowboys shooting and gangsters shooting and Huns shooting. Joe was thinking that the pictures were exciting but not very real because you never saw things like that in Fashion Street. He started to think then how it would be if when he got back to Fashion Street a whole lot of horrible monsters were trying to get into the greengrocer's shop to eat Mavis, and her overalls were torn. When he looked round, the Cannibal King was gone, which again went to show how cunning he was . . .

Joe sighed. He could tell from the way his stomach felt, that it was dinner time, and since the old cannibal was nowhere to be seen, he might just as well go home. He would have gone straight home, except that he noticed the big chocolate advert over the railway bridge and being so near, thought he might as well have a look at Itchy Park to see if any flowers were coming up yet.

Itchy Park was an old graveyard which, though full up, had hedges and a few big old trees. Flowers grew up round the graves which were so covered with grass that without the gravestones and monuments you would think it was a real park. There were two iron benches painted dark green for your convenience, should you happen to be tired, and in nice weather old men used to meet there to talk politics, while mothers pushed their babies in prams, and children played Release round the graves. With its white stone pillars with iron fences between them, the iron all black and green, the stone all white and black and grey patches from the rain and smoke, it was like ancient Greece. In nice weather, a pleasant place for a short outing.

At Itchy Park the sun made the white stone pillars and whitened headstones shine like alabaster, and Joe dawdled between the graves on his way to one which, last spring, was covered with crocuses. He spelt out some of the shorter words which could still be read on the stones, because even if he didn't go to school yet, Mr. Kandinsky told him, there was no need for him to be ignorant. He stopped at the memorial with the split angel on it to see if it had split any more lately. It had only one wing and the tip of that was missing, so that if it did split there wouldn't be much of that angel left, and Itchy Park was already short of angels because they got knocked off so easily. Fortunately, the split angel was no worse, so Joe went over to the crocus grave.

Some of the crocuses were shooting and striped dark green leaves showed through the grass which was winter thin and short. One of the crocuses was quite large but it looked as if it would never flower and felt stone cold. In spite of the sun, blasts of wind cut through the graveyard like wet stone knives. It was no wonder if the flowers were frozen stiff, and the grass thin, and the angels splitting. Standing up to breathe on his fingers Joe saw the Cannibal King.

Why he didn't see him straight away Joe couldn't imagine, because he was sitting on one of the iron benches with his sack beside him, drinking from his bottle. If Itchy Park was his lair, it was certainly a cold one, although maybe one of the graves opened secretly and the king crept into it at night. Joe knelt down again behind the headstone on the crocus grave to watch.

Between taking long drags on the bottle, the king grunted and coughed, not a short dry cough like a dog, but a large wide wet rackety cough, as if his whole chest and stomach coughed with him. The choker round his throat opened and his neck showed loose skin red and raw. There was spit all round his mouth, and his eyes ran with water. As he drank and coughed he only looked like an old man in a graveyard with a bad cough in the cold time of the year.

Joe was creeping round the back to go home, when suddenly the Cannibal King gave an enormous cough which shook his whole body so that his face turned purple. While he was getting his wind back, his face turned white making his beard look dark and thick. He closed his eyes and sank back on the bench, and the open bottle, which was still in his hand, dipped over so that some of the spirit poured on to his coat.

When he got home, Joe's mother and Mr. Kandinsky were full of questions about where he had been and how cold he was. Joe didn't tell them about the old Cannibal King. It would have been too difficult to explain why he wasn't a cannibal or a king any more, just because of the cold.

(from *A Kid for Two Farthings* by Wolf Mankowitz)

Comprehension and Discussion

1. In the end the Cannibal King is a sick, harmless tramp, so what might explain his "cunning behaviour" earlier on, looking into Mr. Kandinsky's shop and giving Joe the slip?

2. What is the game of "Release"?

3. Can *you* explain why the tramp seemed to Joe no longer like a cannibal or a king? Why did Joe find this too difficult to explain at home?

4. What might have been in the tramp's bottle? Do you think he was really ill?

5. Why were Joe's mother and Mr. Kandinsky so full of questions when he returned?

6. Comment on the words and the comparisons chosen for the description in the paragraph beginning: "Some of the crocuses were shooting . . ." What makes this effective description?

7. Do you know some "full up" graveyards? Should such old town graveyards be turned into parks for children to play in and for people to enjoy themselves in, or is this disrespectful or sacrilegious?

8. Would you expect to find similar book and magazine covers in a magazine shop today?

9. Name the most exciting books you know. Are they about "real" people and events, or obviously imaginary characters?

10. As a child, did you build up a terrifying picture of any adult, as Joe did? When, and why, did you cease to be frightened of him?

For Written Answers

1. What time of year was it and how do you know this?

2. What was the weather like? Again give reasons.

3. Why did Joe turn to look into the magazine shop and was this in fact a mistake?

4. Explain why Itchy Park was "like Ancient Greece".

5. What is "alabaster" and why is it mentioned in connection with the sunshine?

6. What details about Itchy Park suggest that it was a town graveyard, not a country one?

7. Why do you think Joe took so long to notice the Cannibal King in the park?

8. What evidence is there in this passage that Joe is only six years old?

The Hunchback in the Park

The hunchback in the park
A solitary mister
Propped between trees and water
From the opening of the garden lock
That lets the trees and water enter
Until the Sunday sombre bell at dark

Eating bread from a newspaper
Drinking water from the chained cup
That the children filled with gravel
In the fountain basin where I sailed my ship
Slept at night in a dog kennel
But nobody chained him up.

Like the park birds he came early
Like the water he sat down
And Mister they called Hey mister
The truant boys from the town
Running when he heard them clearly
On out of sound

Past lake and rockery
Laughing when he shook his paper
Hunchbacked in mockery
Through the loud zoo of the willow groves
Dodging in the park keeper
With his stick that picked up leaves.

And the old dog sleeper
Alone between nurses and swans
While the boys among willows
Made the tigers jump out of their eyes
To roar on the rockery stones
And the groves were blue with sailors

Made all day until bell time
A woman figure without fault
Straight as a young elm
Straight and tall from his crooked bones
That she might stand in the night
After the locks and chains

All night in the unmade park
After the railings and shrubberies
The birds the grass the trees the lake
And the wild boys innocent as strawberries
Had followed the hunchback
To his kennel in the dark.

DYLAN THOMAS

Discussing the Poem

1. Dylan Thomas remembers the tramp and the park from childhood; how does he express the child's idea that the park only really existed during the day? What other ideas in the poem represent a child's-eye view?

2. What was the park like, and which people and animals were frequent visitors?

3. How and why did the boys mock the hunchback?

4. How did the hunchbacked tramp make up for his ugliness, his poverty and the cruel taunts of the children? Is the way he used his imagination at all similar to the way the children used theirs, in their games?

Method Exercises

Exercise 1. When the author of the passage writes:

> The only thing to do was to . . . tell the sweetshop man, the informer, who would then tell the police.

he uses the verb "would tell" instead of "will tell", because he is referring to the future in the past tense: at that time (in the past) he *would* (later) tell the police. The various tenses formed with "would" (and "should"), instead of "will" and "shall", are sometimes called "future in the past tenses," or (more commonly) CONDITIONAL TENSES, since they are used in "if" clauses that state an uncertain possibility.

> One of the crocuses was quite large but it looked as if it would never flower.

When used as "future in the past", the verbs still imply a condition. They suggest that this was something that *would* happen in the future, if we were correctly predicting, not otherwise.

126

e.g. 1. I *shall go* to Norfolk next week.

2. Last week, I said I *would go* to Norfolk this week, but that was before the train strike.

Implied condition: if nothing happened to prevent me.

(a) What is the implied or actual "condition" in each of these examples from the passage?

(i) He started to think how it *would be* if, when he got back to Fashion Street, a whole lot of horrible monsters were trying to get into the greengrocer's shop.

(ii) He *would have gone* straight home, except that he noticed the big chocolate advert over the railway bridge.

(iii) Without the gravestones and monuments you *would think* it was a real park.

(iv) There were two iron benches painted dark green, for your convenience, *should* you *happen* to be tired.

(v) It *would have been* too difficult to explain why he wasn't a cannibal or a king any more.

(b) Rewrite the following table of tenses of the verb "to go", completing all ten gaps:

	SIMPLE	CONTINUOUS	PERFECT	PERFECT CONTINUOUS
PRESENT	He goes	—	he has gone	—
PAST	—	—	—	he had been going
FUTURE	—	—	he will have gone	—
CONDITIONAL	—	he would be going	—	he would have been going

(Turn back to page 41 if you still need help with these tenses.)

Exercise 2 (a) The following ten sentences illustrate some further conventions in using the *apostrophe*. Discuss every use of the apostrophe here, and be prepared to explain each case.

1. I like Thomas and Brown's products.
2. I would also enjoy Thomas's and Brown's incomes.
3. Thomas and Brown's, the boatbuilders', is in Water Street.

4. Thomas and Brown, the boatbuilders' yard, is very well equipped.

5. It's only a stone's throw from here.

6. In the telephone directory, you find them among the T's, not the B's.

7. This year's orders for boats may yield a profit in two years' time.

8. Mr. Brown has been looking at the others' boats.

9. Someone else's products often seem more attractive than one's own.

10. M.P.s may soon be discussing a J.P.'s duties; Mr. Thomas is one of the local J.P.s.

(b) Rewrite the following, inserting the 14 apostrophes, 15 capital letters and one set of inverted commas required:

ten minutes walk from the towns centre, on ones way to the station, is longmills and brents beautiful longmills park. the parks committees plan for the boroughs main park included the parks superintendents ideas and his senior deputys suggestion for a hilltop restaurant. mr. bliss, the deputys suggestion was for a revolving restaurant for both residents and visitors enjoyment; but after a months argument they were openly insulting each others ideas and the superintendent called this one bliss folly.

Exercise 3. (a) Look at the poems on pages 12, 25, 85 and 124 from the point of view of their use of *rhyme*. Each verse in *Lesson In Murder* (p. 12) has the following pattern of rhymes at the ends of lines: a, b, a, b. What is the usual pattern in *The Ballad of Billy Rose* (p. 25)? Is it ever varied? Would you say that any of the rhymes are imperfect or *half-rhymes*? Is there any use of rhyme at all, at the ends of lines or within verse lines, in *Humming-Bird* (p. 85)? Finally, how does Dylan Thomas use rhymes in *The Hunchback in the Park* (p. 124)? Notice the irregular pattern of full rhymes (such as "park" and "dark") and the numerous half-rhymes (like "water" and "enter"). Can you explain why "rockery" and "mockery" or "cup" and "up" seem to be full rhymes, while "shrubberies" and "strawberries" is only a half-rhyme, even though the last part of both words sounds the same?

(b) Do you remember from Book Two what *alliteration* is? What are the repeated consonant sounds in the following?

(i) But above ... more like dead and dried specimens than actual living creatures, sat the horrible males, absolutely motionless save for the rolling of their red eyes ...

(ii) It was a wonderful sight to see at least a hundred creatures of such enormous size and hideous appearance all swooping like swallows with swift, shearing wing strokes above us.

(iii) Innumerable rounded gray summits, ghostly hummocks, billows of snowy substance, stretching crest beyond crest into the remote obscurity, gave us our first inkling of the distance of the crater wall.

(iv) They were mounds and masses of frozen air.

(v) They showed ... boxers beating one another bloody.

(vi) The king grunted and coughed ... a large wide wet rackety cough ... His neck showed loose skin red and raw.

Can you find further examples of alliteration in the poem *Hunchback in the Park*?

(c) Make up sentences using alliterative phrases (or rhyming words) to describe:

cold drizzling rain; glistening fresh snow; the noise of an aircraft; the motion of a boat; a gale in a wood; a girl with bright eyes and red cheeks; a bulldozer at work; a vacuum cleaner in use; an angry woman; waves breaking over rocks.

Exercise 4. We have seen that the words:

which, that, who, whom

introduce *adjective clauses*, and that they are *pronouns*, and stand for the person, object or idea they describe. They are often called RELATIVE PRONOUNS, since they relate the adjective clause to what it is describing (sometimes called the ANTECEDENT).

In the introduction to the passage from *A Kid for Two Farthings*, we wrote:

Joe, who is only six, has a deformed goat named Africana, which he believes is a unicorn.

What noun does the relative pronoun "who" stand for? If "Joe" is subject of "has" ("Joe has a deformed goat ...") what verb is "who" subject of? What noun does "which" stand for? (Why is it now "which", and not "who"?) What verb is "which" subject of—"believes", or "is"? Notice that the relative pronoun *can* be the object of a verb in the adjective clause:

> Do you like the extract *which* you have just read? (i.e. you have just read *it*—object of verb "have read").

And when the pronoun is "who" (subject) it usually changes to "whom" (object):

> Did you like the author whom you have just met?

In the following examples, adapted from the passage and the poem, what noun does the relative pronoun stand for, and what verb is the relative pronoun subject (or object) of?

(a) The only thing to do was to tell the informer, who would then tell the police.

(b) Itchy Park was an old graveyard which, though full up, had hedges and a few big old trees.

(c) Flowers grew up round the graves which were covered with grass.

(d) Joe dawdled between the graves on his way to one which, last spring, was covered with crocuses.

(e) He spelt out some of the shorter words that he could still read on the stones.

(f) Striped dark green leaves showed through the grass which was winter thin.

(g) Suddenly the Cannibal King gave an enormous cough that shook his whole body.

(h) The open bottle, which was still in his hand, dipped over so that some of the spirit poured on to his coat.

(i) He drank water from the chained cup that the children filled with gravel.

(j) Joe imagines that an old tramp (whom he calls the Cannibal King) intends to steal his pet.

Writing Your Own

1. Choose a particular place you know well and describe it and the people who come there during the day. Take a park, a recreation ground, a village green or common, a market square

or street market, or the local library. Visit the place, if possible. Try to capture the atmosphere in words and concentrate on a few particular people who add a typical touch to the scene. Use the description of Itchy Park and the old tramp who rested there as a model, but be careful to select details that add up to a picture of the place as it usually is, leaving out anything that would be unusual or unlikely. Think of comparisons and vivid phrases (perhaps including some alliteration) to make your description lively, interesting and realistic.

2. Read this poem by a pupil of 14.

The Fall

The tree stood alone, desolate, undisturbed
In the centre of the old woman's garden:
Now it was the only living remnant of her
    lonely life.
Its branches stuck out in misery and dejection,

Stuck out dark, sharp and foreboding.
Its leafy coat had withered months ago,
And now it waited patiently to die,
Like an old woman silently decaying
In the misery of loneliness.

At dawn they found the old woman
Stiff, silent and restful,
Peacefully sleeping in death
In her damp, ugly bed;
And in the garden the fallen tree
Lying in its stagnant bed
Of dead withered leaves.

                                        DAVID

In a sense it is one extended comparison between the old woman and an old tree. Choose any solitary figure you have ever noticed: a tramp, a lonely old man or woman, someone blind or deaf, a cripple, a very poor person, or anyone who seems a lonely figure against his or her particular background. Think what they remind you of, and work out comparisons and descriptive phrases that will help suggest their appearance, their clothes, their habits and movements, and their loneliness. Then try to put these together as a free verse poem.

Oral Work

1. Work out a comic sketch involving some conversation and action between two (or more) tramps. Other characters (such as a policeman) might be involved. The sketches should be fully rehearsed and then performed to the class.

2. Discuss the whole matter of tramps, beggars, unemployable people and gipsies. First, can we draw any clear distinction between those who are forced into this kind of life, those who positively choose it and prefer it, and those who are mentally or physically fit for no other life? Consider each separately. What can and should be done for those who find themselves poor and unemployed (through no fault of their own)? Is enough done already (a) in this country and (b) in other parts of the world? Does having generous unemployment pay and various free services in fact encourage people to be lazy and not to work? What is the attraction of a wandering life of poverty to those who choose it? Are gipsies similar to tramps in their way of life, or would they prefer to be absorbed as ordinary members of society? What should be done for the down-and-outs who are too ill (for instance, the alcoholics) or too unintelligent or mentally unbalanced to fit into a normal life with a job to do?

Activities and Research

1. Prepare a paragraph or short talk on each of the following: the dole, vagrants and vagrancy laws, the Poor Law, work-houses, Bedlam beggars, gipsies, hobos, hitch-hiking, jumping trains (including "riding the rods"), W. H. Davies and George Borrow, pedlars and tinkers, the Salvation Army, National Assistance.

2. Visit your local park or common (perhaps before tackling either of the pieces of work in *Writing Your Own*), with a note-book or a sketch-book, specifically to look for new ways of seeing the scene. Pick on objects such as a dead tree or a withered leaf, or the earliest shoots of spring growth. Sketch them in words or drawings. Notice the people, the animals, the plants and trees, the weather and the whole atmosphere of the place. Search for accurate comparisons to describe what you really see.

Further Reading

A Kid for Two Farthings by WOLF MANKOWITZ (Deutsch; Heinemann)
This book is a very realistic child's-eye view of life in London's East End before the Second World War, culminating in a lively description of the wrestling match between Mr. Kandinsky's assistant, Shmule, and "the Python". In an unexpected way, this helps the "unicorn" to grant Joe's wishes.

Huckleberry Finn by MARK TWAIN (various publishers)
Like *Tom Sawyer*, this is a classic story of poor lads by the Mississippi River, in the days before the abolition of slavery. Huck, who is every boy's ideal of the young truant, careless of all authority, sets off downstream on a raft, with the runaway negro, Jim.

Ginger and Batty Billy by PRUDENCE ANDREW (Lutterworth)
Ginger, the likeable young cockney in *Ginger Over the Wall*, is in this story standing up for his cousin Marj and even the town's "down-and-out" Batty Billy, against the jeering cowardly children in a small Welsh town. There is plenty of entertaining action, even if the characterisation is rather superficial.

The Autobiography of a Super-Tramp by W. H. DAVIES (school edition, Allen & Unwin)
The poet W. H. Davies took to tramping in America, where he learned to beg and to "ride the rods", and met some fascinating "professionals". He worked his passage on Atlantic cattle-boats and later set off on the Klondyke gold rush. He gives a first hand picture of a down-and-out's life on both sides of the Atlantic. (920)

Supplementary Exercises

We have seen that nouns and parts of verbs can both sometimes act as adjectives. They are then shown in *graphic analysis* in the adjective positions. For example, what noun and what part of a verb are used as adjectives in this sentence, and what nouns do they qualify?

A running tap can sometimes cause a water shortage.

In graphic analysis, this would be set out as follows:

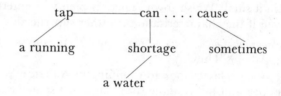

Analyse the following sentences on this pattern. (Some have complements or indirect, as well as direct, objects.)

(a) We sell growing plants.

(b) Many people are growing their own pot plants.

(c) Next week our autumn flowers should bloom.

(d) Beautiful blooms are uncommon in winter.

(e) A flourishing tree blooms every spring.

(f) Spring vegetables are often expensive.

(g) Were any plant stalks broken?

(h) Broken stalks give the growers much trouble.

(i) Most market gardeners own their own market gardens.

(j) Where will you find a better vegetable market?

(a) We saw in Book 2 that adjective and adverb *phrases* can be shown in graphic analysis, as complete units, in the same positions as single adjectives or adverbs. For example, reconstruct the sentence that has been analysed here:

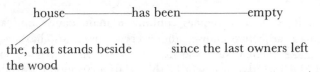

people————————should not participate

with slow reactions   in high-speed motor racing

Analyse the following sentences graphically:

i. The speed limit on the Oxford Road was introduced for a very good reason.

ii. Several cars without speedometers were breaking the speed limit on the Oxford Road.

iii. At the Council's last meeting, some members proposed a change in the speed limit.

iv. The rest of the Council's business was rather dull.

v. What will you do with all your money?

vi. The house beside the wood has been empty since 1970.

(b) Since adjectives and adverb *clauses* have the same function as single adjectives or adverbs, they too can be analysed in the same way, standing as complete units in the graphic analysis. For example, reconstruct the following sentence:

house————has been————empty

the, that stands beside   since the last owners left
the wood

Analyse the following sentences graphically; each contains at least one adjective or adverb clause.

i. What will you do when you get the money?

ii. When the Council last met, some members proposed a change which would affect the speed limit.

iii. The speed limit which was in force on the Oxford Road was introduced because there had been several accidents there.

iv. Several cars that had no speedometers were breaking the speed limit where it was particularly dangerous to do so.

*Analysis Exercise 3

In analysing sentences that contain a main statement and adjective or other *subordinate* clauses, it is usual to use a system of CLAUSE ANALYSIS using columns, rather than make a more detailed graphic analysis. In columns, the last sentence in Exercise 2 (b) would have been analysed like this:

	CLAUSE	KIND	FUNCTION	RELATIONSHIP
A	several cars . . . were breaking the speed limit	Main clause		
a¹	that had no speedometers	Subordinate clause	Adjective	Qualifies noun " cars" in main clause "A"
a²	where it was particularly dangerous to do so	Subordinate clause	Adverb of place	Modifies verb "were breaking" in main clause "A"

Notice that a main clause has no other function or relationship, and also that it is usual to say that adjective clauses *qualify* nouns or pronouns, while adverb clauses *modify* verbs. Now rule some columns similar to those shown here for use in analysing the following sentences.

Each of these sentences contains a main clause and a subordinate adjective clause, and every clause must have a verb. To make them easier, the first five have the verbs underlined and the introductory word (the relative pronoun introducing the adjective clause) in italics.

(a) Anne Frank was a girl *who* knew her own mind.

(b) In Amsterdam you can still see the house *in which* Anne Frank lived.

(c) Anne Frank was a girl *whom* we all admire.

(d) The diary *that* she kept has now become quite famous.

(e) The inventor showed me a machine *that* he had just completed.

(f) The machine which he showed me was quite revolutionary.

(g) It could do anything that you told it to.

(h) A man who controlled an army of these machines could make himself dictator.

(i) The secret was in an electronic brain which was extremely sensitive.

(j) The inventor is worried about a machine whose power is so complete.

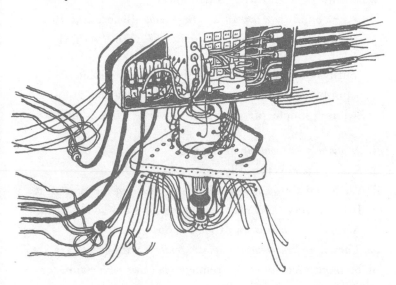

Revision Exercise 1

Punctuate and set out the following conversation correctly. It includes several uses of apostrophes and inverted commas, and single inverted commas inside double ones.

Now that youve got your pony said Phils mother at the breakfast table next morning what are you going to call him Phil swallowed a mouthful of toast and said I was thinking of calling him Gabby Gabby Whatever made you think of that Jean exclaimed Perhaps hes got the gift of the gab suggested Phils dad with an ironic smile No Phil replied firmly Im not joking He is to be called Gabby after Jodys pony Gabilan in Steinbecks story The Red Pony

The following sentences use the made-up words "scrunch", "mirn(y)", "squibble" and "wint". Like ordinary English words they appear in varying forms and as different parts of speech.

(a) State whether each of the italicised words in these sentences is a noun (is it then subject, object, indirect object or complement?), an adjective (what does it then describe?) or a verb (what tense is it, and what is its subject?).

> e.g. You always *scrunch* a *mirny squibble* before it *wints*.
>
> scrunch = simple present tense of verb "scrunch", subject "you";
>
> mirny = an adjective, describing noun "squibble";
>
> squibble = a singular noun, object of "scrunch";
>
> wints = simple present tense of verb "wint", subject "it".

  i. A *squibble was winting* in the *mirn*.
 ii. *Squibbles wint* very easily.
iii. We found this *winting squibble* and *scrunched* the *mirn* off it.
 iv. It was a very *mirny squibble* and we gave it a good *scrunch*.
  v. A *squibble scrunch* is an expensive business.
 vi. They *were scrunching* the *winted squibble* with great care.
vii. *Scrunching* machines can remove *squibbles' mirn* stains.

(b) Write out a table of tenses for the verb "to wint" similar to that on page 41 or page 127.

(a) In the following sentences, a number of commas should be replaced by semicolons. Rewrite the sentences, making the necessary changes.

  i. The last of the members left the clubhouse, the light was switched off, it was very dark outside.

ii. I watched the schoolboys' team play, and felt they might do very well, however, they still need practice.

iii. Not all the selectors feel as I do, several are very dissatisfied, but others still want to see the youngsters, who are still inexperienced, given a chance.

iv. The secretary, Joe Brown, was searching for new talent, he failed to find it, of course.

v. We need to understand the rules of the game, we need to keep really fit, we need to study the style of past experts, we need, above all, the will to succeed.

vi. He kicked the ball with all his might, there was a loud, shattering crash of broken glass.

(b) Explain the difference in meaning between the following three versions of the same short passage, which differ only in punctuation. Then make up two further variations of it by altering the punctuation.

i. The reply was that there were no more in the kitchen where the rest were. Nobody knew what then was the answer. To go and get some?

ii. The reply was that; there were no more in the kitchen; where the rest were, nobody knew. What then was the answer? To go and get some?

iii. The reply was that there were no more. In the kitchen, where the rest were, nobody knew. What then? Was the answer to go and get some?

Revision Exercise 4

(a) Turn the italicised verbs in the following passage from the passive to the active voice, making any other *necessary* changes. Begin your answer: "New building methods are making . . ."

Great and exciting changes *are being made* in our environment by new building methods. Very tall blocks *can be built* by us if piles *are driven* into the ground and the structure *is supported* on pillars. When much of the accommodation *is lifted* up in the air by our architects, the ground level *is left* free for more spacious planning. On the ground, large areas *can* easily *be flattened* or *landscaped* by new, more powerful earth-moving machinery, and roads, bridges, underpasses, fly-overs and raised pedestrian precincts *are* all quickly and cheaply *constructed* by contractors today. Much muddle and squalor *has been created* by technical limitations in the past; this *will* soon *be swept* away by architects of the future.

(b) Rewrite each of the verbs in (a) in the equivalent past tense. Do this twice in each case, once to give the past tense of the passive voice, and once to give the past of the active voice. Note that "will" becomes "would". Here is the first verb as an example:

> changes are being made—changes were being made
> building methods are making changes—building
>   methods were making changes

Revision Exercise 5

(a) Make up three short sentences using each of the following words first as a noun, then as an adjective and thirdly as a verb.

e.g.: command

noun: The sergeant-major shouted a sharp *command*.
adjective: The actors gave a *command* performance of their play.
verb: They *were commanded* to give it by the Queen.

base	fire	ground	return	sound
deal	fish	light	round	stable

(b) *Antonyms* can be formed from the following words by adding one of the following prefixes: dis-, im-, in-, ir-, un-.

e.g. agree—disagree; recoverable—irrecoverable.

approve	continue	fit	perfect	reverent
believe	decent	healthy	proper	reversible
conclusive	effective	mature	rational	satisfied
constant	fasten	mobilize	refutable	wise

Revision Exercise 6

(a) Set out the following business letter correctly with all the necessary punctuation:

wendle secondary school eastern road wendleton surrey
1st may 19..... the manager the true-scale models co ltd
23 nosuch road wimbledon london s w 19 6 x p dear sir i am
writing on behalf of the wendle school junior scientific
society to ask if it is possible to arrange for about twenty
of our members to visit your factory in wimbledon during
our half-term holiday which is the week from june 3rd to
june 7th we should be very grateful for such an opportunity
to visit your works and see your scale toys being made
alternatively perhaps you could send someone to speak to
one of our after-school meetings here yours faithfully
peter smith secretary

(b) Imagine that you received a reply to this letter inviting your
party on Tuesday, 4th June at 2.30 p.m., and that the visit was
a great success, and included a complete tour and a free tea.
Write a letter on behalf of the society, thanking the manager
for his generous hospitality.

Revision Exercise 7

The following three passages require commas, full stops and
apostrophes to complete their punctuation. Rewrite them
correctly.

(a) "Its not fair" he said "I dont have a chance I mustnt do
this and I cant do that because its dangerous Im not even
allowed to go to the grocers and I havent a hope of going
on Wednesdays outing if Dads in this mood"

(b) In a months time Shackles and Green the rod-makers
factory in St Jamess Road will be sold by auction Mr
Shackles share of the proceeds will go to the Widows
Housing Trust and theyre going to build some old peoples
flats where elderly ladies can enjoy one anothers company
and yet have the privacy that is everyones right even in
ones old age

(c) A number of MBEs OBEs CBEs and KBEs were created in
last years Queens Birthday Honours List in spite of several
newspapers criticisms of the Governments policy in award-
ing honours

In 1891 Henri Becquerel discovered accidentally that uranium had the same effect on a photographic plate as sunlight. This started the Curies on their famous search, which led to the discovery of radioactivity and the new element, radium.

CHAPTER TEN

Scientific Discovery

The news of Becquerel's findings regarding uranium reached the Curies. They were strongly interested, Marie as a skilled chemist, Pierre as a skilled physicist. They wondered about the mineral that spontaneously gave out these rays which not only fogged photographic plates but also took off the charges from electrified bodies. The uranium-containing mineral was chemically quite complex. Was the energy coming from the uranium atoms? Or could it be from some other kind of atom in the complex mineral? Marie, in a well-planned way, set out to get the answers. She analyzed carefully all the uranium-containing minerals that were available in the museum collection of the University of Paris. She determined the quantity of uranium in each, and found the chemical combinations in which the element was held. Pierre tested the various minerals by the rate at which electrified bodies brought near them lost their charges. After several weeks of intense effort the first results appeared. The intensity of the surprising radiation from uranium minerals had a direct relation to the quantity of uranium present and was not affected by the chemical combinations of the uranium with atoms of other kinds. Nor was it affected by lighting or temperature.

There remained the *possibility* that some well-known element, present along with the uranium, was the source of the strange radiation. The matter could be decided by using each element in its pure state or in some compound. Beside uranium they found one element, and one only, that had the power of giving off rays spontaneously. This was the metal *thorium*. For the property these metals possessed, Marie proposed to use the term *radioactivity*; these two metals were *radioactive elements*.

Pitchblende, a mineral of Bohemia, contains both uranium and thorium. Marie had made no analysis of it, since no sample had been available. She received some through the mail. She expected that the radioactivity would be that of the uranium present and the thorium present added together. The result was *about four times as great*, so Pierre thought that some error had

143

been made. Marie checked and rechecked *her* experimental findings; there was no error. He checked and rechecked the radioactivity *he* had measured; there was no error. Where did this excessive or abnormal radiation come from? To Marie there was only one answer—and Pierre agreed. *Pitchblende must contain a powerfully radioactive element.* Since it had been missed completely in her analysis, she and Pierre had estimated that such an element could not be present as more than a hundredth of the entire weight of the mineral. Actually it was to be but a millionth of that weight.

In a communication sent to the French Academy of Science and published in the *Proceedings* on April 12, 1898, she announced the probable presence in pitchblende of a new element endowed with powerful radioactivity. She knew that the world of science would expect her to follow up the announcement by experimentally obtaining a pure substance that was a compound of the element. Then she would have to produce the element itself. These steps were needed before she could state positively, "It exists."

It was at this point that Pierre gave up his own research work to help Marie in her search. He was a lecturer at the University of Paris, so could not give full time; he did, however, do all the radioactive testing and, later, helped chemically by preparing the special compounds of the new element. That complete co-operation lasted for eight years—a period that was brought to a tragic close by Pierre's death in a traffic accident on a busy thoroughfare of Paris.

The pitchblende for the experimental work was supplied by the Austrian government from its uranium mines in Jachymov, Bohemia. The Curies had to pay only for the transportation— but even that was a strain upon the family purse. A more difficult matter was finding a place for Marie's laboratory in which tons of material would have to be worked over just to get the crystals that could be held on the tip of a penknife blade. They wanted a suitable workroom. All that Pierre could get was a little room facing the courtyard. On the other side of the yard was a wooden shack and an abandoned shed with a leaky skylight roof. The Faculty of Medicine of the University of Paris had formerly used the place as a dissecting room. The shed had a dirt-floor, some worn kitchen tables, and an old cast-iron stove with a rusty pipe. The shed had one advantage. It was so untempting, so miserable, that no one thought of refusing them its use or of charging rent . . .

By the end of the year they had a communication for the *Proceedings* that carried these lines:

> The various reasons we have enumerated lead us to believe that a second new radioactive substance obtained from pitchblende contains a new element to which we propose to give the name *radium*. This substance certainly contains at present a very strong proportion of barium; yet in spite of that its radioactivity is considerable. The radioactivity of pure radium must be enormous.

The days of work stretched out into months and years of effort. Little by little the "imperceptible traces" became visible as tiny crystals . . .

These tiny crystals were dangerous, however. A single one in a little sealed tube, the tube in a small metal box, the box in the pocket of her laboratory apron for the half-hour she was eating lunch, produced a red spot on Marie's skin and a sore that took a month to heal. But radium also was a saver of life. By destroying diseased cells, a crystal of such a radium compound cured growths, tumors, and certain forms of cancer; the epidermis, partially destroyed by the action, formed again in a healthy state.

(from *Men of Chemistry* by Keith Gordon Irwin)

Comprehension and Discussion

1. What does "spontaneously" mean? Why was it important that uranium's effects were "spontaneous"?

2. Why was it necessary to obtain a pure sample of the new element before they could convince the world of science?

3. What is "analysis"? What was Marie aiming to do when she "analyzed carefully all the uranium-containing minerals that were available"?

4. Why did Marie *first* send for a sample of pitchblende from Bohemia?

5. What is "the epidermis", and why is it significant that it "formed again in a healthy state"?

6. What is the difference between a chemist and a physicist? How is the difference illustrated here?

7. What would the distinction be between Pierre's "research work" and his lecturing?

8. Why *do* scientists go on with their work when it is expensive, uncomfortable or tedious to do so?

9. What other constructive and destructive uses for radio-active materials do you know of? Would it have been better if mankind had never made these and later discoveries about radioactivity and atomic physics?

10. Why are research results, like those of the Curies, usually published in learned journals? Should all research results be published, or are there circumstances when they can (or should) be kept secret?

For Written Answers

Except for No. 5, answers should be full sentences in your own words.

1. Was Becquerel right to assume that it was the uranium alone that fogged photographic plates on that occasion?

2. Why and how did Marie coin the word "radioactivity"?

3. What practical use was the fact that radioactive materials "took off electric charges"? How did Pierre in fact measure radioactivity?

4. Why did the Curies check and recheck their findings about the radioactivity of pitchblende?

5. Write out the sentence in the passage that explains why a large quantity of pitchblende was needed to get even a tiny sample of the new element.

6. What illustration does the passage give of the destructive power of radioactivity in radium? Recount this in your own words.

7. What sacrifices did the Curies make for their research?

8. In what ways was radium a saver of life?

Method Exercises

Exercise 1. The passage about the Curies twice refers to com-munications about their progress in the "Proceedings of the French Academy of Science".

(a) The first reference is given in *reported* or *indirect speech*:

> *She knew* that the world of science *would* expect *her* to follow up the announcement by experimentally obtaining a pure substance that *was* a compound of the element. Then *she would* have to produce the element itself. These steps *were* needed before *she could* state positively, "It exists."

We have printed every word that would need changing, if it were direct speech, in italics. Rewrite this as direct speech, beginning:

> "I know that . . ."

(b) In the second reference, we are given the exact words of the communication, i.e. it is in *direct speech*:

> "The various reasons *we have* enumerated *lead us* to believe that a second new radioactive substance obtained from pitchblende *contains* a new element to which *we propose* to give the name 'radium'. *This* substance certainly *contains* at *present* a very strong proportion of barium; yet in spite of that its radioactivity *is* considerable. The radioactivity of pure radium must be enormous."

Again, we have put into italics each word that would require altering, in order to make a report of this passage. Rewrite it in reported speech beginning:

> Professor and Madame Curie stated that the various reasons they . . .

Exercise 2. A study of the passages in Exercise 1 should illustrate most of the basic RULES FOR REPORTED SPEECH. They are as follows:

1. First and second person pronouns (and possessive adjectives) become third person. Use names to avoid any confusion of pronouns.

2. All present tenses become the equivalent past tense; and all future tenses become the equivalent conditional. Existing past and conditional tenses remain unchanged.

3. "This" becomes "that"; "these" becomes "those"; "here" becomes "there"; and so on.

4. Any mention of time or place will usually require to be altered.
   (The table of tenses on page 127 may help with Rule 2.)

The following sentences illustrate these rules (progressively and in the same order). Rewrite them in reported speech, beginning each in the way suggested:

(a) "In my next experiment I wanted to show you my latest discovery," the research assistant told the professor.
   The research assistant told the professor that . . .

(b) "After studying your apparatus, I applied your principles to something I thought of myself."
   After studying the professor's . . .

(c) "I hope you know what you are doing," the professor commented.
   The professor commented that . . .

(d) "I have seen some serious accidents in my years as a scientist," he added.
   He added that . . .

(e) "Young people just will not take the precautions I should consider essential."
   Young people just . . .

(f) "I am sure this apparatus I have here will prove safe enough," replied the assistant.
   The assistant replied that . . .

(g) "In the next few minutes I hope I shall convince you," he said.
   He said that in the following few . . .

(h) "After what you did last week," said the professor slowly, "I need a lot of convincing."
   The professor said slowly that after . . .

Exercise 3. (a) An etymological dictionary has the following entry for "radium":

Rad'ium, n. 1898. (f. L. *radius*, ray, RADUS + -IUM.)
A metallic element found in small quantities in combination in pitchblende.

What does "etymological" mean? Where in this entry is the etymology of "radium" given? Discuss the significance of all the signs and abbreviations, and of variations in type, used, in this entry.

The Curies had to create new words for *radium, radioactivity,* and another new element they called *polonium.* In each case they adapted existing root words. Thus the word *polonium* they made from *Polonia* (Latin for Poland), because Marie was originally Polish. Look up what *uranium* and *thorium* were named after.

(b) Find out the meaning of the following Latin and Greek prefixes (and one suffix), all of which have frequently been used to build up English words. For each one, find three English words that incorporate it.

Latin	Greek	Latin	Greek
ante-	anti-	mal-	-logy
ex-	auto-	retro-	micro-
extra-	bio-	trans-	photo-
inter-	cyclo-	sub-	poly-
intra-	hypo-	super-	tele-

(c) New words are constantly being added to any living language.

(i) In English, they are frequently made from basically Latin or Greek root-words. Recent examples are:

cosmonaut aerosol automation stereophonic megaton

Find five more new words of this kind, using a good dictionary to check that they have been introduced within the last twenty years.

(ii) Other words are made by combining or adapting existing English words:

e.g. count-down hovercraft to tape (v.) panel-game off-beat

Find five more words of this kind, again checking etymologies and dates in a dictionary.

(iii) Some words enter the language from current slang or jargon, or from passing fashions and interests, e.g.:

blitz evacuee quisling barrage-balloon firewatcher

These were all Second World War terms: have they become permanent additions to the language? The following are post-war examples:

scampi rock'n-roll teddy-boy brainwashing beatnik

Add five more (even more recent) examples, and comment on how likely these are to become permanent parts of our language.

(d) Attempt dictionary definitions of the meaning of some (or all) of the recent words given as examples in (c).

Exercise 4. (a) As revision of the difference between verbs taking *objects* and those taking *complements,* study the following three sentences:

> The tramp seemed tired and old.
> The tramp seemed a tired old man.
> The tramp was tiring his companion out.

Find in these examples an adjective complement, a noun complement, and an object, and discuss the difference between object and complement.

(b) State which pattern each of the following sentences follows, i.e. is it:

> subject—verb—adjective complement,
> subject—verb—noun complement,
> or subject—verb—object?

  (i) The two old men were obviously tramps.
 (ii) They had no place to sleep.
(iii) The children were being a nuisance to them.
 (iv) They drank milk from an old bottle.
  (v) It tasted very unpleasant.
 (vi) It had turned sour in the sun.
(vii) Some people may always remain poor from choice.
(viii) These men had had no chance to choose.
 (ix) Are all tramps as pathetic as that?
  (x) They had gradually become resigned to the life.

(c) Compare these newspaper headlines:

> SUMMERS GETS BETTER
>   (subject—verb—adjective complement)
> SUMMERS GETS THE CUP
>   (subject—verb—object)
> SUMMERS TURNS PROFESSIONAL
>   (subject—verb—noun complement)

Find, or make up, any five headlines that follow the first of these patterns, another five (not necessarily at all related to the first five) following the second pattern, and five following the third pattern.

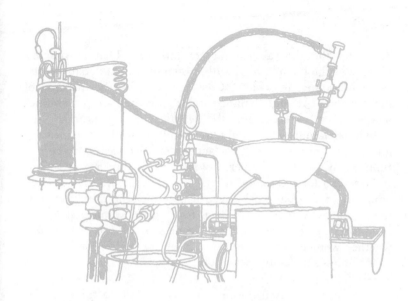

Writing Your Own

1. Choose any outstanding scientist, inventor or engineer whom you admire and do some research into the facts of his (or her) life and work. This composition could be similar in plan to your account of a sportsman (page 32), but concentrate here more on the importance of the man's contribution to progress, perhaps, in fact, recounting the story of his one greatest achievement, and the difficulties he had to overcome, rather than writing a short biography. Your composition needs to be planned and paragraphed with care, and it is important to see that all the facts are correct.

2. Write a clear and accurate account of any experiment you have performed, or seen demonstrated or read about recently. Remember to write for an intelligent layman, and therefore to explain in clear terms the purpose of the experiment and the apparatus required. Set out the steps of the process in logical order, explaining how the result demonstrates the point to be proved. Your style should be impersonal and clear—you are *not* telling the story of a personal adventure in the laboratory! You may include diagrams if you wish, but these should be additional illustrations, and not a substitute for explanation in words.

Oral Work

1. Under the general heading, or motion, "That a woman's place is in the home", hold a discussion or formal debate on the place of women in society. Consider not only the question of how women should balance their domestic responsibilities against their careers, but also whether the government (or individual families) are right to spend as much on educating girls as on boys. (Do girls in fact get equal educational opportunities?) Consider whether any careers or jobs are, or should be, reserved for men only, whether women should always have equal pay for equal work (even if they have no family to support), and why there have been fewer great women scientists, composers, artists or political leaders than men. Consider whether women with careers are liable to be less feminine, or to make less satisfactory wives and mothers.

2. After some research, be prepared to explain to the class the difference between a hypothesis, a theory, and a proven fact. Illustrate your explanation with examples.

Activities and Research

1. Prepare a short explanation of the field covered by some or all of these sciences:

aeronautics	chemistry	meteorology
anthropology	cybernetics	physics
astronomy	economics	psychology
biology	electronics	sociology
botany	geology	zoology

2. Look up the following and discuss whether they should be classed as sciences at all:

alchemy; astrology; necromancy; palmistry; graphology; phrenology; theology.

3. Find out how the ancient Greeks and Romans counted up to one hundred, in Greek and Latin, and find as many English words as you can that are derived from these numbers:

e.g. centenary, from Latin *centum*, 100.

Further Reading

Men of Chemistry by KEITH GORDON IRWIN (Dobson)
This book surveys the history of chemistry from Ancient Egypt to the nuclear age and includes the contributions of all the outstanding chemists, sometimes in their own words. (540)   To find out more about Marie Curie, read *The Radium Woman* by ELEANOR DOORLY (Heinemann). (920)

The Radar Man (The Story of Sir Robert Watson-Watt) by JOHN ROWLAND (Lutterworth)
One of a series of biographies that investigate the personal background of scientists who have shaped modern science, this book also explains the nature and importance of discoveries about radar. (920)

The Scientist by H. MARGENAU and D. BERGAMINI (Time-Life)
The world of science has become impossible for any one man to understand in detail. But this beautifully illustrated book tries to draw the threads of science together by looking at scientists, their backgrounds, their instruments, their methods, their interaction with each other and the world at large, and their greatest achievements and honours. This is a fascinating book to browse through. (500)

Men and Women Behind the Atom by SARAH R. RIEDMAN (Abelard-Schuman)
Eleven short biographies and much scientific information are to be found in this very readable account of the development of atomic physics up to 1957. (925)

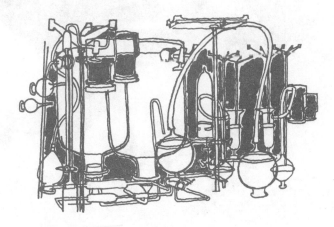

The mysterious stranger, Shane, has come to live and work with the Starretts on their farm and is involved in their struggle against Fletcher and the cattlemen, who want to drive the farmers off the grasslands. Young Bob Starrett tells the story of how Fletcher's man, Chris, tried to provoke Shane in the Saloon at the local store.

CHAPTER ELEVEN

The West

I dashed into the store side, over to the opening between the two big rooms. I crouched on a box just inside the store where I could hear everything and see most of the other room. It was long and fairly wide. The bar curved out from the opening and ran all the way along the inner wall to the back wall, which closed off a room Grafton used as an office. There was a row of windows on the far side, too high for anyone to look in from outside. A small stairway behind them led up to a sort of balcony across the back with doors opening into several little rooms.

Shane was leaning easily with one arm on the bar, his drink in his other hand, when Chris came to perhaps six feet away and called for a whiskey bottle and a glass. Chris pretended he did not notice Shane at first and bobbed his head in greeting to the men at the table. They were a pair of mule-skinners who made regular trips into the valley freighting in goods for Grafton and other shops. I could have sworn that Shane studying Chris in his effortless way, was somehow disappointed.

Chris waited until he had his whiskey and had gulped a stiff shot. Then he deliberately looked Shane over like he had just spotted him.

"Hello, farmer," he said. He said it as if he did not like farmers.

Shane regarded him with grave attention. "Speaking to me?" he asked mildly and finished his drink.

"Hell, there ain't nobody else standing there. Here have a drink of this." Chris shoved his bottle along the bar. Shane poured himself a generous slug and raised it to his lips.

"I'll be damned," flipped Chris. "So you drink whiskey."

Shane tossed off the rest in his glass and set it down. "I've had better," he said, as friendly as could be. "But this will do."

Chris slapped his leather chaps with a loud smack. He turned to take in the other men. "Did you hear that? This farmer drinks whiskey! I didn't think these plough-pushing dirt-grubbers drank anything stronger than soda pop!"

"Some of us do," said Shane, friendly as before. Then he was no longer friendly and his voice was like winter frost. "You've had your fun and it's mighty young fun. Now run home and tell Fletcher to send a grown-up man next time." He turned away and sang out to Will Atkey. "Do you have any soda pop? I'd like a bottle."

Will hesitated, looked kind of funny, and scuttled past me into the store room. He came back right away with a bottle of the pop Grafton kept there for us school kids. Chris was standing quiet, not so much mad, I would have said, as puzzled. It was as though they were playing some queer game and he was not sure of the next move. He sucked on his lower lip for a while. Then he snapped his mouth and began to look elaborately around the room, sniffing loudly.

"Hey, Will!" he called. "What's been happening in here? It smells. That ain't no clean cattleman smell. That's plain dirty barnyard." He stared at Shane. "You, farmer. What are you and Starrett raising out there? Pigs?"

Shane was just taking hold of the bottle Will had fetched him. His hand closed on it and the knuckles showed white. He moved slowly, almost unwillingly, to face Chris. Every line of his body was as taut as stretched whipcord, was alive and somehow rich with an immense eagerness. There was that fierce concentration in him, filling him, blazing in his eyes. In that moment there was nothing in the room for him but that mocking man only a few feet away.

The big room was so quiet the stillness fairly hurt. Chris stepped back involuntarily, one pace, two, then pulled up erect. And still nothing happened. The lean muscles along the sides of Shane's jaw were ridged like rock.

Then the breath, pent in him, broke the stillness with a soft sound as it left his lungs. He looked away from Chris, past him over the tops of the swinging doors beyond, over the roof of the shed across the road, on into the distance where the mountains loomed in their own unending loneliness. Quietly he walked, the bottle forgotten in his hand, so close by Chris as almost to brush him yet apparently not even seeing him, through the doors and was gone.

I heard a sigh of relief near me. Mr. Grafton had come up from somewhere behind me. He was watching Chris with a strange ironic quirk at his mouth corners. Chris was trying not to look pleased with himself. But he swaggered as he went to the doors and peered over them.

"You saw it, Will," he called over his shoulder. "He walked out on me." Chris pushed up his hat and rolled back on his heels and laughed. "With a bottle of soda pop too!" He was still laughing as he went out and we heard him ride away.

"That boy's a fool," Mr. Grafton muttered.

Will Atkey came sidling over to Mr. Grafton. "I never pegged Shane for a play like that," he said.

"He was afraid, Will."

"Yeah. That's what was so funny. I would've guessed he could take Chris."

Mr. Grafton looked at Will as he did often, like he was a little sorry for him. "No, Will. He wasn't afraid of Chris. He was afraid of himself."

(from *Shane* by Jack Schaefer)

Comprehension and Discussion

1. Who were Mr. Grafton and Will Atkey? What job did each do? Which of them was more intelligent and discerning?

2. Is it true that Chris and Shane were "playing some queer game"?

3. Do you agree with Shane that Chris's insults were "mighty young fun"?

4. What does the phrase "taut as a stretched whipcord" imply? Why is the word "rich" used in the next part of that sentence?

5. What does the description of Shane's jaw tell us about him and his thoughts?

6. Judging from phrases like "almost unwillingly", and from the way Shane looked beyond Chris towards the mountains, what do you think was going on in Shane's mind at that critical moment?

7. What would have happened if Shane had not walked out?

8. What do the following terms and phrases mean?
   mule-skinners; freighting in; a stiff shot (of whiskey); a generous slug (of whiskey); leather chaps; ironic quirk; pegged Shane for a play like that.

157

9. How is Chris's choice of words to describe farmers made insulting? Suggest some words and phrases Shane *might* have used to insult cattlemen in reply.

10. Is this incident typical of "Western" novels, films and plays? Would you call the characters and situation hackneyed? Does the style of writing make use of any slang or worn-out words and phrases, either where young Bob Starrett is supposed to be telling the story, or in the conversation?

For Written Answers

Give full answers in your own words. (Remember *not* to begin answers with "Because . . .")

1. Why might Shane have been disappointed that Chris seemed not to notice him at first?
2. Why do you think Shane sent for a bottle of soda pop?
3. Is it important that it was *this* bottle he gripped so fiercely?
4. Why did Mr. Grafton sigh with relief?
5. Why hadn't young Bob noticed him come up?
6. Does Will Atkey or Mr. Grafton seem to understand Shane better? What does each think about Shane's behaviour?
7. Why did Mr. Grafton think Chris a fool?
8. Explain in your own words what probably made Shane "afraid of himself".
9. Describe in your own words the layout of the bar-room as indicated here. Also draw a sketch-plan of it.

Beeston, the place, near Nottingham;
We lived there for three years or so.
Every Saturday at two o'clock
We queued up for the matinée,
All the kids for streets around
With snotty noses, giant caps,
Cut down coats and heavy boots,
The natural enemies of cops
And schoolteachers. Profane and hoarse
We scrambled, yelled and fought until
The Picture Palace opened up
And then, like Hamelin children, forced
Our bony way into the Hall,
That much is easy to recall;
Also the reek of chewing-gum,
Gob-stoppers and liquorice,
But of the flickering myths themselves
Not much remains. The hero was
A milky, wide brimmed hat, a shape
Astride the arched white stallion.
The villain's horse and hat were black.
Disbelief did not exist
And laundered virtue always won
With quicker gun and harder fist
And all of us applauded it.
Yet I remember moments when
In solitude I'd find myself
Brooding on the sooty man,
The bristling villain, who could move
Imagination in a way
The well-shaved hero never could,
And even warm the nervous heart
With something oddly close to love.

VERNON SCANNELL

Discussing The Poem

1. Recall or re-read Robert Browning's poem *The Pied Piper of Hamelin*, and then discuss why these children entering the cinema were "like Hamelin children".

2. Discuss the words and phrases chosen to describe (a) the "kids", and (b) the "hero". Look particularly at striking expressions like "we . . . forced our bony way" and "laundered virtue always won".

3. What did Vernon Scannell feel about "the bristling villain"? Does this tell us anything about the Western films, or anything about the kind of child the poet was? (Note that the poem is entitled " *Autobiographical Note*".)

Method Exercises

Exercise 1. The following is a *reported* (or *indirect*) *speech* version of part of the passage from Shane, beginning:

> He turned to take in the other men. "Did you hear that? . . .

Chris turned to take in the other men and asked them whether they had heard what Shane said. Chris expressed surprise that the farmer drank whiskey and exclaimed that he did not think those "plough-pushing dirt-grubbers" drank anything stronger than soda pop.

Shane replied, friendly as before, that some of them did. Then he was no longer friendly, and in a voice like winter frost he told Chris that he had had his fun, and that it was very young fun. He then told Chris to run home and tell Fletcher to send a grown-up man next time. Turning away, he called to Will Atkey to ask if he had any soda pop, and said that he would like a bottle.

Compare this closely with the original, direct speech version

Notice how, in addition to the four rules given on page 147, the following three RULES FOR REPORTED SPEECH are applied here:

5. Questions become statements, usually introduced by the words "if" or "whether".

6. Exclamations also become indirect statements, worded to suggest the pain, surprise, pleasure, scorn, etc. implied in them.

7. Commands and requests become appropriate statements, using adverbs such as "politely" to suggest the word "please", and so on.

Turn the following into reported (or indirect) speech, beginning in the way suggested in each case.

(a) "Do you like Western books and films?" the teacher asked the class.
    The teacher asked the class whether . . .

(b) "Which are the best Westerns you have ever seen or heard?" he continued.
    He continued by asking them which . . .

(c) "What! Is it true you have never seen a single Western film, Smith?" he exclaimed in surprise.
    He expressed surprise and asked Smith if . . .

(d) "Right, be quiet! I shall now read this extract from 'Shane' to you all," the teacher said.
    The teacher ordered the class to . . .

(e) "Goodness! Have you seen this paper, dear?" said the professor's wife. "There's a report of your death on the front page."
    The professor's wife exclaimed . . .

(f) "Oh, really," the professor replied without looking up from his book; "then don't forget to send a wreath, my dear."
    Without looking up from his book, the professor casually . . .

(g) "Hey, Will!" Chris called. "What's been happening in here? It smells. That ain't no clean cattleman smell. That's plain dirty barnyard."
    Chris called loudly to ask Will . . .

(h) Chris stared at Shane. "You, farmer. What are you and Starrett raising out there? Pigs?"
    Chris stared at Shane, and, calling him a . . .

Exercise 2. Words have associations and suggestions beyond their basic meaning. When Chris wants to insult Shane, he calls him a "plough-pushing dirt-grubber". If he had talked of "farm-workers on the arable lands" or of "skilled ploughmen and sons of the soil", the meaning would have been similar, but the implications quite different.

Many words are EMOTIONALLY TONED; they suggest particular feelings and attitudes. Consider all the words for a *smell*:

perfume, fragrance, scent, aroma, odour, fume, stink, stench. Notice how these suggestions range from something delicate and delightful to something repellent and disgusting. Where would we place the word "smell" itself in this range?

(a) Advertisers are particularly aware of the power and importance of emotionally toned words. Each of the following advertiser's phrases in the left-hand column could be matched in basic meaning with one phrase in the right-hand column, but they are very different in implication. Pair them off, and comment on the difference.

e.g. "tough quality" is equivalent to "coarse strength".

Complimentary	Uncomplimentary
tough quality	unusually stupid countryman
generous size	long-term expense
compact, traditional cottage	rude and vulgar
gay colours	dull cream paint
soft, natural tone	a slippery shine
easy payments	a bewildering variety
a trend-leading breakthrough	inconvenient bulk
a polished, glossy surface	gaudy appearance
a wide range	an untried invention
quaint old rustic personality	small, old-fashioned house
frank and outspoken	coarse strength

(b) Write two short descriptions of each of the following, so that one is favourable and the other insulting or critical.

e.g. The smell in a cowshed.

(i) The rich, country odour of decomposing manure.

(ii) The sickening stench of rotting dung.

A man's beard	Warm sunshine	Snakes
A long journey	Fried food	A fast car
A strong, alcoholic drink		An old building
A manual worker		Snow in a town

Exercise 3. Look up the term CLICHÉ and discuss how metaphors, similes and other phrases become the clichés of conversation and writing. Slang, weak words and phrases, and clichés are found most often in conversation and ill-considered writing. The following examples come from the passages in Chapters Two, Five, Seven and this chapter. Why should they be more common in these particular passages?

Rewrite the following sentences, replacing the weak parts (in italics) with clearer, more lively and more original phrasing.

(a) The conversation stopped *for a split second*.
(b) I was about *to call it a day* when I *had a sudden urge* to try once more.
(c) I'll do my best *to straighten you out* if you want me to.
(d) *It's up to you* now, son.
(e) I knew *deep down inside of me* that he had only my interests at heart.
(f) That is *where you came unstuck*.
(g) The German left full-back *had you worried*.
(h) Let's *put the wind up* Broccoli.
(i) He takes it all so seriously and *this lays him open to attack*, a *shot in the back*.
(j) I liked being *out of the swim*.
(k) Now I come *to the root of the matter*.
(l) I'm *scared to death* that we shall be discovered.
(m) I wish *like anything* that one of our protectors could sleep here.
(n) Will hesitated, *looked kind of funny*, and scuttled past me into the store room.

Exercise 4. What is the difference between a *phrase* and a *clause*? Both phrases and clauses can act as adverbs, and three common kinds of *adverb phrases and clauses* are those of place (saying where something happened), those of time (saying when something happened), and those of manner (saying how something happened). Study these examples:

(i) *Adverb phrase of place:*

Chris was standing still by the rail.

(ii) *Adverb clause of place:*

I crouched where I could hear everything.

(iii) *Adverb phrase of time:*

Chris did not notice Shane <u>at first</u>.

(iv) *Adverb clause of time:*

Shane was leaning easily on the bar <u>when Chris came to perhaps six feet away</u>.

 (v) *Adverb phrase of manner:*

Shane was leaning <u>with one arm on the bar</u>.

(vi) *Adverb clause of manner:*

He said it <u>as if he did not like farmers</u>.

   In the following sentences, adapted from the passage, some adverb phrases and clauses have been printed in italics. In each case, state whether it is a phrase or a clause, whether it is acting as an adverb of time, of place or of manner, and what verb it modifies (or describes).

(a) Chris stalked up *on the porch*.

(b) I crouched *where I could see most of the other room*.

(c) Will came back *right away*.

(d) Shane was leaning easily on the bar *when Chris called for a whiskey bottle and a glass*.

(e) Shane was leaning easily *with his drink in his other hand*.

(f) Mr. Grafton looked at Will *as he did often*.

(g) He sucked on his lower lip *for a while*.

(h) He began to look *around the room*.

(i) *In that moment* there was nothing in the room for him.

(j) Chris rolled back *on his heels*.

Writing Your Own

1. Consider again the qualities of the outstanding sportsman you wrote about in Chapter Two, and of the outstanding scientist you described in Chapter Ten. How do they compare with the "heroes" of books, and those in history and legend? Is there a "stock" or conventional idea of a hero in all the books you have read and the films and plays you have seen? Can an

author make a hero out of a criminal or someone who is weak and unsuccessful? What do you think about Vernon Scannell's feeling that heroes are sometimes too good or too successful to be interesting, while the villains can command our sympathy?

Taking as your examples some heroes you remember well, write an essay on "The Hero in Books and Films", discussing what seem to be his essential qualities, and whether the conventional idea of a fictional hero is just an unreal ideal that is never matched in real life.

2. Write two short, clear descriptions of "wanted" persons, in a style suitable for a police announcement. Choose two contrasting subjects, such as a hardened criminal and a missing child. Here are twenty-two headings used by the police when compiling a description. Using these as a guide, make yours as complete a word picture as possible.

(a) Full name and place of birth.
(b) Date of birth (if known) or age (apparent).
(c) Occupation (any known previous occupation to be included).
(d) Height.
(e) Build (stout, medium, thin, erect, stoops, etc.).
(f) Face (long, round, broad, smiling, scowling, wrinkled, etc.).
(g) Complexion (fair, dark, pale, sallow, fresh, made up, etc.).
(h) Hair on face (colour, quantity, style, clean shaven, etc.).
(i) Hair (colour, quantity, parting, bobbed, shingled, waved, cut, etc.).
(j) Forehead (high, low, bulging, vertical, receding, etc.).
(k) Eyebrows (colour, thick, thin, shape, pencilled, plucked, etc.).
(l) Eyes (colour, large, small, squint, peculiarities, glasses [if any] etc.).
(m) Nose (large, small, hook, straight, flat, broken, turned up, etc.)
(n) Mouth (large, small, open, close shut, droops at corners, etc.).
(o) Lips (thick, thin, upper or lower protruding, rouged, pale, cracked, etc.).
(p) Teeth (white, discoloured, prominent, gaps, false, etc.).
(q) Chin (receding, projecting, dimpled, double, etc.).
(r) Ears (large, small, close to head, protruding, pierced, long or short lobe, etc.).
(s) Marks (scars, warts, birth-marks, pimples, tattoos, etc.).
(t) Peculiarities (stammer, accent, gait, deformities, etc.).
(u) Habits (fond of racing, games, smoking, drinking, women, speaks of . . . , etc.).
(v) Dress.

Discuss Western books, films and television programmes. Some members of the class should collect evidence for these criticisms:

that the scenes, characters and situations are hackneyed and repeated too often;

that the heroes are admired for their toughness and self-confidence, and not for really admirable qualities like sympathy, intelligence or generosity;

that the stories look upon Indians, Negroes and foreigners as inferior to the American heroes;

that the stories glamorise gambling, drinking and searching for wealth, when these are actually sordid and degrading;

that it is wrong to base law and order on violence and the use of force;

that the over-simplified picture of independent heroes and treacherous villains is so unreal that it is wrong to go on portraying it.

Other members of the class must prepare to defend Westerns by pointing out the good qualities of the best of them.

Activities and Research

Find out about the factual history of the American West, including something about the dates and importance of the following:

Davy Crockett; The California Gold Rush; Henry Wells, William Fargo and the American Express Co.; The Pony Express; The Union Pacific Railway; Lt.-Col. George Custer and his "last stand"; the Sioux and Apache Indians and the Indian Wars; Jesse Chisholm's Trail; Wild Bill Hickok, Wyatt Earp and "Doc" Holliday.

Each member of the class should make up two suitable questions as a contribution to a class quiz on this theme.

How does the true history of these people and events match the representation of them in books and films, as far as you can tell?

Shane by JACK SCHAEFER (Deutsch; Penguin; Corgi; Heinemann)
The feud between the cattle ranchers and the farmers gradually
worsens until at last Fletcher calls in a professional killer,
Wilson. This step forces Shane to revert to his former role of
gunfighter. This book is distinguished from many other Western
novels by its sympathetic treatment of "good" and "bad"
characters, and the delicate handling of the personal relationships that arise.

O. Henry Westerns by O. HENRY (selected by Patrick Thornhill)
  (Methuen)
Short, humorous, often thrilling, these are short stories by a
man, himself for many years a cowboy, who was a master of the
twisted plot and the unexpected ending.

The Ranger and Other Stories by ZANE GREY (Hodder & Stoughton)
Here are four tales of the old American West by one of its
classic storytellers, whose style is gripping and whose characters
are straightforward and uncomplicated.

Pictorial History of the Wild West by J. D. HORAN AND P. SANN
  (Spring Books)
This book gives a true and very full account of the outlaws of the
Old West, and of the men who fought them to establish law
and order. Here are the stories of legendary figures such as
Butch Cassidy, Buffalo Bill, Billy the Kid and Wyatt Earp,
vividly recounted and excitingly illustrated. (937.6)

Gerald Durrell spent part of his childhood on the Greek island of Corfu. A crumbling, old, plaster-covered garden wall at their villa proved a particularly rich hunting ground for the young naturalist.

CHAPTER TWELVE

A Young Naturalist

But the shyest and most self-effacing of the wall community
were the most dangerous; you hardly ever saw one unless you
looked for it, and yet there must have been several hundred
living in the cracks of the wall. Slide a knife blade carefully under
a piece of the loose plaster and lever it gently away from the
brick, and there, crouching beneath it, would be a little
black scorpion an inch long, looking as though he were made
out of polished chocolate. They were weird-looking things, with
their flattened, oval bodies, their neat, crooked legs, the enormous crab-like claws, bulbous and neatly jointed as armour,
and the tail like a string of brown beads ending in a sting like
a rose-thorn. The scorpion would lie there quietly as you
examined him, only raising his tail in an almost apologetic
gesture of warning if you breathed too hard on him. If you kept
him in the sun too long he would simply turn his back on you
and walk away, and then slide slowly but firmly under another
section of plaster . . .

Then one day I found a fat female scorpion in the wall, wearing what at first glance appeared to be a pale fawn fur coat.
Closer inspection proved that this strange garment was made
up of a mass of tiny babies clinging to the mother's back. I was
enraptured by this family, and I made up my mind to smuggle
them into the house and up to my bedroom so that I might
keep them and watch them grow up. With infinite care I
manoeuvred the mother and family into a matchbox, and then
hurried to the villa. It was rather unfortunate that just as I
entered the door lunch should be served; however, I placed the
matchbox carefully on the mantelpiece in the drawing-room,
so that the scorpion should get plenty of air, and made my way
to the dining-room and joined the family for the meal. Dawd-
ling over my food, feeding Roger surreptitiously under the table
and listening to the family arguing, I completely forgot about
my exciting new captures. At last Larry, having finished,
fetched the cigarettes from the drawing-room, and lying back
in his chair he put one in his mouth and picked up the match-

box he had brought. Oblivious of my impending doom I watched him interestedly, as, still talking glibly, he opened the matchbox.

Now I maintain to this day that the female scorpion meant no harm. She was agitated and a trifle annoyed at being shut up in a matchbox for so long, and so she seized the first opportunity to escape. She hoisted herself out of the box with great rapidity, her babies clinging on desperately, and scuttled on to the back of Larry's hand. There, not quite certain what to do next, she paused, her sting curved up at the ready. Larry, feeling the movement of her claws, glanced down to see what it was, and from that moment things got increasingly confused.

He uttered a roar of fright that made Lugaretzia drop a plate and brought Roger out from beneath the table, barking wildly. With a flick of his hand he sent the unfortunate scorpion flying down the table, and she landed midway between Margo and Leslie, scattering babies like confetti as she thumped on the cloth. Thoroughly enraged at this treatment, the creature sped towards Leslie, her sting quivering with emotion. Leslie leapt to his feet, overturning his chair, and flicked out desperately with his napkin, sending the scorpion rolling across the cloth towards Margo, who promptly let out a scream that any railway engine would have been proud to produce. Mother, completely bewildered by this sudden and rapid change from peace to chaos, put on her glasses and peered down the table to see what was causing the pandemonium, and at that moment Margo, in a vain attempt to stop the scorpion's advance, hurled a glass of water at it. The shower missed the animal completely, but successfully drenched Mother, who, not being able to stand cold water, promptly lost her breath and sat gasping at the end of the table, unable even to protest. The scorpion had now gone to ground under Leslie's plate, while her babies swarmed wildly all over the table. Roger, mystified by the panic, but determined to do his share, ran round and round the room, barking hysterically.

"It's that bloody boy again . . ." bellowed Larry.

"Look out! Look out! They're coming!" screamed Margo.

"All we need is a book," roared Leslie; "don't panic, hit 'em with a book."

"What on earth's the *matter* with you all?" Mother kept imploring, mopping her glasses.

"It's that bloody boy . . . he'll kill the lot of us . . . Look at the table . . . knee-deep in scorpions . . ."

"Quick . . . quick . . . do something . . . Look out, look out!"

· "Stop screeching and get a book, for God's sake . . . You're worse than the dog . . . Shut *up*, Roger . . ."

"By the Grace of God I wasn't bitten . . ."

"Look out . . . there's another one . . . Quick . . . quick . . ."

"Oh, shut up and get me a book or something . . ."

"But *how* did the scorpions get on the table, dear?"

"That bloody boy . . . Every matchbox in the house is a deathtrap . . ."

"Look out, it's coming towards me . . . Quick, quick, do something . . ."

"Hit it with your knife . . . *your knife* . . . Go on, hit it . . ."

Since no one had bothered to explain things to him, Roger was under the mistaken impression that the family were being attacked, and that it was his duty to defend them. As Lugaretzia was the only stranger in the room, he came to the logical conclusion that she must be the responsible party, so he bit her in the ankle. This did not help matters very much.

(from *My Family and Other Animals* by Gerald Durrell)

Comprehension and Discussion

1. What does "self-effacing" mean? In what way were the scorpions self-effacing? Why were they rarely seen?

2. How closely did Gerald "examine" the scorpion when he says "he would lie there quite quietly as you examined him"?

3. What is an "almost apologetic gesture"? In what sense could the scorpion's warning be "apologetic"?

4. It was unfortunate that Gerald was called to lunch on his way into the house. What else was unfortunate, or foolish, about his behaviour that meal-time? What does "oblivious of my impending doom" mean?

5. Whereabouts on its body is a scorpion's sting and how serious is its sting? Was all the panic justified?

6. What evidence has Gerald got for his assertion that the scorpion meant no harm?

7. Go through the conversation in this passage, deciding who said which line in each case where it is not clearly indicated. What picture emerges from this incident of the different personalities of Gerald's brothers, Larry and Leslie, of his sister Margo and his mother?

8. How would you have reacted to the scorpion? What is the best way to deal with potentially dangerous wild creatures? Would you agree that the Durrell family illustrate how *not* to react?

9. Discuss what is humorous about this incident and the way it is told.

10. Discuss whether it is sometimes right to use swear-words (like "bloody") in writing conversations or in writing stories.

For Written Answers

1. (a) Find *one* word in the passage that clearly shows that the scorpions were one among many kinds of creatures living together in the wall.

   (b) Find *one* word which indicates that Gerald was strictly forbidden to carry such creatures into the house.

2. Did these scorpions like the sun? How is this indicated in the passage?

3. Where did Gerald intend to keep his family of scorpions and why was he so determined to defy his family's rule in this way?

4. What does "surreptitiously" mean, and why should Gerald be feeding Roger in this way?

5. How does a scorpion hold its sting when it is ready to attack?

6. List all the comparisons Gerald Durrell uses in this passage, considering the effectiveness of each one. You will have to decide whether, "a scream that any railway engine would have been proud to produce", is a kind of comparison.

7. Write in your own words a brief account (of several sentences) of the size, shape, appearance and habits of the scorpion, as far as can be gathered from this passage.

Method Exercises

Exercise 1. The following words appear in this order in the passage from *My Family and Other Animals*. Six are used as nouns, six as verbs (or parts of verbs), six as adjectives, six as adverbs.

> self-effacing, lever, bulbous, apologetic, gesture, enraptured, smuggle, manoeuvred, surreptitiously, oblivious, impending, glibly, scuttled, confetti, thoroughly, emotion, desperately, promptly, bewildered, chaos, peered, pandemonium, advance, hysterically.

Write them out in four columns, starting like this:

Nouns	*Verbs*	*Adjectives*	*Adverbs*
gesture	lever	self-effacing	surreptitiously

Find the meaning of each word, and make up a sentence using it as the same part of speech and with a similar meaning.

Exercise 2. Larry was particularly prone to *exaggeration* in the incident in the passage. It is doubtful if he literally means to say about Gerald:

> "He'll kill the lot of us."

What other two exaggerations does he use in the rest of his outburst? Exaggeration for the sake of effect is known as HYPERBOLE (find out how to pronounce this word). It is frequently found in the form of comparisons, and is often a sign of a rather weak style.

The opposite of hyperbole is LITOTES (How is this word pronounced?), or intentional understatement. Colloquial English is full of sayings like "not so bad" and "he is no fool", where we intentionally understate in order to convey the opposite meaning, i.e. that something is "very good" or someone is "clever".

Decide whether each of the following examples represents litotes or hyperbole, and discuss (i) what each means and (ii) whether the word or saying is a hackneyed one, i.e. a *cliché*, or whether it seems genuinely original.

(a) Thousands of scorpions were to be found in the crevices of the wall.

(b) Larry was not exactly pleased to find a scorpion in a match-box.

(c) The scorpion was naturally just a little annoyed at being shut up like that.

(d) She shot like lightning across the table.

(e) Roger's hysterical barking did not really help matters.

(f) Fantastic bargains: five new pence in the pound off all the goods in the window!

(g) By no means all of our goods are shoddy, madam.

(h) Bono brings you the whitest white wash of all.

(i) This tobacco is worth its weight in gold.

(j) "We're having a little trouble with the men," the manager told the Chairman of the Board, as the workers set fire to the factory.

(k) Climbing Everest is not quite the same as planning a Sunday School outing.

(l) He is so tall he stands out like a giant, a Colossus among men.

(m) Every time you turn around, you cost me money!

(n) You brainless zombie, watch what you're doing!

(o) My dear fellow, I cannot thank you enough!

Now make up a sentence using hyperbole, and another using litotes, to describe each of the following. Avoid clichés and weak language as far as you can.

An angry woman	A very shy boy
A fast, modern car	A large number of gnats
A good income	A flood
A dog howling	The pain from a small cut
The noise in a street market	A stormy sea

Exercise 3. We have already discussed the joining words called *conjunctions*, and how words like:

if, although, because, as, where, when, until, while, before, after, whenever, wherever,

are used to join together *clauses* (groups of words making partial sense, and each with a verb of its own). Conjunctions show the relationship of a subordinate part of a sentence, (telling us how, why, when or where something happens) to the main statement.

But there are other joining, or introductory, words called

PREPOSITIONS; these link *phrases* to the main statement.

e.g. in, on, under, over, behind, before, in front of, through, inside, outside, into, out of, by, from, to.

All these words establish a relationship in *place* between a particular noun or pronoun and the rest of the sentence:

e.g. Mr. Smith does his work *in* that building.

"Building" is linked to the rest of the sentence by "in". He might possibly have worked on, under, behind (etc.) the building. Each preposition thus establishes a different relationship.

Prepositions also establish relationships in *time*:

before, after, during, until, at, till, throughout, etc.

can all be used to indicate a time;

e.g. Mr. Smith does his work *during* the lunch-break.

Here, again, "during" shows us what "lunch-break" has to do with Mr. Smith's doing his work.

Other prepositions, such as:

of, for, by, like, on, about, to, etc.

are used to establish more abstract relationships;

e.g. I have no further information *about* Mr. Smith.

Notice that it would mean something quite different to say:

I have no further information *for* Mr. Smith.

Why should these words be called "prepositions"? Notice that they are often said to *govern* the nouns or pronouns they precede; alternatively these are called *objects of the preposition*.

(a) The same word may be a preposition when it introduces a phrase (i.e. governs a noun or pronoun), and a conjunction when it introduces a clause. State whether the words in italics in the following sentences are prepositions or conjunctions, writing out the phrase or clause each introduces.

1. Gerald Durrell waited *until* dinner was over.

2. I shall wait *until* next Thursday.

3. *After* dinner there was quite a family panic.

4. *After* he had found the scorpion, he put it in a matchbox.

5. You must understand how dangerous scorpions are *before* you learn to pick them up.

6. *Before* the Second World War, villas on Corfu were cheap.

7. I asked him *for* an answer, *for* he knew all the answers.

175

(b) The same word, following a verb, may be a preposition when it introduces a phrase (i.e. governs a noun or pronoun), and an adverb when it stands by itself, modifying the verb:

e.g. He returned *before* last Sunday. (preposition)

He had returned *before*. (adverb)

State whether the italicised words in the following sentences are prepositions or adverbs, and in each case make up another sentence of your own, using the preposition as an adverb, or the adverb as a preposition.

1. I was knocked *over*.
2. The band preceded the procession and the children ran *after* the column.
3. My friend walked casually *by*.
4. All the children ran *about* the village without shoes on.
5. Some had plenty and others did *without*.
6. *Throughout* the night there were frightening noises.
7. I have read *through* it all.
8. I will go *on* while you stop here.

(c) What are the prepositions that usually complete the following popular phrases? Use each phrase in a sentence of your own to illustrate the meaning of the phrase.

e.g.—the last resort

Answer: *In* the last resort we shall have to give in, but we shall do all we can to avoid this.

—the whole	—hook or—crook	——the hilt
—a doubt	—thick and thin	—you and me
—the weather	——sight——mind	—the balance
—top—the world	—one fell swoop	—vain
—the other hand	—the most part	—a premium

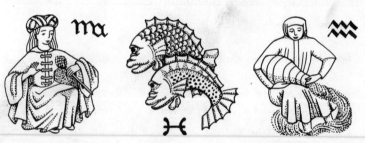

Exercise 4. In Chapter 11, we studied adverb clauses of time and place. Which words in the following sentences form an adverb clause of time, and which an adverb clause of place?

> Gerald levered the plaster away where he expected to find a scorpion. The scorpion would lie there quietly as he examined it.

Notice that the adverb clause of place could instead be introduced by "wherever", and that the conjunctions "when, while, until, before, after" can also introduce adverb clauses of time.

Complete each of the following sentences so that it contains a complete adverb clause, and then underline the adverb clause, stating whether it is of time or of place.

(a) Gerald and his family lived where the weather . . .

(b) He was surprised when . . .

(c) Gerald forgot about the scorpion in the matchbox until . . .

(d) He left the box on the mantelpiece while . . .

(e) Before he . . . Gerald put the box on the mantelpiece.

(f) Gerald watched Larry interestedly as . . .

(g) He had put the box where . . .

(h) After the female scorpion . . . she hid under a plate.

(i) Whenever . . . Roger barked more hysterically.

(j) Wherever he . . . Gerald was always collecting animals.

Writing Your Own

1. Write a short story incorporating either a *comic* encounter with an animal or animals, or an exaggerated and amusing domestic disaster or panic. Think first about what elements in a story help to make it funny· surprise, vivid and even eccentric

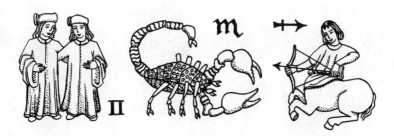

characters, incongruous situations (such as a very dignified person in a ludicrous predicament), sudden changes of mood lively conversation with exaggerated reactions to events, and even a cynical or resigned attitude in the writer. Discuss examples of these and other comic devices, and plan your own story carefully before you begin.

2. Attempt a short account of the appearance, habitat, food and life-cycle of any insect or small bird or mammal. You will probably need to consult reference books, but try to choose a creature you know well or can observe for yourself.

Although it is not a complete or "scientific" account, Gerald Durrell's picture of the scorpion in the passage in this chapter will give you some hints as to the kind of information to include, and how to use comparisons and accurately chosen words to convey the exact appearance of the creature you choose. Plan the composition, dealing with each topic (e.g. where it lives, what it eats, how it reproduces) in a separate paragraph.

Oral Work

1. The incident from *My Family and Other Animals* should provide a starting point for improvising a play, in which the actors must convey the very different characters and reactions of members of Gerald's family.

Similar comic incidents could also be worked out in play form (not necessarily with a full script) by groups of the class. Remember how important timing and character acting are to comic plays: some rehearsal will be necessary to achieve any really humorous effect.

2. Individual members of the class could choose short passages from books that they have found particularly amusing and prepare these for reading aloud to the class. You will soon realise that to do justice to the humour demands fluent reading with a good sense of timing and some variation in your voice (especially if conversation is included). Practise these.

Activities and Research

1. Illustrate the accounts of insects written by the class (Writing Your Own, 2) and collect them together to form a folder of work.

2. The Scorpion (Scorpio) is one of the twelve ancient Signs of the Zodiac. These are shown in the illustrations on pages 176-9. Write an illustrated article about these signs, where to see them in the night sky and what importance was attached to them by ancient astronomers. Refer to what you found out about astrology in Chapter Ten. Look at the modern use of horoscopes in newspapers and magazines today.

Further Reading

My Family and Other Animals by GERALD DURRELL (Allen & Unwin; Penguin)
This is the boyhood life of the famous naturalist and writer, full of delight in the rich natural life of Corfu and comic character-isation of his family and their eccentric friends. Try his other popular books, like *The New Noah* and *The Bafut Beagles*. (591.9)

Zoo Quest for a Dragon by DAVID ATTENBOROUGH (Lutterworth; U.L.P.)
David Attenborough gives a full account of a naturalist's expedition to Java, Bali, Borneo and Komodo, with as much interest in the peoples and customs of these places as in the strange animals he wanted to film. Try the other *Zoo Quest* books, by this well-known television personality. (591.9)

The *Instructions to Young Naturalists* series (Museum Press)
The topics covered in this series include "Amphibians and Pond Dwellers", "Insects", "Mammals", "Fossils" and ornithology, and they are dealt with by such well-known authorities as Brian Vesey-Fitzgerald and L. Hugh Newman. (560-590)

Wild Life in Danger by ALAN C. JENKINS (Methuen)
A fascinating, fully illustrated account of the world-wide struggle to save nearly extinct animals and preserve the precious balance of nature.

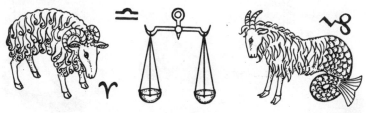

*The Moonfleet smugglers have captured Mr. Maskew, the local magis-
trate, spying on them: Elzevir Block, therefore, has in his power the
man who killed his son, David. John Trenchard, the young smuggler
who tells the story, owes his life to Elzevir, but he is also in love with
Maskew's daughter, Grace.*

CHAPTER THIRTEEN

Justice

At last he spoke again, but the brave words were gone, and the thin voice was thinner. He had dropped threats, and was begging piteously for his life. "Spare me," he said; "spare me, Mr. Block: I have an only daughter, a young girl with none but me to guard her. Would you rob a young girl of her only help and cast her on the world? Would you have them find me dead upon the cliff and bring me back to her a bloody corpse?"

Then Elzevir answered: "And had I not an only son, and was he not brought back to me a bloody corpse? Whose pistol was it that flashed in his face and took his life away? Do you not know? It was this very same that shall flash in yours. So make what peace you may have with God, for you have little time to make it."

With that he took the pistol from the ground where it had lain, and turning his back on Maskew, walked slowly to and fro among the bramble-plumps.

Though Maskew's words about his daughter seemed but to feed Elzevir's anger, by leading him to think of David, they sank deep in my heart; and if it had seemed a fearful thing before to stand by and see a fellow-creature butchered, it seemed now ten thousand times more fearful. And when I thought of Grace, and what such a deed would mean to her, my pulse beat so fierce that I must needs spring to my feet and run to reason with Elzevir, and tell him this must not be.

He was still walking among the bushes when I found him, and let me say my say till I was out of breath, and bore with me if I talked fast, and if my tongue outran my judgment.

"Thou hast a warm heart, lad," he said, "and 'tis for that I like thee. And if thou hast a chief place in thy heart for me, I cannot grumble if thou find a little room there even for our enemies. Would I could set thy soul at ease, and do all that thou askest. In the first flush of wrath, when he was taken plotting against our lives, it seemed a little thing enough to take his evil life. But now these morning airs have cooled me, and it goes against my will to shoot a cowering hound tied hand and foot, even though he had murdered twenty sons of mine. I have thought if there be any way to spare his life, and leave this hour's agony to read a lesson not to be unlearned until the grave. For such poltroons dread death, and in one hour they die a hundred times. But there is no way out; his life lies in the scale against the lives of all our men, yes, and thy life too. They left him in my hands well knowing I should take account of him; and am I now to play them false and turn him loose again to hang them all? It cannot be."

Still I pleaded hard for Maskew's life, hanging on Elzevir's arm, and using every argument that I could think of to soften his purpose; but he pushed me off; and though I saw that he was loth to do it, I had a terrible conviction that he was not a man to be turned back from his resolve, and would go through with it to the end . . . and I knew that the final act was not far off.

Maskew knew it too, for he made his last appeal, using such passionate words as I cannot now relate, and wriggling with his body as if to get his hands from behind his back and hold them up in supplication. He offered money; a thousand, five thousand, ten thousand pounds to be set free; he would give back the *Why Not?*; he would leave Moonfleet; and all the while the sweat ran down his furrowed face, and at last his voice was choked with sobs, for he was crying for his life in craven fear.

He might have spoken to a deaf man for all he moved his judge; and Elzevir's answer was to cock the pistol and prime the powder in the pan.

Then I stuck my fingers in my ears and shut my eyes, that I might neither see nor hear what followed, but in a second I changed my mind and opened them again, for I had made a great resolve to stop this matter, come what might . . .

Elzevir looked full at Maskew, and raised his pistol; but before he had time to take aim, I dashed upon him like a wild cat, springing on his right arm, and crying to him to stop. It was an unequal struggle, a lad, though full-grown and lusty, against one of the powerfullest of men, but indignation nerved my arms, and his were weak, because he doubted of his right. So 'twas with some effort that he shook me off, and in the struggle the pistol was fired into the air.

Then I let go of him, and stumbled for a moment, tired with that bout, but pleased withal, because I saw what peace even so short a respite had brought to Maskew. For at the pistol shot 'twas as if a mask of horror had fallen from his face, and left him his old countenance again; and then I saw he turned his eyes toward the cliff-top, and thought that he was looking up in thankfulness to heaven.

But now a new thing happened; for before the echoes of that pistol-shot had died on the keen morning air, I thought I heard a noise of distant shouting, and looked about to see whence it could come. Elzevir looked round too, forgetting to upbraid me for making him miss his aim, but Maskew still kept his face turned up towards the cliff. Then the voices came nearer, and there was a mingled sound as of men shouting to one another, and gathering in from different places. 'Twas from the cliff-top that the voices came, and thither Elzevir and I looked up, and there too Maskew kept his eyes fixed. And in a moment there were a score of men stood on the cliff's edge high above our heads. The sky behind them was pink flushed with the keenest light of the young day, and they stood out against it sharp cut and black as the silhouette of my mother that used to hang up by the parlour chimney. They were soldiers, and I knew the tall mitre-caps of the 13th, and saw the shafts of light from the sunrise come flashing round their bodies, and glance off the barrels of their matchlocks.

I knew it all now; it was the Posse who had lain in ambush. Elzevir saw it too, and then all shouted at once.

"Yield at the King's command: you are our prisoners!" calls the voice of one of those black silhouettes, far up on the cliff-top.

"We are lost," cries Elzevir; "it is the Posse; but if we die, this traitor shall go before us," and he makes towards Maskew to brain him with the pistol.

"Shoot, shoot, in the Devil's name," screamed Maskew, "or I am a dead man."

Then came a flash of fire along the black line of silhouettes, with a crackle like a near peal of thunder, and a fut, fut, fut of bullets in the turf. And before Elzevir could get at him, Maskew had fallen over on the sward with a groan, and with a little red hole in the middle of his forehead.

(from *Moonfleet* by J. Meade Falkner)

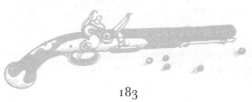

Comprehension and Discussion

1. How do we know (from this extract) that it was not Elzevir and John alone who had captured Maskew?

2. Why did John Trenchard (the narrator in this story) think it "now ten thousand times more fearful" for Maskew to be shot? Was he thinking only of Grace Maskew?

3. What was ironic about Elzevir's choice of a weapon to kill Maskew? (What does "ironic" mean in this case?)

4. In what ways does it become clear that Elzevir himself had doubts about killing Maskew? Did he believe that death itself was necessary because Maskew would never learn his lesson? If he didn't, why did Elzevir persist in the plan to kill Maskew?

5. What does it mean to "cock the pistol and prime the powder in the pan"? What is a "matchlock"? In approximately what period of history was this kind of weapon in use?

6. What is a "posse"? Why were the men apparently "gathering in from different places"?

7. Whose fault was it that Maskew was shot?

8. What do the following words and phrases mean? "bramble-plumps"; "(Elzevir) bore with me"; "poltroons"; "to play them false"; "he was loth to do it"; "in supplication"; "in craven fear"; "indignation nerved my arms"; "he doubted of his right"; "to upbraid me"; "the sward".

9. In what ways is the style of this passage old-fashioned? (*Moonfleet* was first published in 1898.) What period is the story set in? Was the author deliberately adopting an old-fashioned style, e.g. in using "thou" as well as "you"?

10. Which of these three characters, Maskew, John or Elzevir, do you most sympathise with, and why?

11. Is revenge *ever* justified? Who was *originally* in the wrong in this case? Do you agree with the principle of "an eye for an eye and a tooth for a tooth"?

For Written Answers

Give *full* answers, in your own words.

1. Why did Maskew begin by threatening and then change to pleading for his life?

184

2. Apart from the motive of revenge for his son, David, what was Elzevir's *second* reason for killing Maskew?

3. How, apparently, did they prevent Maskew from running away during this incident?

4. *Was* Elzevir in fact "looking up in thankfulness to heaven" after the gun had fired into the air?

5. Who shot Maskew?

6. What time of day was it when Maskew was shot?

7. The *Why Not?* was a public house that Elzevir used to run. Why is it printed in italics? How should you write it in hand-writing?

8. Sum up, in a few sentences of your own, the characters of (a) Maskew, (b) Elzevir and (c) John, as you interpret them from this passage.

Method Exercises

Exercise 1. Study the following uses of SEMICOLONS in the passage.

(i) "Spare me," he said; "spare me, Mr. Block . . ."

(ii) Still I pleaded hard for Maskew's life, hanging on Elzevir's arm, and using every argument that I could think of to soften his purpose; but he pushed me off; and though I saw he was loth to do it, I had a terrible conviction that he was not a man to be turned back from his resolve . . .

(iii) He offered money; a thousand, five thousand, ten thousand pounds to be set free; he would give back the *Why Not?*; he would leave Moonfleet; and all the while the sweat ran down his furrowed face . . .

Notice that the semicolon after "he said" is followed by a *small* s-. Notice that a semicolon can be used in addition to the words "and" and "but", if the break between main state-ments needs to be emphasised. What justification is there for the first semicolon in (iii)? Compare this with the use of semi-colons in question 8 of *Comprehension and Discussion*.

Now study the uses of the COLONS (:) in this passage.

(iv) Then Elzevir answered: "And had I not an only son . . .?"

(v) "But there is no way out: his life lies in the scale against the lives of all our men, yes, and thy life too."

(vi) "Yield at the King's command: you are our prisoners!"

Basically the colon is an *introductory* punctuation mark. It is most often used in modern writing to introduce a list of things, people or ideas; but it can also be used to introduce direct speech, and to introduce an explanation or comment. In this use it marks a stronger pause than a semicolon.

(a) Rewrite the following sentences, inserting all the *colons* and *commas* that you think necessary:

1. The usher an impressive man in uniform stood up and shouted "Silence in court!"

2. All the court officials were there magistrates clerks ushers witnesses jurymen lawyers and policemen.

3. An old "lag" if ever there was one Grimes had committed almost every offence in the book larceny burglary forgery perjury robbery with violence and even blackmail.

4. There was no other possible verdict the accused was found guilty.

5. The judge pronounced sentence as follows "Herbert Smith this court finds you guilty of driving dangerously while under the influence of alcohol and hereby disqualifies you from holding or obtaining a driving licence."

6. Capital punishment can take several different forms hanging beheading by guillotine the electric chair shooting the gas chamber and even drinking hemlock.

7. There are widely different degrees of what we simply call "corporal punishment" they range from severe deliberate and premeditated beating with a cat-o'-nine-tails to a light slap on a naughty child's leg.

(b) To complete the punctuation, the following passage requires at least seven commas, four semicolons, three full stops, two pairs of inverted commas, one colon and one apostrophe. Rewrite it with correct punctuation.

The figure of Justice is blindfolded to show her impartiality she holds a balance to show that she weighs up the case for and against us with care and she holds a sword with which to execute punishment on the guilty All this makes her a forbidding figure an unsympathetic symbol she is without mercy or consideration for the wrong-doer she takes no account of a criminals motive or provocation Many wise men including Shakespeare in plays like The Merchant of Venice and Measure for Measure have seen that without forgiveness and understanding very few of us would be innocent enough to escape just punishment none of us after all is perfect

Exercise 2. In Chapter Twelve we saw that *prepositions* "govern" nouns and pronouns, i.e. these are often *objects* of prepositions. Where pronouns have a separate object form, therefore, this is used after any preposition:

> e.g. before me, after them, towards her, by us.

Mistakes can occur when two objects follow a preposition:

> It is left to you and her (not "she") to decide.

Other confusions arise between certain similar prepositions (e.g. "of, from, off"), and between prepositions and conjunctions (e.g. "like" is a preposition, "as" is a conjunction).

(a) Rewrite the following sentences, choosing the correct word from those given in brackets, and being prepared to justify that choice in discussion afterwards.

1. Between you and (I, me), there is no hope of a favourable verdict.

2. He has made it possible for John and (I, me) to visit our friend in prison.

3. For you and (he, him) to be involved in this feud would be as great a mistake as for (I, me) to seek revenge myself.

4. When all the lost property has been taken (off, of) the coaches, they have an auction (off, of) all the unclaimed articles.

5. The customs men brought to the shore some contraband (off, from) the boat.

6. The duty to be paid is a matter of great importance to you and (I, me).

7. There are not many smugglers (like, as) (they, them) today.

8. (Who, Whom) were you working for; and do you know (who, whom) you were paid by?

(b) Different prepositions indicate different relationships, and there is therefore a difference between "to play with" and "to play for".

(i) John plays football with his friends down the road during the week.

(ii) On Saturdays John plays for the local boys' team.

Make up sentences to indicate the different meanings of:

to agree with	to provide for	to share between
to agree to	to provide with	to share among
	concerned with	grateful to
	concerned about	grateful for

Exercise 3. Lawyers have to be very careful to express themselves so that there is no possible cause for misinterpretation of their legal documents. They try to define all their terms and to avoid any ambiguities, especially any depending on the punctuation. (Why, do you think?) Legal language on forms, agreements and lists of rules is often complicated, and can usually be put much more clearly and briefly:

> e.g. This policy shall be null and void if it shall have been obtained through any fraudulent or wilful misrepresentation or concealment or through any knowingly untrue averment.

This means:

> This policy will be invalid if it was obtained by giving false information.

Try to make up clear yet brief explanations of the following statements:

(a) Poems by deceased writers are eligible under the conditions of entry for the Society's poetry competition only within twelve months from the date of the writer's decease.

(b) No claim in respect of injury or loss to the goods transmitted, arising from theft, fire, accidental damage or the negligence of the Company's servants, or from any cause whatsoever, can be entertained by the Company.

(c) It should not be assumed that no allowance will be payable by the employer when there are fewer than two children in the family of the employee.

(d) The Licensee shall pay to the Authority a sum not exceeding that which he paid heretofore, provided always that the terms of his licence have not been altered by the Schedule attached hereto.

(e) A strict compliance with these regulations is urgently requested, as any deviation from them is liable to occasion much inconvenience to all concerned.

(f) With regard to the fact that he has not complied with the regulations, we shall not in fact take any serious measures at this stage.

(g) Notwithstanding anything herein contained to the contrary, it is hereby declared and agreed that the Company shall only be liable for the excess of £10 for each and every claim made.

(h) It is further agreed that should the vehicle not be repairable owing to parts being unobtainable the liability of the Company shall be limited to an amount which is equivalent to the estimated cost of the repairs rendered necessary by the accident not exceeding the Insured's estimated value as stated in the Policy.

*Exercise 4. *Adverb clauses of time* answer the question, "When did it happen?":

e.g. He was still walking among the bushes <u>when I found him</u>.

Adverb clauses of place answer the question, "Where did it happen?":

e.g. The pistol lay <u>where Maskew would see it</u>.

Adverb clauses of cause (or *reason*) answer the question, "Why did it happen?"; they are usually introduced by the words "because, as, since":

e.g. His arms were weak <u>because he doubted of his right</u>.

Adverb clauses of manner answer the question, "How did it happen?"; they are usually introduced by "as, as though":

e.g. I shall shoot him in the face <u>as he shot David</u>.

You will notice that the words "as" and "since" can introduce different kinds of adverb clauses.

(a) What is the adverb clause in each of the following sentences? What kind of adverb clause is it?

1. He let me say my say till I was out of breath.
2. They heard voices where the soldiers were assembling.
3. Elzevir looked at Maskew as though he hated him.
4. Elzevir had to shoot Maskew because he was the enemy of the smugglers.
5. It was several months since I had seen Grace.
6. Since I liked Grace, I could not bear to see her father murdered.
7. As the sun rose, the soldiers appeared on the cliff-top.
8. As he had no other hope, Maskew told them to shoot.
9. They primed their weapons as they had been taught to do.
10. Before Elzevir could get at him, Maskew had fallen over on the sward with a groan.

(b) Two short sentences can often be joined in several ways, so that one becomes an adverb (or adjective) clause telling us more about the other:

e.g. He went out. I came in.

(i) *Adverb of cause:* He went out because I came in.

(ii) *Adverb of time:* When (As, After, Before) he went out, I came in.

(iii) *Adverb of place:* He went out where I came in.

(iv) *Adverb of manner:* As I came in, so he went out.

Rewrite the following, joining them in the various ways suggested; for help with adjective clauses, turn to page 115. Use only the introductory words suggested on pages 90, 129, or 177.

1. The magistrate fined the man. He had been stealing. (Adjective clause; adverb clauses of time and cause.)
2. The smugglers hid the booty. The officers could not find it. (Adjective clause; adverb clauses of place, cause and time.)
3. Maskew pleaded for his life. Elzevir was determined to have revenge. (Adverb clauses of cause and time.)
4. Maskew expected to die anyway. He shouted to the soldiers to shoot. (Adverb clauses of time and cause; adjective.)
5. Maskew behaved like a coward. One might expect this. (Adverb clause of manner.)

Writing Your Own

1. Study the picture above. Consider the characters of the police-man and the child as their faces reveal them, and what might perhaps be going on. Now write a short story for which this might be an illustration.

2. The first job of any court of justice or police investigation is to get a clear and correct picture of all the facts. Yet it is in fact rare for any two witnesses to agree on the details of any event, since people's memories are short, their minds are often clouded by preconceived judgments and emotional reactions, and they frequently have great difficulty in expressing themselves.

An accurate, complete and clearly expressed account of an accident or crime can therefore be invaluable to the police. Imagine that you are a witness of some accident or of some crime; choose a likely situation that is not too sensational, and keep yourself as a *witness*, rather than imagining you are some sort of hero in the drama. Make very careful notes, perhaps based on a sketch-map, of all you saw and heard, including details like the weather, how light it was at the time, the exact time and place of the events. Your account will be credible only if it is consistent—you cannot see events from two places at once, remember. Put your final account down in a clear, logical order and simple, unemotional language. There must be no confusion of facts with opinions or irrelevant emotions.

Oral Work

1. Arrange to hold a "mock trial". Most of the class can be involved as judge, jury, counsel, witnesses, accused, ushers, clerks, etc., but it is extremely important to work out a story in advance and let each of the witnesses know exactly who they are and what they are supposed to have done and seen. Usually, only the accused person is allowed to lie: everyone else must know his story and honestly keep to it. The following is a possible outline story:

Christopher Woodland's motor scooter has been stolen from outside his house, 10 Armitage Lane, Wilston. A neighbour, Mr. Pole (of number 6), while waiting at the bus-stop, saw Albert Prestwick standing near the scooter. A few minutes later Mr. Pole caught the 8.50 a.m. bus. When Woodland came out of his house at 8.55 a.m., the scooter had gone. He informed the police, who asked at number 6 and, as a result of Mr. Pole's information, P.C. Richardson went to 13 Plough Road, Prestwick's house, and found the scooter in the path that runs behind the houses in Plough Road. Mrs. Prestwick denied all knowledge of the scooter and said her husband had left for work at 8.15 a.m. while she was still in bed feeling unwell. At Smiths' Warehouse, where Mr. Prestwick is a packer, the Manager, Mr. Deal, stated that he did not arrive until 10.15 a.m. Prestwick claimed that he had been late because he had gone to Brocks, the High Street supermarket, intending to get the shopping for his wife, who had felt ill that morning. He had not purchased anything, however, since he had forgotten his money.

2. Discuss the cases for and against (a) capital punishment, (b) corporal punishment, (c) treating all prisons as places of reform and rehabilitation and not as places of punishment.

Activities and Research

1. Find out what you can about prisons and punishment past and present. What were: the Poor Law, the Workhouse and the Debtors' Prisons? What offences were punishable by hanging in the 18th century? What kinds of punishment were: transportation, ducking, the pillory, the stocks, the treadmill, the cat-o'-nine-tails, the rack? Find out about the life and work of John Howard, Elizabeth Fry and other prison reformers and what prison life is like today. This information could be collected into an interesting illustrated folder.

2. What is the difference between:
   libel and slander; larceny and burglary; blackmail and threatening behaviour; forgery and fraud; a solicitor and a barrister; a leading question and a cross-examination; circumstantial evidence and conclusive evidence; on remand and on probation?

Further Reading

Moonfleet by J. MEADE FALKNER (Arnold; Penguin)
This story has all the ingredients of exciting adventure: secret tunnels, smugglers' hide-outs, lost treasure, conflicting loyalties and a touch of romance. It is a classic among tales of smugglers.

The Land God Gave to Cain by HAMMOND INNES (Collins; Fontana)
When an invalid radio amateur in England picks up an S.O.S. from the wilds of Labrador, only his son believes him, and the story of the son's journey to the desolate scene, to find the truth and see justice done, involves an exciting and dangerous chain of coincidences. This is a book by an accomplished modern story-teller.

Stories of Famous Detectives by LEONARD GRIBBLE (Barker)
These stories of famous detectives in Western Europe and North America make up a fascinating picture of developing police methods in the fight against crime. (351.74)

You and the Law by EWAN MITCHELL (Max Parrish)
The author, a barrister-at-law, gives advice on a wide variety of legal problems which teenagers might encounter. These include trespass, stealing, licence difficulties, and giving and receiving injuries. (347)

The narrator is a nurse in her first year of training in a war-time hospital. She and Chris, a senior nurse, are on night duty on a women's ward.

CHAPTER FOURTEEN

In Hospital

They had had several operation cases in the late afternoon and evening, and the last one, an old lady of seventy, had come back from the Theatre only just alive. "She won't last long," said Sister, getting up again to feel her barely perceptible pulse. "I've rung up her people, but I doubt whether they'll get here in time." Automatically, she straightened the sheet over the dying woman and left us. There was nothing more she could do.

Sister Adams was off that night, and Sister Gilbert came tiptoeing up at ten o'clock with Mrs. Colley's relations. The husband was a humble old man with faded blue eyes and the walk of a man who has spent his life with horses. His daughter was thin and tired-looking, her face blotched with crying, but she had put on her best coat and hat and was clutching an enormous battered handbag.

"I've brought Mum's bag along," she whispered. "She can't bear to be parted from it, but they took her off in such a hurry." They stood by the bed and looked speechlessly at the old lady, her nose high and pinched in her waxy face, the collar of the white gown much too big for her.

Chris wanted to look at her dressing, and the husband and daughter went obediently to wait in Sister's sitting-room. The old man sat forward in his chair, his elbows on his knees, turning his cap round and round in his hands, and the daughter sat politely, with her hands in her lap as if she were making a call.

Chris had her hand on Mrs. Colley's wrist, frowning.

"Not long," she said. "Christ, I hate to stand by and let someone just slip off like this. Here—stay with her a minute. That Appendix'll be out of bed if I don't give her her morphia."

The green-shaded light over the bed fell on the old woman's face. You could trace the outline of every bone in her skull and her nose was typically sharp and prominent, as if the face had fallen away from it. Her skin was cold and faintly damp, and her pulse no more than a tremor and then not even that. I listened for her breathing and called Chris over. "She's dead."

"I wouldn't swear to it," she said, and stood pensively tapping her foot. "Look, get the hypo. syringe and the coramine. It couldn't hurt to give her a shot."

"I suppose I'd better call her people in," she said despondently, when she had given the injection. "Oh, damn, here's Chubby. What the hell does he want?" Chubby was Mr. Soames, the little new House Surgeon, just out of the egg, with fluffy hair that never would lie down on his round head. He was on for all surgical cases to-night, and was just going round to see if it was all right for him to go to bed. As we watched Mrs. Colley, one of her eyelids fluttered and for a moment her breathing was audible.

"My God," said Chris suddenly, "I wonder——." She clutched hold of Chubby's arm. "Listen," she whispered urgently, "couldn't we give her an intravenous? Couldn't we try it? Sister said it wasn't any use, but I don't know—*Please*, Mr. Soames, do let's try. It seems awful just not to do anything when she's still alive."

Chubby ran his fingers through his hair. "I don't know," he said hesitatingly, "it's not much good——." Chris's eyes were sparking at him, her face alive with urgency. "All right," he said and laughed nervously, "I'll have a shot if you like."

"I'll go and lay up the trolley," she gabbled. "Don't go away —I'll have it ready by the time you've scrubbed up. You put the electric heat cradle over her," she told me, "and tell her people they can't come in for a sec."

"Is she——?" asked the daughter, getting up as I went into the sitting-room. "We're going to try something," I said. "It might not be any good, but——." The old man was watching me like a trusting dog.

I wanted to stay and watch Chubby cut down into Mrs. Colley's vein, where the saline was going to run in through the needle, but half the ward chose to be awake and kept me running about for the next half-hour. Mrs. Davenport fussed and fretted and had me yanking her leg up and down five or six times. "What's all that light at the top of the ward for?" she grumbled. "A person can't sleep with all this running about."

"We're trying to save someone's life," I snapped.

"Poor soul," she said. "But me leg isn't right yet, Nurse, I don't know how it is——." I said something quite rude to her, I can't remember what, but it shocked her into silence, although she kept up a rhythmic, insistent moaning for as long as she could keep herself awake.

I went to hold Mrs. Colley's arm for Chris, while she bandaged it to the splint to keep it still. Mr. Soames was regulating the drip of the saline, his face flushed with excitement, for it was the first intravenous he had done since he had been here. Sister Gilbert came along to see why we had not rung her yet to say that Mrs. Colley had died.

"I'll do the round while I'm here," she said. "All right, don't bother to come with me, Nurse," and she tiptoed off down the ward alone.

When she came back, she found the three of us wild with excitement. Mrs. Colley's skin was still cold, but it was no longer clammy. You could hear her breathing now; you could distinctly feel her pulse.

"Of course, it might be only a momentary rally," Sister said doubtfully, but she obviously didn't think that.

"Keep her warm," said Chubby, putting on his white coat, his chick's hair on end. "I'll come back when I've finished my round. Let me know at once if anything happens, and for God's sake keep that drip running."

"Tidy her up," said Sister, "and let her people come in." While I was rearranging the sheets to hide a little blood that Chubby had spilt in his haste, I kept touching Mrs. Colley, to feel her skin gradually losing its marble chill. Suddenly she opened her eyes and looked at me accusingly. "Me arm," she whispered, "what you done to me arm?"

"Now you've got to keep that arm still, d'you hear? Don't you dare move it." She raised a grizzled eyebrow at me.

"Hoity-toity," she said faintly.

The husband and daughter came in, breathless with hope, glancing uneasily at the bandaged arm rigidly outflung and the gibbet-like saline apparatus. "She may not know you," whispered Chris, and Mrs. Colley unhooded one eye. "Think I don't know Dad?" she mumbled. " 'Ere, where's me 'andbag?"

(from *One Pair of Feet* by Monica Dickens)

Comprehension and Discussion

1. Discuss the description of Mrs. Colley's face throughout this extract; how does the author emphasise both her age and how ill she was?

2. What does Chris mean by saying:
"That Appendix'll be out of bed"? Why the capital "A"?
Does this manner of speaking of them tell anything about
her attitude to her patients, and would you criticise the
attitude?

3. What does "just out of the egg" mean when applied to
Mr. Soames? Can it be connected with his hair or remarks
later in the passage, about the intravenous? Why is he
called *Mr.* Soames and not *Dr.* Soames?

4. Does Mr. Soames show signs of being nervous, and has he
any reason to be nervous?

5. What do you think "coramine" is? What, apparently, are
an "intravenous" and "saline apparatus"?

6. Why is the handbag an important detail in this incident?

7. Discuss the meaning of the following in this passage:

the Theatre; her dressing; surgical cases; scrubbed
up; gibbet-like; barely perceptible pulse; the hypo.
syringe; the electric heat cradle; hoity-toity.

8. At breakfast after this incident, Chris says:
"Often I wonder why anyone is a Nurse—all the sordid
part, and the drudgery, and the impossible women, and
all that. Then something like this last night happens, and
you see exactly why."
Discuss this comment. What are the satisfactions and difficulties of being a nurse? Why do people take up this job?
Do they deserve more pay or better conditions than other
professions? Is nursing a career for women only?

9. Imagine yourself a nurse, and discuss the ideal patient and
the difficulties you might expect to have with different
patients, or with doctors, surgeons, sisters, etc.

10. Were the visitors—Mr. Colley and his daughter—well
treated when Mrs. Colley was critically ill? How much
freedom should patients have to receive visitors? Should
parents be able to visit children in hospital at any time, or
even stay with them?

For Written Answers

1. Which sister rang up Mrs. Colley's relations, the Day Sister or Sister Gilbert?

2. "Her nose was typically sharp and prominent"—typical of what, do you think?

3. In what ways did Mr. Colley and his daughter show their nervousness and embarrassment?

4. Why did Mr. Soames hesitate to give an "intravenous"?

5. Describe what an "intravenous" is like, so far as you can tell from this extract.

6. What did Sister Gilbert mean by a "momentary rally"? Why did she make this remark when she "obviously didn't think that"?

7. Was Nurse Dickens (the author) right to shock Mrs. Davenport into silence?

8. What kind of patient do you think Mrs. Davenport was?

Method Exercises

Exercise 1. When applying the rules for reported speech (see Chapters Ten and Eleven), it is important to use your common sense in interpreting what a speaker meant to say, and it is usual to correct or modify any strong or incorrect language that the speaker used. For example, these remarks from the passage might be reported in the following way:

Direct: Chris had her hand on Mrs. Colley's wrist, frowning.

"Not long," she said. "Christ, I hate to stand by and let someone just slip off like this. Here—stay with her a minute. That Appendix'll be out of bed if I don't give her her morphia."

Reported: Chris had her hand on Mrs. Colley's wrist, frowning, and said that she would not last long. Then she swore and added that she hated to stand by and let someone just slip off like that. She called to Monica to stay with Mrs. Colley for a minute, because the appendix patient would be out of bed if she did not give her her morphia.

199

Notice how "Not long", "Christ", "Here", and "That Appendix" are reported.

Write reported speech versions of the following conversations from the passage, beginning in the way suggested in each case. Always turn the "I" in the passage into "Monica".

(a) From: I listened for her breathing and called Chris over . . .
    To: . . . What the hell does he want?"

Begin: Monica listened for Mrs. Colley's breathing and called Chris over to tell her that . . .

(b) From: Chubby ran his fingers through his hair . . .
    To: . . . The old man was watching me like a trusting dog.

Begin: Chubby ran his fingers through his hair and hesitatingly said that he did not know about an intravenous, . . .

(c) From: Mrs. Davenport fussed and fretted and had me yanking her leg . . .

    To: . . . as long as she could keep herself awake.

Begin: Mrs. Davenport fussed and fretted and had Monica yanking her leg . . .

Exercise 2. The following three *anecdotes* are given in note form. In each case, write them out twice in full form, (a) using some direct speech for the conversation, and (b) using reported speech, reporting what is said. Study the conversation in the passage if you are not sure of the punctuation rules. Remember to start a new paragraph for each new speaker in the direct speech version, although this is not necessary in reported speech.

(i) Pretty girl selling poppies—man asks about her job—nurse—if bought poppy, could he be patient in her hospital?—unlikely—why?—Queen Anne's Maternity Hospital.

(ii) Anti-smoking exhibition—exhibit marked "Cured cancerous lung"—visitor stared, puzzled, long time—finally, doctor in attendance asked what puzzled by—if patient was cured, why is lung in bottle?

(iii) Patient: scared—first operation.
     Doctor: sympathise—mine too.

Exercise 3. Condense the following information into note form. Use suitable sub-headings, such as: Entry qualifications, Applications, etc. Under such headings put all important information in note-form (similar to the notes given in Exercise 2). Make up a suitable title for the whole passage, and put this at the head of your notes.

The minimum age for beginning any course in nursing, leading to State Registration, is 18 years (although it is possible to prepare beforehand by taking a pre-nursing course). Candidates must have a good general education, and suitable examination qualifications, although the most important quality nursing requires is an interest in people. Anyone wishing to take up nursing as a career must follow a course of training in a hospital approved by the General Nursing Council as a training school. The first step is to apply by letter to the Matron. If accepted, the candidate enters upon a three- or four-year course. The first eight to twelve weeks are spent in a preliminary training school, after which there is a further trial of about two months as a student nurse in the hospital wards. The Preliminary Examination is generally taken after twelve months and the Final Examination after three years. Once these have been passed the name of the nurse can be placed on the State Register. There is a simpler alternative to this full course which consists of one year's training followed by one year's nursing practice. This qualifies one to become a State-Enrolled Nurse. No fees are required for these training courses.

Exercise 4. In addition to adverb clauses of time, place, manner and cause, there are also adverb clauses of CONDITION:

     e.g. That Appendix'll be out of bed *if I don't give her her morphia.*

The clause gives the condition on which something happens, i.e. on which the appendix patient will be out of bed. Adverb clauses of condition are usually introduced by: "if, provided that, unless".

There are also adverb clauses of CONCESSION. What does the word "concession" normally mean? Adverb clauses of concession say in spite of what something happens:

     e.g. It shocked her into silence *although she kept up a rhythmic, insistent moaning.*

These adverb clauses are usually introduced by "although, though, even if, even though".

(a) All but two of the following sentences include an adverb clause of condition or concession. The remaining two contain other kinds of adverb clauses. Write out the adverb clauses stating what kind each is.

1. I'll have a shot if you like.
2. Let me know at once if anything happens.
3. Though Maskew's words about his daughter seemed to feed Elzevir's anger, they sank deep in my heart.
4. If it had seemed a fearful thing before, it seemed now ten thousand times more fearful.
5. Elzevir bore with me if I talked fast.
6. I cannot grumble if thou find a little room there even for our enemies.
7. It goes against my will to shoot a cowering hound, even though he had murdered twenty sons of mine.
8. Though he was loth to do it, he was not a man to be turned back.
9. The daughter sat politely as if she were making a call.
10. Chubby laughed as though he was rather nervous.

(b) The same basic sentences can be varied to include adverb clauses of time, condition or concession, e.g.:

Time: Sister Gilbert thought it hopeless when they tried the saline drip.

Condition: Sister Gilbert thought it hopeless if they tried the saline drip.

Concession: Although Sister Gilbert thought it hopeless, they tried the saline drip.

What is the difference in meaning in each case, and what is the main clause and what the adverb clause in each?

Find the main clause and the adverb clause of time in each of the following, and rewrite the sentence twice, once to include an adverb clause of condition, and once to include an adverb clause of concession, as in the above examples:

1. As we watched Mrs. Colley, one of her eyelids fluttered.
2. I went to hold Mrs. Colley's arm for Chris, while she bandaged it to the splint.

3. I'll do the round while I'm here.

4. When she came back, she found the three of us wild with excitement.

5. I'll come back when I've finished my round.

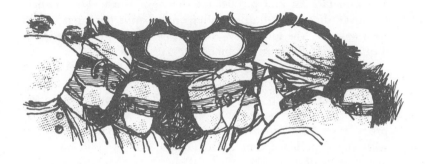

Writing Your Own

1. As good a test as any of friendship is the trouble we take to keep in touch with friends who are ill in hospital or at home. When we cannot easily visit them, our friends and relatives will particularly appreciate a personal letter: "For who can hear and feel himself forgotten?" as W. H. Auden says at the end of his poem *Night Mail*. Sick people, however, deserve special sympathy and understanding. Our letters have to try to keep them in touch with all that is going on, and what their friends are doing, without letting them feel jealous or unwanted. Discuss how one might strike the right balance, and the kind of news that one should emphasise.

Write a letter to a sick friend or relative, in which you describe events (such as a visit, a sports match or a school occasion) that they would want to hear about, as vividly and fully as you can to help them share the experience.

Practise the correct setting out of a personal letter. Discuss the position and punctuation of your address and the date, and the appropriate opening and conclusion for a personal letter, as you learnt last year.

2. Everyone has experienced pain and most people will have had at least one quite serious illness. It is not always easy to find the right words to describe these experiences, but they are usually associated with vivid memories: the bottles of medicine

by the bed, the noises from the world outside, the smells of a hospital ward or a sick room, the close-up faces of people clustered around you after an accident, or of a dentist bent over your teeth, or perhaps a vivid dream while you lay sweating out a high temperature. Search your mind for comparisons and associations, and puzzle out the right word. Thus Laurie Lee once described the pain after one's hands have been dead with cold as "the long, slow torment as our hands thawed out, a quiet agony of returning blood".

Describe *any* experience of pain or illness, from intense cold to blistering heat, from toothache to sprained ankle, or from a serious operation to a feverish cold. Make your description either a free verse poem, or a piece of very vivid and personal prose. Include the memories and associations that you connect with the experience, but avoid clichés like "a splitting head-ache" or "stiff as a poker".

Oral Work

1. Discuss the popularity of television serials and plays with a hospital setting or a medical interest. How many examples have there been over the last year or more? What are the "ingredients" of the successful series; i.e. what kinds of nurses, doctors, patients, and so on; what stock scenes and situations?

Now compare and contrast these fictional representatives with the facts of illness, hospital life and the life and work of nurses and doctors, as far as you can judge. Can the television series be said to do any harm, or any good?

2. A group of the class might prepare a short comic play which is a *parody* of the silliest or most obvious of the stories discussed in 1. above, with exaggerated characters and absurd situations.

Activities and Research

1. (a) Find out what the following people contributed to the development of modern medicine: William Harvey, Florence Nightingale, Edward Jenner, Lord Lister, Louis Pasteur, Sir Alexander Fleming, Sigmund Freud.
(b) What kind of medical work do the following do?

A general practitioner (G.P.), surgeon, consultant, house surgeon, paediatrician, dental surgeon, psychiatrist, oculist, chiropodist, medical officer of health (M.O.H.), matron, sister, staff nurse, medico-social worker, health visitor, midwife, S.R.N., physiotherapist, radiographer, pathologist. This information might be the basis for a class quiz, for which members of the class could make up suitable questions.

2. (a) Write a clear interpretation *in words* of the facts and conclusions to be drawn from the following two graphs or tables, one below and the other on page 207:

The continuous line shows the number of deaths from lung cancer per million of population in England and Wales, each fifth year from 1920 *to* 1970.
The dotted line shows the weight of tobacco sold as cigarettes in the United Kingdom in those years, in thousands of tonnes.

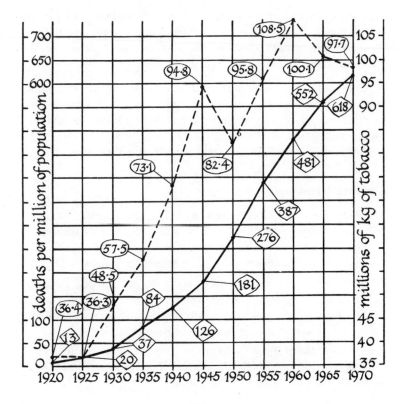

(b) Write business letters (one on behalf of the whole class in each case), asking for further information about smoking and health from:

> The Publications Department,
> The Health Education Council,
> Lynton House,
> 7-12 Tavistock Square, W.C.1.

and: The Public Relations Department,
> The Chest and Heart Association,
> Tavistock House North,
> Tavistock Square, W.C.1.

and: The Public Relations Department,
> Department of Health and Social Security,
> Alexander Fleming House,
> Elephant and Castle, S.E.1.

Your Local Education Authority may also be able to supply information.

Ask for display material as well as pamphlets, and pin up this information on the notice board, while several members of the class can report back to the rest on the contents of the pamphlets and booklets you receive.

3. Collect from newspapers and magazines all the examples you can find of advertisements that use people's desire for good health, fear of illness, or respect for the authority of doctors, nurses and other medical experts, as a means of selling goods to the public. Discuss these, and how effective they are.

Further Reading

One Pair of Feet by MONICA DICKENS (Penguin; Joseph)
Monica Dickens describes her first and only year of training as a war-time nurse with humour, sympathy and observation, and conveys the satisfactions and the irritations in a nurse's life.

Doctor in the House, etc. by RICHARD GORDON (Joseph; Penguin)
Some of the language and the references in these books are at times rather adult, but you will probably still enjoy this lively, comic series about the lighter side of medicine.

Sue Barton, Student Nurse by HELEN DORE BOYLSTON (Bodley Head)
This is the first of a lively, colourful (if rather superficial) series of books for girls on careers in nursing.

Medical Scientists and Doctors by NORMAN WYMER (O.U.P.)
These eight short biographies of leading figures in medicine
include Elizabeth Garrett Anderson and Albert Schweitzer, as
well as the work of the great pioneers of medical research. (926.1)

Milestones in Medicine by GEORGE BANKOFF, M.D., F.R.C.S.
  (Museum Press)
This account, by a surgeon, of the development of modern
medicine, including dissection, vaccination, anaesthesia, anti-
biotics, etc., links each "milestone" with the man who made
the discovery. (610.9)

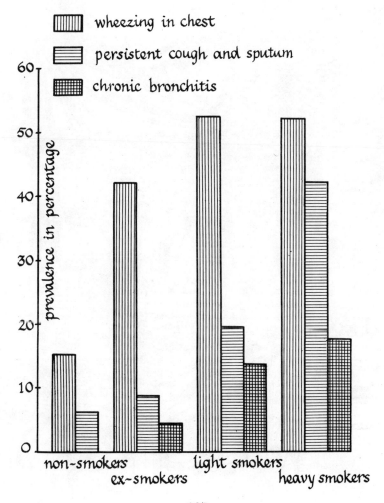

Although he later became a distinguished writer, Howard Spring began life in a poor street in Cardiff with little education and less money. He recalls those days in his autobiography.

CHAPTER FIFTEEN

People and Places

There were many ways of adding small sums to a family's income. Joe Blain, who brought ghostly complication to the simple game of Rap-tap-ginger, had a handcart made of a box fixed to the wheels of a perambulator. On the side he had painted

J. BLAIN

Dealer in White Rats
and
Old Iron

Joe had discovered the fecundity of rats and the irresistibility of the pink eyes that looked out over the soft pointed snouts. Any boy who coveted one of Joe's rats had to pay heavily in junk: any sort of old iron, jam jars, rags, bones or bottles. These he conveyed in his handcart to the marine-store dealer's.

We, lacking his imagination and enterprise, acted on the simple commercial principle of buying a thing and then selling it for more than it had cost. Behind the high wall which made our end of the street a *cul de sac* there was a sawyer's yard, presided over by a patriarchal man whose flowing beard was always powdered with sawdust. It was a good place to visit, that woodyard, with its rich resinous scents, its chugging steam-engine, its whining circular saw, and its good-natured old proprietor who was always willing to give sawdust for nothing to boys who owned rats, mice or rabbits. His son, who ran the engine, was something of a celebrity with us because once, taking the saw in his father's absence, he had sliced one of his fingers clean off.

There we bought wood: planks sawn into pieces that were approximately a foot square. Our only contribution to increasing their value consisted in chopping each piece into a dozen sticks and tying the sticks into bundles. There was always a perambulator knocking about the house, and that made a good enough hawker's cart. From door to door in the better-class streets that were not far away we would hawk our firewood and add about fifty per cent to the capital invested in the enterprise.

Rhubarb, in its season, was another line of ours, and one that I preferred, because it meant an early call at the market gardens where everything smelt fresh and dewy. To sell rhubarb, you had to be an early bird—earlier than the orthodox greengrocers who came about the streets with their carts. So we would go to the gardens before breakfast, and we were always told to pull our own supplies. That was an agreeable thing to do, sinking your hands deep amid the wet lush leaves and pulling at the stalks that came away with a ripe sucking sound. Then home to breakfast, a hasty bundling of the rhubarb, and off on the round.

When winter set in I became engaged as a regular Saturday errand boy at the greengrocer's and fishmonger's. Before there was light in the sky I would be at the shop where a natty little pony was pawing the ground, harnessed to a light cart. The greengrocer was a woman, and a devil of a driver. Already she would be waiting, reins in her fingers, and no sooner had I leapt up beside her than we were off with a jingle of harness and a brisk cloppity-clop of the pony's hoofs.

I loved those rides, though to this day I can feel the bitter tingling in my feet that did not reach down to the friendly straw strewn on the floor. The sharp air cut like whips, but what of that when such a gallant drive was forward! Over the river bridge we went before a soul was stirring, and into the heart of the town. There in Custom House Street, which is Cardiff's Covent Garden, I held the pony while the woman chaffered over boxes of kippers and crates of oranges, sacks of potatoes and all the ingredients of her picturesque calling.

Dead though the city might be elsewhere, Custom House Street was wide awake, full of champing horses, and rattling harness, and shouting men; and the pavements exhaled into the still frosty air their unforgettable smell of trodden vegetable garbage.

Back then we would rattle as briskly as we had come, the lash lightly stroking the pony's flank as he tore past the grey face of the workhouse behind the elms that were winter-bare. Then, after a cup of tea in the parlour behind the shop, we would open up for business, and the day degenerated into a prosaic lugging of baskets about the streets, delivering the threepenn'orths of this and that which housewives were too lazy or too proud to carry for themselves.

At eleven p.m., while the gas-flares were still sizzling in the shop, I would be sent home after a sixteen hour day with a shilling for wages and a couple of herrings for charity. I had no complaints to make, for a sumptuous midday dinner was thrown in, too.

I liked that job, but lost it through ambition. A scholarship examination was held one Saturday, and in order to sit, my employer having refused me permission, I took French leave. I did not win the scholarship, but I was given the sack.

(from *Heaven Lies About Us* by Howard Spring)

Comprehension and Discussion

1. Can you explain the game of Rap-tap-ginger?
2. Was Joe Blain's sign appropriate? What is "fecundity"?
3. What does "add about fifty per cent to the capital invested in the enterprise" mean? Is this phrase connected with the "simple commercial principle" already mentioned? Is there an element of humour in using such language about their activities?
4. What does "Cardiff's Covent Garden" mean? Is the market in fact "Cardiff's Billingsgate" as well?
5. What would you imagine the scholarship examination was for? Does this incident seem unfair to the boy?
6. Discuss the meaning of the following:

a patriarchal man	the pavements exhaled
something of a celebrity	gas-flares
we would hawk our firewood	a sumptuous midday
to be an early bird	dinner
champing horses	I took French leave

   the day degenerated into a prosaic lugging of baskets
7. List all the details in this description that seem old-fashioned: what period is Howard Spring describing, do you think?
8. How does the author make his description of (a) the wood-yard, (b) the rhubarb picking, and (c) Custom House Street, vivid and full of atmosphere?

9. Examine the author's use of comparisons, and his choice of words: e.g. "the friendly straw", "the sharp air cut like whips", "the lash lightly stroking the pony's flank", "the grey face of the workhouse", etc.

10. Why did Howard Spring work at these jobs, and why do school pupils and students do part-time work today? Was Howard Spring working too hard, and should there be limits to the hours young people spend working, the money they can earn and the age at which they can start earning? Should schools restrict their pupils' part-time work? What are the best jobs for young people in your area today?

For Written Answers

1. Was Howard Spring earning money to spend on himself? (Justify your answer.)

2. What is a "cul de sac" and how did the woodyard wall make the street one?

3. Why did you need to be up early to make money out of rhubarb? What is the season for picking rhubarb?

4. Why did the author's feet tingle when he was riding on the greengrocer's cart?

5. Why was the greengrocer's job a "picturesque" one?

6. What did Howard Spring do for the greengrocer most of the day? Does he imply anything about the customers he worked for?

7. In what ways was the greengrocer "a devil of a driver"? Use examples from the passage.

8. Explain in your own words how the author lost his job "through ambition".

Method Exercises

Exercise 1. Examine the following statements:

1. Howard found a job.
2. The job was a hard one.
3. He found his friend a hard job.

4. He found the job hard.

5. He found the job hard work.

What is the subject and verb in each case?

Which sentence has (a) a complement, (b) a direct object, (c) an indirect as well as direct object?

Examples 4 and 5 will not fit completely into these patterns: here "hard" (adjective) and "work" (noun), while not being subjects, objects or complements of the verb, still refer to the object "job". These are called OBJECT COMPLEMENTS (the complement in example 2 is a *subject complement*). Verbs like:

make, find, elect, paint, call, keep, think,

quite often have complements to their direct objects. What do the code letters (S, SC, IO, etc.) mean in the following examples?

6. Joe painted his cart. (S - V - DO)

7. Joe painted his cart black. (S - V - DO - OC)

8. His cart became black. (S - V - SC)

9. Joe painted me a picture. (S - V - IO - DO)

10. Joe painted his cart with black paint. (S - V - DO - ADV)

(a) Find the object complements in the following sentences, stating whether they are adjectives or nouns (possibly with adjectives), or pronouns.

1. The straw kept their feet warm.

2. The frosty air made his feet cold.

3. He considered this job a good one, but he found it tiring. (2)

4. We should hardly think that greengrocer generous today.

5. The housewives thought themselves too good to carry home their own shopping.

6. The greengrocer had some of the vegetables delivered.

7. They named Custom House Street the Covent Garden of Cardiff.

8. Joe Blain called himself a dealer.

9. How does the author make his description vivid and full of atmosphere?

(b) Complete the following so that each becomes a complete sentence containing an object complement:

1. The voters elected him . . .
2. The children coloured the . . .
3. His behaviour leaves me . . .
4. Keep this country . . .
5. I would call . . .
6. The committee appointed . . .

Exercise 2 (a) What are the main subjects and verbs of the following sentences from the passage?

1. On the side he had painted "J. BLAIN . . ."
2. Behind the high wall which made our end of the street a *cul de sac* there was a sawyer's yard . . .
3. There we bought wood: planks sawn into pieces that were approximately a foot square.
4. From door to door in the better-class streets that were not far away we would hawk our firewood . . .
5. To sell rhubarb, you had to be an early bird—earlier than the orthodox greengrocers . . .

In each case, the sentence begins, not with a subject, but with what is basically an adverb or an adverb equivalent. This kind of sentence structure throws some emphasis on to the adverbs and adverb phrases, and helps to vary the style of the passage.

(b) Find *ten* more examples in the passage of similar constructions, where an adverb, or a phrase (sometimes an adjective phrase) or clause, precedes the subject and verb. Write these out, underlining one subject word in each sentence.

(c) Make up the most interesting and vivid sentences you can on this pattern, beginning at least five of them in the ways suggested below:

1. Lost in the deep, mysterious woods . . .
2. From London to Birmingham, from Birmingham to Manchester, from Manchester to the Lake District . . .
3. Over mountain passes and down steep valleys, through thick forests and by wide grasslands, across treacherous marshes and beside deep rivers . . .
4. Under the inspector's sharp eyes . . .
5. There, under the pile of garden rubbish . . .

214

Exercise 3. The following might be found in a dictionary:

down 1. *n.* Open high land, esp. chalk uplands.

down 2. *n.* Fine, soft, short hair or feathers.
      downy *adj.* (-ier, -iest; -iness, *n.*)

down 3. *adv.* Towards, to or in a lower position; from earlier to later period; away from central or important place; towards completion.
    prep. Downwards with or along; outwards from.
    adj. (not compared) Descending; dejected; directed downwards; travelling away from (train terminus).
    v.t. (coll.) Bring, put, throw or knock down.
    n. (usu. pl.) Reversal of fortune; (coll.) grudge.

(a) Discuss all the abbreviations used here, together with the setting out and punctuation. Explain the difference between an *adv.* and a *prep.*, and between a *v.t.* and a *v.i.* What does "coll." stand for? Why is **downy** indented from the left-hand margin? What does "downy" in fact mean and what noun is formed from it? Explain the -ier, -iest after "downy" and the note "not compared" after **down** *adj.*

(b) Using the dictionary information above, give the part of speech and the meaning of the word *down* in each case in the following passage.

    When I am feeling *down*, I take a *down* train from Waterloo *down* to Sussex, where I look up to the beautiful *downs*, and, in spite of all the ups and *downs* of my business life, I feel refreshed deep *down* into my very heart. Over the hills and *down* the chalky paths I stride, swishing the *down* from thistles with my stick as I pass, until I return to the village to *down* an honest pint with the locals, and finally set these thoughts *down* in my diary on the way home.

(c) Make up seven short sentences that would serve as good examples to show the seven main uses of the word "down", as given in the dictionary entry, together with one sentence for "downy", one for the comparative of "downy", and one for the noun derived from "downy".

Exercise 4. Study these sentences:

1. Howard Spring earned money because his family was poor.

2. Howard Spring earned money so that his family should not be poor.

3. Howard Spring earned money so that his family was no longer poor.

The first clearly includes a reason (an adverb clause of cause) why he earned money. The second is not so clearly a reason, and is rather an aim; and the third is certainly not a reason, it is a result. The clause "so that his family should not be poor" is called an adverb clause of PURPOSE. The clause "so that his family was no longer poor" is called an adverb clause of RESULT. Example 3 might have been written:

4. Howard Spring earned so much money that his family was no longer poor.

Adverb of purpose clauses are usually introduced by: "so that, in order that, lest". Adverb of result clauses can be introduced by "so that", but more often the "so" is in the main clause, and the adverb clause of result begins with "that".

(a) All the following sentences include an adverb clause: most of them are adverb clauses of result or purpose, but two are different kinds of adverb clauses. Write out the adverb clauses and state what kind each is:

1. Joe called himself a "dealer" so that he could make money out of junk.

2. He bought so much junk that he was bound to get some money for it.

3. We bought things in order that we might sell them at a profit.

4. If you wanted to sell your rhubarb, you had to be an early bird.

5. We always tried to be early so that we could sell our rhubarb easily.

6. I held the pony so that she could bargain for the stock.

7. She drove so fast that she got quite a reputation.

8. I took French leave that I might sit the examination.

9. Although I did not pass, I got the sack.

10. I was so ambitious that I risked losing my job.

(b) By slight changes, especially in the verbs of the introductory words, or both, many adverb clauses of result can be
changed to purpose, or vice-versa: e.g.

I tired myself out so that I might fall asleep quickly. (PURPOSE)

I tired myself out so that I fell asleep quickly. (RESULT)

Rewrite each of the following with enough alteration to
change the adverb clause from purpose to result or result to
purpose:

1. They sold many bundles of firewood so that they could
make several pounds.

2. He got up so early that he could do his paper round in
comfort.

3. He worked half-heartedly in order that he might fail the
examination.

4. I held the horse firmly lest it should run away.

5. They had so much pocket-money that they did not need a
Saturday job.

Writing Your Own

1. Describe your own town, or area, for the benefit of a stranger.
Perhaps you might imagine you are writing (in English!) to a
pen-friend in a foreign country, and the composition could then
be in proper letter form. But work out first the kind of information that it is important and interesting for your correspondent
to have, to be able to picture your town or village: its size and
how densely populated it is, what the main local industries or
occupations are, and where it is in relation to other parts of
the country and road and rail communications, etc. Then
choose certain places, buildings, parks, etc. for closer description,
so that he can begin to form an imaginary picture of them.
Finally, try to convey some of your own feelings about your
home town. Describe some of the people and places as you know
them, on your way to school, or through a part-time job, or at
holiday times and week-ends. This personal description, for which
you should get many hints from Howard Spring's account, will
help give your description life and personality.

Whether you write a letter or a straightforward description,
pay attention to paragraphing and clear arrangement of your
material.

2. Study the following table of figures concerning the average income of some 400 imaginary school pupils.

	Years Old	Average Pocket Money (weekly from parents)	Average Earned Income (regular, weekly)	Average Total Income (all sources)	% of pupils contributing to clothes or keep.
BOYS	12	30p	15p	48p	2%
	14	40p	·48p	95p	6%
	16	72p	95p	£1·80	30%
	18	£1	£1·50	£2·50	66%
GIRLS	12	30p	15p	52p	0%
	14	35p	30p	78p	6%
	16	65p	60p	£1·40	25%
	18	85p	95p	£1·90	55%

Sums of money are given to the nearest 1p and percentages to the nearest 1%. All amounts of money are averages from approximately 50 answers to questionnaires.

Make notes of some conclusions to be drawn from these figures. Remember that average incomes may seem small when just a few boys or girls get a lot of money and the rest get nothing. Ask yourself questions like:

(a) How much better off for pocket money are the boys than the girls at each stage? Why might this be?

(b) How much better off for earned money are the boys than the girls, and why?

(c) Why does total income sometimes exceed the total of pocket money from parents plus earned money? Where is this not true, and why?

(d) Which groups have the most financial responsibility? How and why do these percentages vary?

(e) Where do any of the figures rise steadily and where (and why) are there sudden jumps?

Imagine that a survey in your own or in local schools has provided you with this table of results. Write a short explanation (suitable for the school magazine) to *accompany* the figures. Do not quote all the figures again, but try to draw the readers' attention to all the interesting rises, falls, comparisons and contrasts that you can see in them, and to give some possible explanations for these variations.

Oral Work

1. Discuss the point of view that young people today have too much money to spend, that too many of them spend too much of their time and energy earning money (and then wasting it), and that this has led to serious exploitation of young people by advertisers and salesmen, who try to make them a separate part of the community with a different sense of values.

For this discussion certain members of the class must make an honest attempt to see the situation from the point of view of an adult who, when young, had little pocket money and could only earn small wages, even when he first went to work full-time, let alone earn good money from a part-time job. What is he likely to feel? Might he have good reasons for his views?

2. Prepare and give a talk on the facilities in your area (a) as they are now, and (b) as they should be, in your opinion. Consider the whole range of facilities for recreation, entertainment (including eating out, dancing, cinemas, theatres, and all sporting events), transport, and quiet relaxation. Consider the needs of different age-groups, but do not ignore the question of who should pay for any improvements.

Activities and Research

1. The class or an interested group should make a survey of pocket money, part-time jobs and money earned, based on your own class, the whole school, or possibly two or more schools. The table of imaginary figures on page 218 might suggest some basic questions and how these could be worded on a questionnaire, and it is important to plan questions in such a way that the answers can be quickly analysed and turned into averages or percentages. In any case, it is going to be more interesting if the same series of questions can be answered by different groups: girls as opposed to boys, sixth-formers as opposed to first-formers, those with practical rather than academic interests.

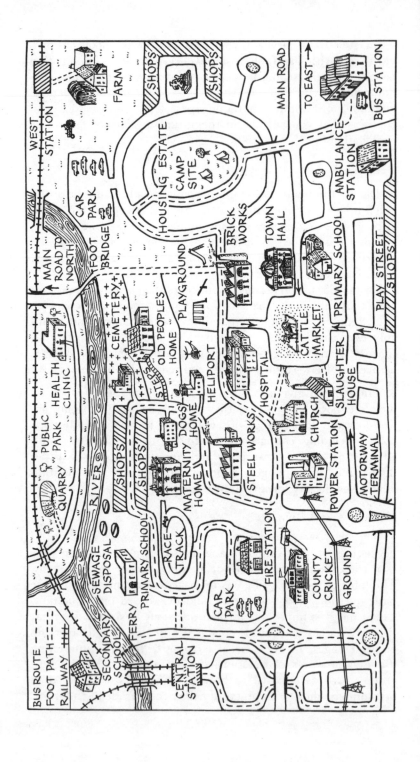

If this information is to be presented as part of a tape-recorded magazine programme, then it would be interesting to reinforce the facts with interviews about them in which staff, parents, and pupils of different views are encouraged to comment on the whole question of money and young people.

2. Study the town plan opposite and note all the examples of bad planning you can see. For instance, do children have to cross a main road to reach the local school? Either list in writing the improvements you would make, or redraw the map with the necessary alterations.

Further Reading

Heaven Lies About Us by HOWARD SPRING (Collins)
In a short but delightful autobiography, the writer recalls his poor but happy childhood and youth in Cardiff at the end of the nineteenth century. (920)

The Boy from Hackston N.E. by REGINALD TAYLOR (Hamish Hamilton)
The story deals with the problems Joe Grazier has to solve and the fights he has to win in the streets of Hackston, where temptation, crime and violence are never far away. More suitable for boys than for girls, it is an easy book to read; the characterisation is simple and clear cut; the action is exciting.

Maidens' Trip by EMMA SMITH (Penguin)
This tells the story of three girls in their late teens who worked a pair of canal boats on the London to Birmingham route, during the war. The book gives a realistic and amusing account of the boat people and all those connected with canals.

People and Places by MARGARET MEAD (Blackie)
Margaret Mead is an anthropologist, famous for her studies of primitive races in the Pacific. In this book, however, her first for young people, she deals with all kinds of people from all over the world, the conditions in which they live, their customs and attitudes and how these change. She also explains how an anthropologist sets to work. This fascinating book is highly recommended. (572)

Liam O'Flaherty, the author of this short story, was born on the Aran Islands off the coast of Galway and knew well the fishermen's bitter struggle with the sea and its inhabitants.

CHAPTER SIXTEEN

Animal Encounters

He was eight feet long. At the centre of his back he was two feet in circumference. Slipping sinuously along the bottom of the sea at a gigantic pace, his black, mysterious body glistened and swirled like a wisp in a foaming cataract. His little eyes, stationed wide apart in his flat-boned, broad skull, searched the ocean for food. He coursed ravenously for miles along the base of the range of cliffs. He searched fruitlessly, except for three baby pollocks which he swallowed in one mouthful without arresting his progress. He was very hungry.

Then he turned by a sharp promontory and entered a cliff-bound harbour where the sea was dark and silent, shaded by the concave cliffs. Savagely he looked ahead into the dark waters. Then instantaneously he flicked his tail, rippling his body like a twisted screw, and shot forward. His long, thin, single whisker, hanging from his lower snout like a label tag, jerked back under his belly. His glassy eyes rested ferociously on minute white spots that scurried about in the sea a long distance ahead. The conger eel had sighted his prey. There was a school of mackerel a mile away . . .

He roamed about for half an hour, a demented giant of the deep, travelling restlessly at an incredible speed. Then at last his little eyes again sighted his prey. Little white spots again hung like faded drops of brine in the sea ahead of him. He rushed thither. He opened his jaws as the spots assumed shape, and they loomed up close to his eyes. But just as he attempted to gobble the nearest one, he felt a savage impact. Then something hard and yet intangible pressed against his head and then down along his back. He leaped and turned somersault. The hard gripping material completely enveloped him. He was in a net. While on all sides of him mackerel wriggled gasping in the meshes.

The eel paused for two seconds amazed and terrified. Then all around him he saw a web of black strands hanging miraculously in the water, everywhere, while mackerel with heaving gills stood rigid in the web, some with their tails and heads both caught and their bodies curved in an arch, others encompassed many times in the uneven folds, others girdled firmly below the gills with a single black thread. Glittering, they eddied back and forth with the stream of the sea, a mass of fish being strangled in the deep.

Then the eel began to struggle fiercely to escape. He hurtled hither and thither, swinging his long slippery body backwards and forwards, ripping with his snout, surging forward suddenly at full speed, churning the water. He ripped and tore the net, cutting great long gashes in it. But the more he cut and ripped the more deeply enmeshed did he become. He did not release himself, but he released some of the mackerel. They fell from the torn meshes, stiff and crippled, downwards, sinking like dead things. Then suddenly one after another they seemed to awake from sleep, shook their tails, and darted away while the giant eel was gathering coil upon coil of the net about his slippery body. Then, at last, exhausted and half strangled, he lay still, heaving.

Presently he felt himself being hauled up in the net. The net crowded about him more, so that the little gleaming mackerel, imprisoned with him, rubbed his sides and lay soft and flabby against him, all hauled up in the net with him. He lay still. He reached the surface and gasped, but he made no movement. Then he was hauled heavily into a boat, and fell with a thud into the bottom.

The two fishermen in the boat began to curse violently when they saw the monstrous eel that had torn their net and ruined their catch of mackerel. The old man on the oars in the bow called out: "Free him and kill him, the brute." The young man who was hauling in the net looked in terror at the slippery monster that lay between his feet, with its little eyes looking up cunningly, as if it were human. He almost trembled as he picked up the net and began to undo the coils. "Slash it with your knife," yelled the old man, "before he does more harm." The young man picked up his knife from the gunwale where it was stuck, and cut the net, freeing the eel. The eel, with sudden and amazing movement, glided up the bottom of the boat, so that he stretched full length.

Then he doubled back, rocking the boat as he beat the sides with his whirling tail, his belly flopping in the water that lay in the bottom. The two men screamed, both crying: "Kill him, or he'll drown us." "Strike him on the nable!" They both reached for the short, thick stick that hung from a peg amidships. The young man grabbed it, bent down, and struck at the eel. "Hit him on the nable!" cried the old man. "Catch him, catch him, and turn him over.

They both bent down, pawing at the eel, cursing and panting, while the boat rocked ominously and the huge conger eel glided around and around at an amazing speed. Their hands clawed his sides, slipping over them like skates on ice. They gripped him with their knees, they stood on him, they tried to lie on him, but in their confusion they could not catch him.

Then at last the young man lifted him in his arms, holding him in the middle, gripping him as if he were trying to crush him to death. He staggered upwards. "Now strike him on the nable!" he yelled to the old man. But suddenly he staggered backwards. The boat rocked. He dropped the eel with an oath reaching out with his hands to steady himself. The eel's head fell over the canted gunwale. His snout dipped into the sea. With an immense shiver he glided away, straight down, down to the depths, down like an arrow, until he reached the dark, weed-covered rocks at the bottom.

Then stretching out to his full length he coursed in a wide arc to his enormous lair, far away in the silent depths.

(from *The Conger Eel*, a short story by Liam O'Flaherty)

Comprehension and Discussion

1. What does "stood rigid" mean? Why were the mackerel in the net like this, do you think?
2. How did the first reaction of the eel to being caught differ from his later behaviour? Why?
3. Which was more panic-stricken, the eel or the fishermen?
4. What do you think the old sailor meant by the "nable"?
5. Why, in the end, did the fisherman fail to kill the eel?
6. Discuss the meaning of the following:

   slipping sinuously; he coursed ravenously; a sharp promontory; concave cliffs; a demented giant; something hard yet intangible; pawing the eel; the boat rocked ominously; their hands clawed his sides; the canted gunwale.
7. Examine the following similes: what is compared to what in each case? Are they effective?
   (a) His black, mysterious body glistened and twirled like a wisp in a foaming cataract;
   (b) rippling his body like a twisted screw;
   (c) his long, thin, single whisker, hanging from his lower snout like a label tag;
   (d) little white spots again hung like faded drops of brine in the sea;
   (e) their hands clawed his sides, slipping over them like skates on ice;
   (f) down to the depths, down like an arrow.
8. Discuss the style of writing in this passage. Consider particularly the description of the mackerel caught in the net ("some ... others ... others") and the use of the words "eddied", "stream of the sea", "strangled in the deep". Note the author's choice of adverbs, especially in interesting constructions like "instantaneously he flicked his tail", "travelled restlessly", "strands hanging miraculously", "he was hauled heavily". Note his use of present participles to give a sense of urgent movement, especially at the beginning of the fifth paragraph. Discuss the repetition in the ninth paragraph and the alliteration in the tenth (or last but one).
9. How is the eel shown to be noble or admirable? Do you sympathise more with him or with the fishermen?

For Written Answers

1. How good was the eel's eyesight, and why did he not see the net?

2. How did the mackerel react to being freed by the eel's struggles, and why did they act as they did?

3. Why did the eel suddenly come to life again in the boat?

4. What did the fishermen fear when he did this?

5. What did the younger fisherman want the knife for?

6. How did the men try to hold the eel down? (Use your own words.)

7. Explain in your own words why the fishermen cursed the eel.

8. How does the author build up our impression of this eel as an exceptional creature?

The Lobster Pot

Who can tell how the lobster got
Into the lobster pot?
When he went in he did not doubt
There was a passage out.
There was not.

JOHN ARDEN

Method Exercises

Exercise 1. Make a summary, in note form, of the main points of the story of the *Conger Eel*. As this is to be in notes, complete sentences in your own words are not necessary. Begin like this:

> Giant conger eel—very hungry—searching sea
> for food—entered harbour—

It should be possible to cover the main facts in the story in between 60 and 100 words of notes.

Exercise 2. (a) It is important to remember that the -*ly* ending is not the best way to recognise an adverb. Many of the commonest single adverbs, such as: "then, now, soon, here, there, up, down, round," etc. do not end in -ly. Examine the first three paragraphs in the story of the *Conger Eel*. There you will find these adverbs in this order (apart from adverb phrases and clauses);

> sinuously, ravenously, fruitlessly, then, savagely, ahead, then, instantaneously, forward, back, ferociously, about, ahead, there, about, restlessly, then, again, again, ahead, thither, up, close, then, then, down, completely.

All these modify verbs or parts of verbs—basically they tell us how, why, where or when something happens. Show that this is so by writing down which word(s) each is modifying here. The first two are given as examples:

> 1. sinuously — modifies present participle "slipping".
>
> 2. ravenously — modifies verb "coursed".

(b) Adverbs are also used in English to modify adjectives or other adverbs, as well as to modify verbs. When Monica Dickens wrote (in the passage in Chapter Fourteen):

... getting up again to feel her barely perceptible pulse.

the adverb "barely" does not tell us how the Sister was going to feel the pulse (as in "She could *barely* feel it."), it tells us *how perceptible* the pulse was. It *modifies the adjective* "perceptible".

Similarly, in the sentence:

Although he was *thoroughly* tired and hungry, the eel searched the bay *very* thoroughly for food.

The first words in italics, "thoroughly", tells us how "tired and hungry" he was, and the second "very", tells us how "thoroughly" he searched. "Very" is an adverb of degree modifying an adverb. What does that adverb, "thoroughly", itself modify?

In *The Conger Eel* we find:

He was *very* hungry.

What word does "very" modify, and what part of speech is this word?

The adverbs:

very, too, quite, so, fairly, more, much, less, just,

are all commonly used as ADVERBS OF DEGREE (as they are called), answering the question "how much?" about adjectives or other adverbs.

Pick out adverbs of degree from each of the following sentences, saying what they modify in each case:

1. Her nose was typically sharp and prominent.
2. Her skin was cold and faintly damp.
3. The collar of the white gown was much too big for her. (2)
4. In the net, the eel was clearly too weak to struggle.
5. A completely satisfactory fishing net has never yet been devised.
6. The fishermen were understandably angry.
7. The only conger eel I ever saw was simply enormous.
8. He judged the short story competition fairly well.
9. I am quite happy with the result of the competition.

Exercise 3. Study the following description of a giant wave, and then answer the questions:

It was nearly high tide. But the sea moved so violently that the two reefs bared with each receding wave until they seemed to be long shafts of black steel sunk into the bowels of the ocean. Their thick manes of red seaweed were sucked stiff by each fleeing wave. The waves came towering into the cove across both reefs, confusedly, meeting midway in the cove, chasing one another, climbing over one another's backs, spitting savage columns of green and white water vertically, when their arched manes clashed. In one monstrous stride they crossed the flat rock. Then with a yawning sound they swelled up midway in the cliff. There was a mighty roar as they struck the cliff and rebounded. Then they sank again, dishevelled masses of green and white, hurrying backward. They rose and fell from the bosom of the ocean, like the heavy breathing of a gluttonous giant.

Then the tide reached its highest point and there was a pause. The waves hardly made any noise as they struck the cliff, and they drivelled backwards slowly. The trough of the sea between the reefs was convulsing like water in a shaken glass. The cliff's face was black, drenched with brine, that streamed from its base, each tiny rivulet noisy in the sudden silence.

Then the silence broke. The sea rushed back. With the speed and motion of a bladder bursting it sprang backwards. Then it rose upwards in a concave wall, from reef to reef, across the cove, along whose bottom the slimy weeds of the ocean depths were visible through the thin sheet of water left to cover the sea's nakedness by the fury of the rising wave.

For a moment the wave stood motionless, beautifully wild and immense. Its base in front was ragged, uneven and scratched with white foam, like the debris strewn around a just-constructed pyramid. Then a belt of dark blue ran from end to end across its face, sinking inward in a perfect curve. Then came a wider belt, a green belt peppered with white spots. Then the wave's head curved outwards, arched like the neck of an angry swan. That curved head was a fathom deep, of a transparent green, with a rim of milky white. And to the rear, great lumps of water buttressed it, thousands of tons of water in each lump.

(from *"The Wave"*, a short story by Liam O'Flaherty)

First discuss, or look up, the meaning of any words you are uncertain of, such as "dishevelled" or "debris". Then write, or discuss, answers to the following questions:

(a) Why does the second sentence begin with "But"? Explain the contrast with the previous statement.

(b) Would you call "until they seemed to be long shafts of black steel sunk into the bowels of the ocean" either a simile or a metaphor? Justify your answer.

(c) What, in the third sentence, is supposed to have "thick manes"—does this make an effective comparison?

(d) Are the "arched manes" mentioned in the fourth sentence the same as the "thick manes" in the third sentence? Is the comparison in the fourth sentence appropriate?

(e) What does "dishevelled" mean and what is it usually associated with? How is it appropriate when applied to these waves?

(f) In what ways were these towering waves before high tide like the breathing of a gluttonous giant? Why "gluttonous"?

(g) Could the sentence "with the speed and motion of a bladder bursting it sprang backwards" be called either a simile or a metaphor? Justify your answer.

(h) Explain in your own words why the "slimy weeds" became visible. Why is the sea's "nakedness" referred to at this point?

(i) How can water be described as "scratched with white foam"?

(j) Discuss the simile "white foam, like the debris strewn around a just-constructed pyramid". What do you imagine such debris to be like, and in what ways is the wave like a pyramid?

Exercise 4. (a) Examine all the similes and metaphors in the passage in Exercise 3. Would it be right to consider some of these as mixed similes and metaphors? e.g. in "Then the wave's head curved outwards, arched like the neck of an angry swan".

When the waves come "towering", "chasing", "climbing", "spitting" and "striding" into the bay, what are they being compared with? This kind of extended metaphor, in which an inanimate thing, like a wave, or a ship, or a vehicle, is given human or animal qualities, as if it could think, feel or move of its own accord, is called PERSONIFICATION (i.e. treating or making something *like a person*). In what ways is the sea personified in the remainder of the passage? Would it be reasonable to say that the cliffs or the reefs are also being personified here?

(b) Which of the following sentences are examples of personification and what is being compared to what in each case?

1. Britain glared angrily at her neighbours across the sea.

2. The wind searched every corner of the grey stone yard and swept the brown leaves into a heap on the far side.

3. Mr. James strutted and crowed and fluffed himself up, for all the world like a bantam cock that had just been proved a champion.

4. An old house stood at the corner, leaning a little, the bricks a mellow brown, its slate roof grey with age, and it seemed to smile benignly on us as we passed.

5. Down the volcano's side slithered hissing snakes of lava, twisting and turning in their search for prey.

(c) Try to make up interesting personifications of: a snow-plough; a small stream; a mountain road; a giant telescope; fog or mist; some flowers (e.g. moving in the wind).

(d) Make up effective similes to describe at least six of these sea-creatures: seagull; crab; jellyfish; shrimp; lug-worm; barnacle; shark; octopus; whale; seal.

Writing Your Own

1. Write a poem or a short story representing any encounter between human beings and animals. *The Conger Eel* and the pupil's poem below may serve as models. Pay particular attention to the feelings of both the person and the animal, and also to the use of appropriate comparisons and vivid words.

Ants

I hate gardening
But bribery can sometimes make me work
And ants are ever a nuisance in my garden.
I had some of that Japanese stuff
And I remember
Smearing it over a stone
Which had been pushed
Deep
Into an unearthed ant's nest.
That was all I had to do
But I lingered on
To see the poison do its work.
The cruelty in animals
Is not only reserved for
Lions and tigers and such like.
They were small and red
And when the spade had brought them to light
It was like London
During the war
When sirens screamed.
For they rushed about in all directions,
Searching for safety from an unseen death.
I stood and watched, perhaps
Half an hour
Until they were all gone
Carrying with them
The deadly poison.
And I felt sorry, ashamed, until
The next day,
Two feet away,
I found them all again
Alive and busy.

ROBIN

2. After some research and preparation, write a factual composition in which you give a clear account of any method of hunting, trapping or catching any animal, including fish and birds. Thus you might give a factual account of fur-trapping, fox-hunting or deer-stalking, or of shooting game, or of various methods of fishing, including trawling, drifting, whaling, lobster-catching, etc. Be sure to collect sufficient information to give a full and clear account of the prey and the best method of catching it.

Oral Work

Discuss (or debate formally) some or all of these provocative remarks:

(i) Hunting with hounds is a barbarous and uncivilised custom that is cruel and inefficient as a method of control and degrading to those who practise it.

(ii) Fishing for sport is one of the most boring and uncreative pastimes ever devised.

(iii) Men are still *hunting* the sea; to use its potential to the full, they should be *farming* it.

(iv) The use of pesticides and poisons to control wild life is a highly dangerous practice which will upset the balance of nature and end by poisoning man himself.

(v) The time has come when all man's efforts and money should be concentrated on preserving animal life, not hunting or destroying it.

(vi) The conditions under which many animals are now reared for food are so abominable that we ought to be ashamed to eat meat at all.

Activities and Research

1. Find out about the life-cycle of any interesting sea-creature, such as the common eel, the turtle, whales, penguins, salmon, sturgeon, seals and sea-lions, and the polyps that form coral.

2. Find out about wild life preservation, nature reserves and protected species of animals. What organisations undertake this work? Write to some of them for information about their current campaigns and research.

3. Find out a little about the life, background and works of these short story writers:

Liam O'Flaherty, O. Henry, Saki (H. M. Munro), Somerset Maugham, V. S. Pritchett, Gerald Kersh, W. W. Jacobs.

Be prepared to give a short talk on one of them.

Further Reading

The Conger Eel from *Short Stories* (Four Square)
The author deals with many aspects of the animal and human worlds, revealing the desirable and undesirable qualities that are to be found in both. These stories are full of interest and contain some fine passages of descriptive writing. A number of them are included in *Contrast I: Short Stories of Bill Naughton and Liam O'Flaherty*, ed. MANSFIELD & NEWSON (Pergamon)

Born Free by JOY ADAMSON (Collins; Fontana)
This is the story of a lioness, reared from infancy by Joy and George Adamson, and returned after three years to the wild. Animal lovers will particularly enjoy this account of a remarkable relationship between an animal and human beings. (599.74)

Kes, A Kestrel for a Knave by BARRY HINES (Joseph; Penguin)
Birds of prey can be trained but not tamed. Billy Casper is in many ways like his kestrel, surrounded by a school and family he hates; his relationship with his pet hawk is the only important thing in his life.

Ring of Bright Water by GAVIN MAXWELL (Longmans; Pan)
This book is mainly the story of the author's pet, Mij, a possibly unique specimen among Asian otters, which he brought back to his beautiful and remote home in the Hebrides. The parts dealing with his attachment to Mij are particularly interesting and moving.

The rich and eccentric Miss Havisham has lived in complete seclusion since she was deserted on her wedding day. Estella is her adopted child. Miss Havisham has summoned Pip, an orphan who lives with his sister and her husband Joe, the local blacksmith, to "play" at her house.

CHAPTER SEVENTEEN

Moods

"Call Estella," she repeated, flashing a look at me. "You can do that. Call Estella. At the door."

To stand in the dark in a mysterious passage of an unknown house, bawling Estella to a scornful young lady neither visible nor responsive, and feeling it a dreadful liberty so to roar out her name, was almost as bad as playing to order. But she answered at last, and her light came along the dark passage like a star.

Miss Havisham beckoned her to come close, and took up a jewel from the table, and tried its effect upon her fair young bosom and against her pretty brown hair. "Your own, one day, my dear, and you will use it well. Let me see you play cards with this boy."

"With this boy? Why, he is a common labouring boy!"

I thought I overheard Miss Havisham answer—only it seemed so unlikely—"Well! You can break his heart."

"What do you play, boy?" asked Estella of myself with the greatest disdain.

"Nothing but beggar my neighbour, miss."

"Beggar him," said Miss Havisham to Estella. So we sat down to cards.

It was then I began to understand that everything in the room had stopped, like the watch and the clock, a long time ago. I noticed that Miss Havisham put down the jewel exactly on the spot from which she had taken it up. As Estella dealt the cards, I glanced at the dressing table again, and saw that the shoe upon it, once white, now yellow, had never been worn. I glanced down at the foot from which the shoe was absent, and saw that the silk stocking on it, once white, now yellow, had been trodden ragged. Without this arrest of everything, this standing still of all the pale decayed objects, not even the withered bridal dress on the collapsed form could have looked so like grave clothes, or the long veil so like a shroud . . .

"He calls the knaves Jacks, this boy!" said Estella with disdain, before our first game was out. "And what coarse hands he has. And what thick boots!"

I had never thought of being ashamed of my hands before; but I began to consider them a very indifferent pair. Her contempt was so strong, that it became infectious, and I caught it.

She won the game and I dealt. I misdealt, as was only natural, when I knew she was lying in wait for me to do wrong; and she denounced me for a stupid, clumsy labouring boy.

"You say nothing of her," remarked Miss Havisham to me as she looked on. "She says many hard things of you, but you say nothing of her. What do you think of her?"

"I don't like to say," I stammered.

"Tell me in my ear," said Miss Havisham, bending down.

"I think she is very proud," I replied in a whisper.

"Anything else?"

"I think she is very pretty."

"Anything else?"

"I think she is very insulting." (She was looking at me then, with a look of supreme disdain.)

"I think I should like to go home."

"And never see her again, though she is so pretty?"

"I am not sure that I shouldn't like to see her again, but I should like to go home now."

"You shall go soon," said Miss Havisham aloud. "Play the game out."

Saving for one weird smile at first, I should have felt almost sure that Miss Havisham's face could not smile. It had dropped into a watchful and brooding expression—most likely when all the things about her had become transfixed—and it looked as if nothing could ever lift it up again. Her chest had dropped so that she stooped; and her voice had dropped, so that she spoke low, and with a dead lull upon her; altogether, she had the appearance of having dropped, body and soul, within and without, under the weight of a crushing blow.

I played the game to an end with Estella, and she beggared me. She threw the cards down on the table when she had won them all, as if she despised them for having been won of me . . .

*   *   *   *   *

I took the opportunity of being alone in the courtyard to look at my coarse hands and my common boots. My opinion of those accessories was not favourable. They had never troubled me before, but they troubled me now, as vulgar appendages. I determined to ask Joe why he had ever taught me to call those picture-cards, Jacks, which ought to be called Knaves. I wished Joe had been rather more genteelly brought up, and then I should have been so too.

She came back, with some bread and meat and a little mug of beer. She put the mug down on the stones of the yard, and gave me the bread and meat without looking at me, as insolently as if I were a dog in disgrace. I was so humiliated, hurt, spurned, offended, angry, sorry—I cannot hit upon the right name for the smart—God knows what its name was—that tears started to my eyes. The moment they sprang there, the girl looked at me with a quick delight in having been the cause of them. This gave me power to keep them back and to look at her; so she gave a contemptuous toss—but with a sense, I thought, of having made too sure that I was so wounded—and left me.

But, when she was gone, I looked about me for a place to hide my face in, and got behind one of the gates in the brewery-lane, and leaned my sleeve against the wall there, and leaned my forehead on it, and cried. As I cried, I kicked the wall, and took a hard twist at my hair; so bitter were my feelings, and so sharp was the smart without a name, that needed counter-action.

(from *Great Expectations* by Charles Dickens)

Comprehension and Discussion

1. If you know the game, explain briefly the point of "beggar my neighbour".

2. In what ways did Miss Havisham appear to have "dropped ... under the weight of a crushing blow"? How had being deserted on her wedding day affected her?

3. Can you think of anything that might explain (a) Miss Havisham's attitude to Estella, and (b) Estella's cruelty to Pip?

4. Is Pip's reaction to his own feelings at the end (a) sensible, (b) understandable? Was he right to blame either Joe or himself?

5. Do you admire Pip or Estella more? Give reasons.

6. Should one be ashamed of crying in public? How do you feel when someone cries in your presence?

7. Is there anything slightly amusing about the style in which parts of this extract are written? Give examples.

8. Why do you think that none of the words—"humiliated, hurt, spurned, offended, angry, sorry"—quite fitted Pip's feelings? Can you express them in a word or a few words?

9. Can you think of other cases, like "Jacks" and "Knaves", where one's choice of words can be used to imply superiority? Discuss:

> afters—pudding—sweet—dessert;
> (high) tea—supper—dinner;
> lounge—sitting room—drawing room;

and add others.

10. How important is it to be good-mannered, well-dressed, at ease in company, and to know the correct words and behaviour to use? Should rules of polite behaviour be systematically *taught*, in school or at home?

For Written Answers

Remember to answer fully and in your own words.

1. Pip had been summoned "to play". What indication is there at the opening of this extract that he had failed?

2. It was afternoon, but the house was kept in gloom. What detail indicates this?

3. What was Miss Havisham wearing?

4. Why did she replace the jewel on the exact spot from which she had picked it up?

5. How are we given the impression that both Estella and Miss Havisham *enjoyed* seeing Pip humiliated?

6. Why was it "natural" for Pip to misdeal?

7. What were Pip's feelings for and about Estella?

8. Did Pip manage to stand up for himself in any way?

Method Exercises

Exercise 1. The punctuation of the passage from *Great Expectations* is perhaps a little old-fashioned, especially in its liberal use of commas. Where, for instance, would commas be unnecessary in the first three paragraphs, by more modern standards of punctuation? But in its use of commas, and also of dashes, to mark phrases or clauses that are *in parenthesis* or *in apposition* (do you remember what these terms mean?), the passage follows modern conventions. A pair of commas, a pair of dashes and a pair of brackets can all be used for this purpose, but the dashes mark more definite pauses than commas, and brackets have the effect of leaving the clause or phrase completely aside from the main statement. Discuss the difference in shades of meaning between these four statements, which differ only in punctuation:

1. The boy who came to play was quite bewildered by the strange house and its occupants.

2. The boy, who came to play, was quite bewildered by the strange house and its occupants.

3. The boy—who came to play—was quite bewildered by the strange house and its occupants.

4. The boy (who came to play) was quite bewildered by the strange house and its occupants.

(a) Compare each of the following sentences with their equivalents in the passage, which differ only in punctuation. How has the meaning been modified?

1. I glanced down at the foot from which the shoe was absent, and saw that the silk stocking on it (once white, now yellow) had been trodden ragged.

2. It had dropped into a watchful and brooding expression, most likely when all the things about her had become transfixed, and it looked as if nothing could ever lift it up again.

3. I was so humiliated, hurt, spurned, offended, angry, sorry—I cannot hit upon the right word for the smart (God knows what its name was)—that tears started to my eyes.

4. So she gave a contemptuous toss, but with a sense (I thought) of having made too sure that I was so wounded; and left me.

(b) Rewrite the following passage inserting all the punctuation that seems necessary. This should include a colon and four apostrophes, and commas for various purposes, including phrases or clauses in parenthesis, but no dashes or brackets. Full stops and capital letters will also be needed.

any boy who coveted one of joes rats had to pay heavily in junk any sort of old iron jam jars rags bones or bottles these he conveyed in his handcart to the marine-store dealers

we lacking his imagination and enterprise acted on the simple commercial principle of buying a thing and then selling it for more than it had cost behind the high wall which made our end of the street a "cul de sac" there was a sawyers yard presided over by a patriarchal man whose flowing beard was always powdered with sawdust it was a good place to visit that woodyard with its rich resinous scents its chugging steam-engine its whining circular saw and its good-natured old proprietor who was always willing to give sawdust for nothing to boys who owned rats mice or rabbits his son who ran the engine was something of a celebrity with us because once taking the saw in his fathers absence he had sliced one of his fingers clean off.

You will find the punctuated version of this on page 209. When you have finished, check your version against the original.

Exercise 2. The passage from *Great Expectations* contains some interesting use of *repetition*. At the simplest level this is for ordinary emphasis in conversation. Miss Havisham repeats, "Call Estella" until Pip finally finds courage to do it. Why does Estella repeatedly call Pip "boy"? Pip's repetition of the same kind of answer:

> "I think she is very proud."
>
> "I think she is very pretty."

is no doubt simply to suggest his nervousness.

But look at how Dickens repeats the patterns of the sentence:

> "As Estella dealt the cards, I glanced at the dressing table again, and saw that the shoe, once white, now yellow, had never been worn."

Examine also the repeated use of "had dropped" or "dropped" in the paragraph beginning:

> "Saving for one weird smile at first . . ."

What effect is he aiming at in these uses of repetition? Do you feel they are successful?

(a) Examine the repetition used in the poem "Hunchback in the Park" on page 124. Does repetition of certain words or phrases seem particularly appropriate or effective in a poem? How successfully has it been used in Geoffrey's poem in this chapter (on page 246)? Does it help to emphasise his mood effectively?

(b) Find some traditional ballads, such as "Lord Randal" or "Sir Patrick Spens", and study their use of repetition, especially where (by slightly altering a basic line or pattern of words) they use the repetition to move the story along step by step. Would repetition have a particularly *practical* value in a song to be remembered and passed on by word of mouth?

(c) Find and read the story of Shadrach, Meshach and Abednego as told in the Authorised Version of the Bible, Daniel, Chapter 3. What effect has repetition there?

Exercise 3. (a) Try to write, in *one* sentence for each, how you feel when you are: bored, excited, ashamed, exhilarated, terrified, calm, apprehensive, spiteful, satisfied, proud. As you have only one sentence, think carefully about what the essential feature of each of these moods is, and what comparisons or choice of words can best express what you honestly feel.

(b) Check that you understand the meaning of each of the following abstract nouns for feelings or states of mind. Then write down the adjective equivalent for each:

> e.g. audacity—audacious

anxiety, arrogance, callousness, courage, cowardice, despair, disdain, envy, humility, indignation, jubilation, loathing, malice, melancholy, optimism, petulance, pity, resentment, serenity, sympathy.

(c) All the following adjectives might be used to describe people. Check their meanings and try to find an *antonym* for each one:

> e.g. elderly—youthful

brawny, cheerful, dainty, delicate, dowdy, filthy, graceful, lanky, lively, plump, ruddy, senile, sickly, slovenly, smiling, squat, tiny, uncouth, unkempt, wrinkled.

Exercise 4. We have already mentioned that phrases and clauses can take the place of nouns, adjectives or adverbs. A NOUN CLAUSE therefore has the function that a single noun would have, and can be subject or object (or complement) of a verb. Thus Pip can say:

I think *that she is very proud*.

What does he think? His thought (the object of the verb "think") is expressed as a whole clause. Similarly, we can say:

Pip's humiliation was *what Miss Havisham wanted*.

or:

What Miss Havisham wanted was Pip's humiliation.

Where is this clause the subject, and where the complement, of "was"?

(a) Write out the noun clause in each of the following sentences, stating what verb it is the subject or object of in each case.

1. I think that she is very pretty.
2. I think (that) I should like to go home.
3. I wished (that) Joe had been rather more genteelly brought up.
4. God knows what its name was.
5. What she had said made me miserable.
6. I thought (that) I overheard something.
7. I noticed that Miss Havisham put down the jewel exactly on the same spot.
8. I saw that the shoe upon it, once white, now yellow, had never been worn.
9. Then I began to understand that everything in the room had stopped.
10. I determined to ask Joe why he had ever taught me to call those picture cards Jacks.

(b) Phrases can also act as nouns, and often one can find a phrase and a clause that are closely equivalent: e.g.

For Pip to be uncomfortable pleased Miss Havisham.

That Pip should be uncomfortable pleased Miss Havisham.

What is the basic difference here between a phrase and a clause? In the following, find the noun phrase and rewrite the sentence with a noun clause that is close in meaning:

1. I determined to ask Joe.
2. Pip wondered what to do.
3. Pip's desperate wish was to be genteel. (2)
4. To play to order proved impossible.
5. Miss Havisham ordered Estella and Pip to play cards.

Writing Your Own

1. Write a description of a person with a very definite or eccentric personality, whether pleasant or unpleasant. Concentrate on what is distinctive or striking about this person, perhaps even exaggerating this into a "caricature". Look again at what Dickens tells us about Miss Havisham, and how her twisted personality comes out in her smile, her speech, her actions, her room, her whole way of life. Concentrate your own account on significant details in this way, as a film director would pick out features for close-up study. Plan your description fully, so that paragraphs are devoted to his or her home or other setting, to physical features generally, to facial features in particular, to clothes and other tastes, to behaviour and mannerisms, with perhaps some typical anecdote to round off the description. But avoid telling a story: your main aim is description. Make full use of interesting words, comparisons and other stylistic effects (such as repetition) as well.

2. Write a poem expressing any strong feelings or definite mood. The first and most important basis for success in this is to be *honest*, completely sincere, so that you write what you really feel and not what you think you ought to feel under the circumstances. Recall any moment of strong feeling: a sad or enjoyable one, one of great exhilaration or triumph, one of boredom or anger or frustration, perhaps one of shame and humiliation as in Pip's case. Recall what you saw and felt and thought. Search for the associations in your mind at such a moment, the details (however irrelevant they may seem) that have become mixed up with the experience. Search for the right comparisons, the right words, and the right form to express them in. Geoffrey, in the poem printed over the page, chose a fairly strict form with some effective repetition—but perhaps his is a repetitive kind of subject?

Boredom

The hours I sit just doing nothing,
    thinking, what can I do?
The hours I waste, staring at nothing,
    wanting to be interested.

The waves of anger that suddenly grip me
    like a biting winter wind.
I want to scream, to rage furiously,
    to fling myself at a wall.

I want to tear and smash and break,
    I want to cause a disturbance.
I want to make a noise,
    to crash my fist through a door.

I want to see a car skid off the road
    and smash against a wall.
I want to break glass, and crush metal
    like a human press.

I want to hit and fight and break,
    I want to kick, and tear at a human face.
I want to damage and destroy,
    I want to madly fling the clock at the floor.

I want to shout and cry.
    Oh! What can I do?
Is there nothing, nothing to interest me?
    Is there nothing a boy can do?

GEOFFREY

Oral Work

1. Have a class debate on co-education. It should be easy enough, even in a co-educational school, to find people prepared to argue the case against it (that it is distracting, that the competition in the classroom is unfair, that schools cannot provide really adequate sports facilities, technical courses, etc. for boys *and* girls, that women teachers are not always the best to teach boys, and so on). But if the class can arrange to debate the matter with pupils from a different kind of school (or of the opposite sex), this may prove particularly interesting.

2. Prepare a reading of the story of Shadrach, Meshach and Abednego (see Exercise 2 (c)), and of some ballads and other poems, for the class.

246

Activities and Research

1. Find out what you can about the life and work of Charles Dickens, including his interest in social reform.

2. Collect examples of different styles of caricature as found in newspaper and magazine cartoon drawings. Study and compare the different styles of cartoonists. The more talented artists in the class might then attempt their own caricatures of other members of the class (or perhaps of members of staff).

Further Reading

Great Expectations by CHARLES DICKENS (various publishers)
This famous novel is an exciting and mysterious story of the Thames marshlands and nineteenth-century London: how Pip helped an escaped convict who was then recaptured and transported, and how, in later life, he was befriended by the convict. The original is rather long, but shortened versions are also available.

An Episode of Sparrows by RUMER GODDEN (Macmillan)
Despite its apparently simple style, this is perhaps one of the most "adult" and sophisticated novels to which you have yet been introduced. Those of you who found "The Boy from Hackston N.E.", for example, too juvenile in its approach to personal problems, will certainly get more satisfaction from parts, at least, of this moving story.

To Clear a River by JOHN BERRINGTON (Penguin)
Tony Finley, who is in the sixth form at a technical school, is very fond of Christine Waite, who goes to a comprehensive school in the same town. They have much in common, but, like many teenagers, they find the course of their relationship is far from smooth. This book is a useful "half-way house" between children's stories and adult novels.

A Waltz Through the Hills by G. M. GLASKIN (Barrie & Rockliff; Heinemann; Penguin)
When their mother dies in Western Australia, Andrew and his sister Sammy resolve to make their own way to their grandmother in England, rather than be sent to an orphanage. How they evade the searching authorities for weeks, aided only by the aboriginal Frank, makes a powerful story, sympathetically told.

Even after he had succeeded in reaching the summit of Everest, the highest mountain in the world, Sir Edmund Hillary still felt he had to climb Scott's Knob, a 2340-metre high mountain in New Zealand which had defeated him on two previous occasions.

CHAPTER EIGHTEEN

A Challenge

Peter Mulgrew and I left camp just before seven, when we had enough light to move freely, and we climbed up the ridge at good speed. The morning was cool and overcast and all the tops of the peaks were in cloud, but we made excellent time.

We swung on to the traverse and climbed up and down through the bluffs, across shingle slopes, and in and out of narrow rock chutes. By ten o'clock we had reached the ridge beyond the knob again and were climbing over a series of precipitous bumps which combined firm snow and steep rock. On one of these bumps we saw a group of seventeen chamois, including some magnificent heads. They all seemed quite indifferent to our presence.

The climbing was getting more difficult and there were tremendous drops on either side. The ridge seemed never-ending and it wasn't until eleven-thirty that we crossed a narrow slot and reached the main face of the peak. Before tackling the problems ahead, we found a comfortable ledge where we could rest and have something to eat. Through the clouds that wreathed the mountain, we could see a twisting ridge climbing up the face until, high up, it ran into a huge rock buttress. From this angle it didn't look easy.

After a short rest, we roped up and I led off along the ridge.

The climbing really started now in earnest. Steep rock pitches were interspersed with narrow snow *arêtes*, and in places we moved one at a time. We made a laborious two hundred feet and then reached a steep rock face which looked too formidable to tackle direct, scrambled down into a snow gully on the right and cut steps up it for a hundred feet, to emerge once more on the ridge, above the obstacle. The snow was firm and safe where it lay in any depth, but crumbled easily when there were only a few inches of it on the slabs. We crossed carefully over another stretch of rock and then I cut a few more steps up some snow to bring us to the foot of the great rock buttress.

The closer we got, the steeper it appeared. I could see no easy way of tackling it, and the only thing was to try it direct.

Peter belayed himself as best he could on the snow slope and I started climbing up a flaw in the face of the buttress. After much grunting and a great deal of zig-zagging backwards and forwards over small holds, I had worked my way up about sixty feet when Peter's cry from below warned me that I was almost out of rope.

A few feet to the left was a narrow ledge and I eased across on to this to rest.

"What's it like?" Peter's voice came floating up.

"Pretty scratchy and rather slow going. Hope you're not too cold in that wind?"

"I'm cold all right, but I can put up with a bit more yet."

I looked above me, then called out again, "Can you give me some rope? I'll see if there's a way out to the left."

There was silence for a while and then Peter's faint reply:

"Can't find another belay, but I've given you a few more feet and that's all you can have."

I debated the matter seriously. It was now after one o'clock; we were still five hundred feet from the top; the weather was looking ominous, and it would be dark at five-thirty. Unless things became a good deal easier, it wasn't going to be worth pushing on.

To save time, I decided to unrope and reconnoitre ahead a few yards. I took off my pack, wedged it into a crack and tied the end of the rope to it. I eased across to the left on small holds, feeling rather lonely without the familiar drag of the rope round my waist, and then made an easier six feet up a broad crack on to another ledge. The wind was freshening and odd wisps of clammy mist were floating by. It was becoming appreciably colder and the holds above me were taking on a thin film of ice.

I carefully eased myself up a few more feet, but didn't like the greasy feeling of the rocks or the way my rubber-soled boots slipped. Somewhat disgruntled, I decided to call it a day. Taking considerable care, I climbed back down to my pack and tied the end of the rope round my waist again.

"We could get up here, Peter," I called, "but it's pretty hopeless at the moment. Ice is forming on the rocks. Time is getting short, so I'm coming down."

It took a long while to descend the icy holds on the face. I was very relieved to join Peter at the bottom.

We were both cold and tired, and the bitter wind gave us no incentive to linger. However, we took particular care as we climbed down our route. Soon after three o'clock we were at the bottom of the face again, but we kept on the rope for the journey over the series of bumps in the ridge.

The snow had hardened considerably under the wind, and some more step-cutting had to be done. We reached the beginning of the traverse at four-thirty, in fading light, and started quickly across it. In our eagerness we went rather high and found ourselves cut off by a big line of bluffs. There was nothing to do but retrace our steps and drop down much lower.

As we scrambled across the loose slope, we could see a group of chamois outlined against the evening sky above us, and suspected they were having a good laugh at us . . .

I was back at Marlborough in May, 1959, hoping, on this occasion to get in ahead of the winter snows. But the weather thought differently and I arrived in the mountains a couple of days after the heaviest snowfall in years. A strong party of six of us tramped up the Branch River and based ourselves a couple of miles past Silverstream, in a new four-man hut that had been flown in by helicopter for the Forestry Department. We were snug and warm there, but frequent gusts of wind during the night indicated that it might be rather unpleasant up top.

I crawled out of my sleeping bag at four a.m. and had a look outside. The stars were sharp and bright above us, but clouds filled the head of the valley and the strong and bitter wind carried stinging ice particles. There was no likelihood of our getting up the north-east ridge in these conditions. But we had to try!

We set off in the dark at six a.m. and fumbled our way through scrub and up shingle chutes into the narrow gorge of Scott Valley. As dawn broke we were clambering over the giant boulders in the bed of the stream and floundering through small snowdrifts. The wind was increasing in strength and it was bitter cold. Above us, the snow-plastered battlements of Scott's Knob were shrouded in fast-moving clouds.

By nine a.m. we were struggling through deep snow on the steep slopes of the top catchment basin of the river, gaining height by going steadily upwards towards the ragged rock buttresses on the upper part of the mountain. At times we were spreadeagled, motionless, as wave after wave of wind-whipped snow lashed against us.

It was hard to be sure just where the true summit of the peak was, and we climbed to the left over some steep, snow-covered slabs, slithering and sliding as the thin layer of snow gave way. It became increasingly difficult to maintain a safe foothold, so we descended fifty feet and I tried again to the right and inched my way up a steep and narrow little snow gully. I reached the crest of the ridge and put my head over into the full force of the wind. It almost plucked me off the slope. On the far side, the ridge dropped abruptly away into thousands of feet of precipices. It was a frightening sight but, despite the wind, I thought we could possibly get along this narrow crest and on to the steep rock tower that cut off from the summit.

My companions were silent. Then an honest voice spoke. "I think the route is technically beyond me."

I looked again and decided that, with these conditions, it was probably beyond all of us.

Though we were reluctant to lose our hard-won height, we carefully descended several hundred feet and then entered a long and steep snow chute that gave a more direct route to the summit. Our feet and hands were bitterly cold and our faces were chafed from the rasping wind. But we struggled upwards and emerged on to the ice-clad summit rocks. Here, mercifully, we were less exposed to the wind.

Gathering up the slack of the climbing rope, we raced up the last hundred feet along a narrow snow ridge, and then on to the broad, windswept summit.

As if in acknowledgement of our victory, the sun broke through the clouds and bathed us in golden light. Not even the wind and cold, or the thought of the downward journey, could subdue my sense of satisfaction at having reached this reluctant summit at last.

(from *The Mountain I Couldn't Conquer* by Sir Edmund Hillary)

Comprehension and Discussion

1. Discuss and explain the technical climbing terms used in this passage: the traverse, the bluffs, shingle slopes, rock chutes, a narrow slot, a rock buttress, we roped up, steep rock pitches, arêtes, a snow gully, cut steps, the slabs, belayed himself.
2. Discuss the main equipment and techniques of rock-climbing with ropes. Why did the climbers "move one at a time" in places?

3. How did Edmund Hillary feel about unroping to reconnoitre? Why did he unrope? Was he taking a foolish risk?

4. What were the main reasons why Hillary abandoned the first attempt described here?

5. Why did they feel they "had to try" to make this ascent when "there was no likelihood of our getting up the north-east ridge in these conditions"?

6. What month normally sees the onset of the New Zealand winter near Marlborough, and about how long is the day at this time of year?

7. How are (a) the chamois, and (b) the weather made to help set the mood of these two attempts on Scott's Knob?

8. Why do men (or women) enjoy such dangerous and uncomfortable pastimes as rock-climbing? What other pastimes pose the same question? Does this passage offer any answer?

9 Have you had similar experiences of the satisfaction of achievement at the cost of real effort and discomfort? Would *you* take an opportunity to undertake any such dangerous enterprise or adventure, if you could?

For Written Answers

1. What kind of creatures are chamois, and what would their "magnificent heads" be?

2. Why do you think Hillary tied his rope to his pack before going on unroped?

3. Explain the importance and meaning of Peter's saying, "Can't find another belay".

4. What kind of boots was Hillary wearing, and did they prove inadequate?

5. Did the successful party in the end go up the "great rock buttress" that had defeated Hillary on his previous attempt? (Give your evidence.)

6. Do you think the wind was any worse on the second than on the first of these attempts? Give reasons.

7. What does "spread-eagled" mean? Why were they like this?

8. Describe in your own words the differences and similarities between the weather conditions for these two attempts, and how far these affected the parties' progress.

253

Breathless

(Written at 21,000 feet on May 23rd, 1953)

Heart aches
Lungs pant
The dry air
Sorry, scant.
Legs lift
And why at all?
Loose drift,
Heavy fall.
Prod the snow
It's easiest way;
A flat step
Is holiday.
Look up,
The far stone
Is many miles
Far alone.
Grind the breath
Once more and on;
Don't look up
Till journey's done.
Must look up,
Glasses are dim:
Wrench of hand
Is breathless limb.
Pause one step,
Breath swings back;
Swallow once,
Dry throat is slack.
Then on
To the far stone;
Don't look up
Count the steps done.
One step,
One heart-beat,
Stone no nearer
Dragging feet.
Heart aches,
Lungs pant
The dry air
Sorry, scant.

WILFRID NOYCE

Discussing The Poem

1. Why do you think the poet repeats the first four lines as the last four lines of the poem?

2. Does the poem *sound* breathless? How are the length of line (and the number of "stressed" syllables), and the rhyme, used to emphasise the climber's state?

3. What is the importance of "the far stone" to the climber?

4. Sum up in plain prose the physical effects of great effort at great heights. Can you explain these effects on the body?

Method Exercises

Exercise 1. (a) The following consists of what should be nine paragraphs, including quite a lot of direct speech, from the passage. Without turning back to the punctuated version, re-write this with all the punctuation you think necessary, beginning a new line for each new piece of direct speech. Then compare your punctuation with that on page 250. (Two paragraphs of the original have been deliberately omitted.)

a few feet to the left was a narrow ledge and i eased across on to this to rest whats it like peters voice came floating up pretty scratchy and rather slow going hope youre not too cold in that wind im cold all right but i can put up with a bit more yet i looked above me then called out again can you give me some rope ill see if theres a way out to the left there was silence for a while and then peters faint reply cant find another belay but ive given you a few more feet and thats all you can have i debated the matter seriously it was now after one oclock we were still five hundred feet from the top the weather was looking ominous and it would be dark at five-thirty unless things became a good deal easier it wasnt going to be worth pushing on we could get up here peter i called but its pretty hopeless at the moment ice is forming on the rocks time is getting short so im coming down it took a long while to descend the icy holds on the face i was very relieved to join peter at the bottom.

255

(b) Now rewrite the extracts from the passage used in (a) as reported speech. Report not only the conversation, but also Sir Edmund Hillary's own narrative, turning everything into third person and past tense. You should begin like this:

A few feet to the left was a narrow ledge and as Hillary eased across on to this to rest, Peter's voice . . .

Exercise 2. Compose short sentences to show the difference in meaning between these rather similar words:

bellow, below; bitter, biter; dinner, diner; dully, duly; fatted, fated; filling, filing; furry, fury; fussing, fusing; hopped, hoped; scarred, scared; sitting, siting; stripped, striped.

Make sure that you understand the difference in pronunciation in each case.

Exercise 3. All the following statements are *ambiguous* for one reason or another. Try to state clearly what two (or more) meanings each can have; and try to explain (using the grammatical terms you have learned in Books One to Three) why the statement was ambiguous:

e.g. I hope I am well on the way up.

could mean: 1. I hope I am in good health for this ascent.

or: 2. I hope I have made good progress towards the top.

In the first case, "well" would be an adjective, complement of "am"; in 2, "well" is an adverb of degree, modifying the phrase "on the way".

(a) The ascent was for experienced climbers only in the summer season.

(b) The Climbing Committee made an alteration in the route that was intended to help beginners.

(c) Edmund found Peter a reliable man to rope with.

(d) The lady climber was a mother with a very young baby who was able to equal the best of the men.

(e) She seems to like rock-climbing better than you.

(f) We could see them on the summit waving a flag from the hotel.

(g) He looked long and hard when he reached the summit.

(h) They were on the highest peak of a mountain range that had never before been conquered.

(i) Their boots were no good on the ice patches because they were so slippery.

(j) Headline:

FAMOUS ROCK CLIMBER HURT ON FACE.

(k) We descended to our companion on the rope.

(l) Headline:

MOUNTAIN GUIDES COACH IN SNOW.

Exercise 4. (a) The following sentences contain, in this order: an adjective clause, an adverb clause of place, an adverb clause of manner, an adverb clause of condition, an adverb clause of purpose, an adverb clause of result, an adverb clause of cause, an adverb clause of time, a noun clause (object of a verb), and an adverb clause of concession. Find and write out each clause, stating what noun it qualifies or what verb it modifies or is the object of.

1. We were climbing over a series of precipitous bumps which combined firm snow and steep rock.

2. The snow was firm and safe where it lay to any depth.

3. Peter belayed himself as best he could.

4. Unless things became a great deal easier, it wasn't going to be worth pushing on.

5. I decided to unrope so that I might reconnoitre ahead a few yards.

6. Time is getting so short that I am coming down.

7. As the snow had hardened considerably under the wind, some more step-cutting had to be done.

8. As we scrambled across the loose slope, we could see a group of chamois outlined against the evening sky.

9. Frequent gusts of wind during the night indicated that it might be rather unpleasant up top.

10. Though we were reluctant to lose our hard-won height, we carefully descended several hundred feet.

(b) The phrase (in italics) describing "way" in:

> I could see no easy way *of tackling it.*

can easily be replaced by an adjective clause:

> I could see no easy way *in which to tackle it.*

Similarly this adverb phrase of purpose:

> I eased across on this *to rest.*

becomes an adverb clause of purpose when "to rest" becomes a true verb with its own subject:

> I eased across on this *so that I might rest.*

Change each of the phrases in italics in the following examples into clauses of the type suggested in brackets.

1. We could see a twisting ridge *climbing up the face.* (Adjective clause.)
2. *After a short rest,* we roped up. (Adverb clause of time.)
3. *To save time,* I decided to unrope. (Adverb clause of purpose.)
4. I decided *to call it a day.* (Noun clause, object.)
5. *In our eagerness* we went rather high. (Adverb clause of cause.)
6. By nine a.m. we were struggling *through deep snow.* (Adverb clause of place.)
7. *Despite the wind,* I thought we could possibly get along this narrow crest. (Adverb clause of concession.)
8. *If forced back,* Hillary would try again. (Adverb clause of condition.)

1. Write an account of any challenging experience, preferably one of your own. Challenges, of course, come in many forms, and are not necessarily as obvious and dramatic as mountains to be climbed, unknown regions to be explored or records to be broken. For many of us they may simply be the determination to learn some new skill, or win some local competition or earn or save the money for something we want. Remember or imagine such an experience and write about it in full, showing why the aim in view seemed important and describing vividly all the struggles required to achieve it. If you can include some set-backs and disappointments in the early stages, these will add interest and help engage the reader's sympathy more.

2. Try to write your own shortened version of the story of Hillary's final and successful expedition to climb Scott's Knob, using *not more than 200 words*. Use mainly your own words, but base your account very closely on the passage, not adding any ideas or details of your own. Include details from the passage of the date, the state of the weather during the climb, the false trails over the snow-covered slabs and along the narrow crest, and the successful route up the snow chute and along the ridge to the top. Write in the *third person* (i.e. about Hillary as "he").

Oral Work

1. The story of men (or women) in a challenging situation should offer opportunities for dramatisation, either as scenes to be acted or as a "radio" drama or a running commentary. Work out a suitable situation in which the reactions of different people to some strain, suffering or physical effort can be shown. Practise the words and movements that seem right to convey a particular kind of physical struggle, for instance, forcing oneself on against strong and bitterly cold winds. If this is to be tape-recorded, consider the use of music and sound-effects to reinforce a realistic atmosphere.

2. Discuss the past year's work in English, saying what you found most interesting and stimulating, and why. Comment on any aspects of the work that seem to you to have been over-emphasised or neglected.

1. Find out about the life and discoveries of the following explorers: Robert Scott, Mungo Park, H. M. Stanley, David Livingstone, Marco Polo, John Cabot, Christopher Columbus, Ferdinand Magellan, Abel Tasman, James Cook, Sir Walter Raleigh, Henry Hudson, Auguste and Jean Piccard, Vasco Da Gama, Sir Martin Frobisher, Francisco Pizarro, Sir Ernest Shackleton, Roald Amundsen.

Each member of the class should then make up two questions based on their lives, suitable for a class quiz later.

2. Find out what opportunities there are today for young people to find challenge and adventure. What are: The Duke of Edinburgh's Award Scheme, Outward Bound courses, Voluntary Service Overseas, International Voluntary Service, the British Schools Exploring Society? How would you set about (a) learning rock-climbing, pot-holing or canoeing, (b) going fell-walking or pony-trekking with organised parties, and (c) planning a tour using Youth Hostels?

3. Prepare a talk or illustrated folder on rock-climbing and mountaineering, including equipment, techniques and some outstanding achievements in this field.

Further Reading

The Mountain I Couldn't Conquer appeared as an article in the short story magazine *Suspense*. A fuller account of Hillary's various exploits, in the Everest expeditions (especially the triumphant 1953 one), and in Antarctic exploration between 1953 and 1958 (when his party made the first tractor trip to the South Pole), can be found in *High Adventure* (Heinemann) (796.52) and in *No Latitude for Error* (Hodder & Stoughton) (919.9), both by SIR EDMUND HILLARY.

Diving to Adventure by HANS HASS (Jarrolds) (797.21); *Men Under the Sea* by EGON LARSEN (Phoenix House) (626); and *Exploring Under the Sea* by J. GORDON COOK (Abelard-Schuman) (627.72). Just as some men have been attracted by the challenge offered by mountains, others like these authors have been attracted by the depths of the sea. Hans Hass recounts his own adventures in many undersea expeditions. The other books trace the history of underwater exploration, describe the expeditions made by the Piccards, and explain about modern equipment used for exploring the ocean deeps.

The Kon-Tiki Expedition by THOR HEYERDAHL (Allen & Unwin; Penguin)
In this extraordinary, real life adventure, the author and five companions proved that a primitive balsa-log raft would drift safely 6900 kilometres across the Pacific to Polynesia, by making the journey as they believed peoples from South America had done centuries before. (910.4)

Journey to the Lost World by STANLEY JEEVES (U.L.P.)
This is an account of a journey to Mount Roraima, the remote plateau-mountain in South America on which Sir Arthur Conan Doyle based *The Lost World*. Three explorers were determined to find out what the "lost world" was really like and journeyed through dense jungle and across rivers and creeks. The search ended in what was very nearly a tragic climax on the rainswept summit. (918.81)

Supplementary Exercises

*Analysis Exercise 4

When we analyse sentences with a main clause and an adverb clause of time or of place (see Chapter Twelve), we specify under the heading "function" which kind of adverb clause it is. Reconstruct the two sentences that are analysed here:

	CLAUSE	KIND	FUNCTION	RELATIONSHIP
1. A	we were reading about Shane	Main clause		
a¹	when we studied Chapter Eleven	Subordinate clause	Adverb of time	Modifies verb "were reading" in main clause "A"
2. A	the extract started	Main clause		
a¹	where Chris was trying to pick a quarrel with him	Subordinate clause	Adverb of place	Modifies verb "started" in main clause "A"

All the following sentences contain a main clause and an adverb clause of time or one of place. To help you analyse them, the first five again have the two verbs underlined, and the introductory word in italics.

(a) The homesteaders had fenced their farms *where* the ranchers wanted to herd cattle.

(b) *When* the ranchers were short of good grass, there was trouble.

(c) *While* Shane was in the valley, the farmers had some protection.

(d) Shane was feared by them all, *until* the gunman came.

(e) *Before* he left for Grafton's store, Shane loaded his gun.

(f) After Shane and Starrett had beaten Fletcher's men, Fletcher sent for Wilson.

(g) There was an uneasy silence as Shane entered the room.

(h) There has been no more trouble since Shane shot Wilson.

(i) Wherever Shane went he carried painful memories.

(j) Whenever Bob saw Shane fight, he felt proud to be his friend.

*Analysis Exercise 5

Each of the following sentences contains a main clause and a subordinate clause: this is either an adjective clause, or an adverb clause of cause or manner (see Chapter Thirteen), time or place. Analyse the sentences in columns.

(a) Smith received a contract that he did not understand.

(b) Because legal documents have to be fool-proof, the wording of them is often complicated.

(c) As Smith did not understand the document, he consulted a lawyer.

(d) As he was leaving the lawyer's office, he noticed another difficult passage in the document.

(e) Since he was there, he asked the lawyer to explain it.

(f) As he had expected, the lawyer charged a small fee.

(g) He has become very suspicious since he heard that explanation.

(h) Wherever he goes, he now expects to be cheated.

(i) He was trusting enough before he had this experience.

(j) He acts as though he trusts no one.

*Analysis Exercise 6

Each of the following sentences contains a main clause and a subordinate adverb clause of concession or condition (see Chapter Fourteen). Analyse them in columns.

(a) If you want to be a doctor you have to train for many years.

(b) Provided that you get the basic qualifications, you can enter medical school.

(c) You will not do well if you are not prepared for hard work.

(d) Unless you study, you will not qualify as a doctor.

(e) Although nurses learn less medicine, their training is also quite difficult.

(f) Most girls love nursing, even if a nurse's life is hard.

(g) Even though they may find it tiring, nursing gives them great satisfaction.

(h) Many nurses are girls, although there are opportunities for boys too.

(i) We can recommend several good books on nursing if you want to know more about it.

(j) This profession, although it is not very highly paid, is a satisfying one with good prospects.

*Analysis Exercise 7

Each of the following sentences contains a main clause and a subordinate clause: most of these are adverb clauses of result or purpose (see Chapter Fifteen), but there are also adverb clauses of reason and condition, and an adjective clause. Analyse them in columns.

(a) Jack took this job so that he might see the world.

(b) He was working so hard that he saw very little.

(c) In order that he should keep up to schedule, he gave up his free time.

(d) As he was earning good money he was not too disappointed.

(e) He was working a lot of overtime so that he did not have much time for regrets.

(f) If he had given up the job in Hong Kong, how would he have got home?

(g) He needed the money that he was sending back to Britain.

(h) So that his mother might have enough to live on, he sent it all back.

(i) She needed it so badly that he did not like to let her down.

(j) He has made great sacrifices so that she should be comfortable.

*Analysis Exercise 8

Noun clauses are often subject, object or complement of the verbs in the main sentence; therefore, when we separate them in analysing that sentence, we are often left with an obviously incomplete main clause (one without a subject, for instance). Take as an example the simple sentence: "Your beliefs affect your behaviour." Both the subject (beliefs) and the object (behaviour) might equally well be clauses—one would then have a sentence analysed in columns as follows:

	CLAUSE	KIND	FUNCTION	RELATIONSHIP
A	. . . affects . . .	Main clause		
a¹	what you believe	Subordinate clause	Noun	Subject of verb "affects" in main clause "A"
a²	how you behave	Subordinate clause	Noun	Object of verb "affects" in main clause "A"

Reconstruct the sentence that was analysed here. Notice that only the word "noun" appears in the function column, while details of whether it is subject, or object or complement are given in the relationship column. Each of the following sentences contains one main and only one subordinate clause: most of these are noun clauses (see Chapter Seventeen), but there are two adverb clauses amongst them. Analyse the sentences in columns.

(a) The fishermen claimed that the rock was haunted.

(b) What they said was not easy to prove.

(c) They stated that they had heard strange noises.

(d) The trouble was that these were heard in stormy weather.

(e) I do not understand how they could hear anything at all.

(f) The stormy gales were so noisy that you could hear nothing else.

(g) Therefore I do not believe what they said about the rock.

(h) One can see why they feared to pass the rock.

(i) It had a bad reputation because so many ships were wrecked there.

(j) What happened to them all is still a mystery.

Revision Exercise 8

(a) Write a reported speech version of the following passage. Begin your answer: "The teacher said that reported speech was commonly . . ."

Reported speech is commonly used in newspapers, when people compile reports of meetings or summaries of letters, and when someone gives an eyewitness account. As the report is referring back to something that was said in the past, all the verbs will go into the past tense; and they will also all be in the third person, because the reporter is not the original speaker. In addition, a report has to try to express in a roundabout way what the speaker may have made clear in his tone of voice—when he uses questions and exclamations and so on. Reported speech can be mainly a matter of common sense—I advise you to imagine yourself a reporter giving a simple, second-hand account of what speakers or authors have said. Is it not simple?

(b) The following is a reported speech version of a conversation between John and Bill. Rewrite it as direct speech with conversation punctuation; that is, try to work out the exact words of the original conversation, and set these out correctly with inverted commas, etc.

Begin your answer:

"I can see I shall have to help you," Bill said.

Bill said that he could see he would have to help John. John asked indignantly why he should; he was managing all right. But Bill went on to say that he, Bill, might be able to manage it better than John. John replied by saying he thought Bill was being rather conceited. Bill had never succeeded where he had failed before, so he did not see why Bill should do so now. Bill told John to pay attention and just let him demonstrate. He politely asked John to give him the knife for a minute and said that what he had to do was to cut the bulge away there and leave the end smoothly rounded. Then it would really be of some use when they took it with them the following day.

Revision Exercise 9

The following sentences include examples of the *figures of speech* you have met so far: simile, metaphor, hyperbole, litotes, repetition and personification. Decide which is an example of which, and be prepared to justify your answer.

(a) The old castle on the hill, with its cold grey stones, seemed like an old man, looking wistfully out to sea.

(b) It had stood on the hill for many years, a sentry on watch over the village below.

(c) Below the cliff the stormy sea boiled among the rocks at high tide.

(d) Innumerable ships had been wrecked on this coast: the lighthouse was worse than useless.

(e) There was no great chance of any ship landing enemy troops on that rocky shore.

(f) Grey walls, grey roofs, grey paving stones; even the woodwork of the castle was grey with age.

(g) Old black cannon round the castle walls yawned casually; one could not imagine that they would be fired again.

(h) Though the caretaker was hardly old, he seemed to fit perfectly into these ancient surroundings.

(i) He looked grim and pale, as if he were the ghost of some past hero of the castle guard.

(j) All the time the sea looked up hungrily at the castle on the cliff, and threw itself in frustrated anger on the rocks below.

(a) Make up short sentences using each of the following words as the different parts of speech suggested.

> For example "since":
>
> as a preposition: He has not been seen since last week.
>
> as a conjunction: He has not been seen since he left.
>
> as an adverb: He has not been seen since.

  i. "after" as a preposition;

 ii. "after" as a conjunction;

iii. "after" as an adverb;

 iv. "through" as a preposition;

  v. "through" as an adverb;

 vi. "over" as a preposition;

vii. "over" as an adverb;

viii. "over" as a noun.

(b) Form adjectives from the following words:

> e.g. skill—skilful; oppose—opposite.

agree ambition ceremony contempt humour mathematics
agriculture apology compare emotion knowledge persuade

(c) Form abstract nouns from the following words:

> e.g. preserve—preservation; ferocious—ferocity.

anxious   cancel   compete   destroy   precise   significant
brilliant   coerce   deceive   generous   recognise   terrify

(a) Explain the difference in meaning between the sentences in the following pairs, which differ slightly in wording or punctuation:

  i. We smelt them cooking: it was not a very pleasant smell.
     We smelt their cooking: it was not a very pleasant smell.

 ii. If we looked closely, we could see him washing in the yard.
     If we looked closely, we could see his washing in the yard.

iii. Could you lend one pound without difficulty?
     Could you borrow one pound without difficulty?

iv. He was rather irresponsible: he was always stopping the car, for instance, whenever he saw a pretty girl.
He was rather irresponsible: he was always stopping the car, for instance whenever he saw a pretty girl.

v. Most of the club members who had not yet paid their subscriptions were asked to resign.
Most of the club members (who had not yet paid their subscriptions) were asked to resign.

vi. The club makes much money from sales and has many individual subscriptions, but there is less this year.
The club makes much money from sales and has many individual subscriptions, but there are fewer this year.

(b) Write sentences that will illustrate the difference between the following pairs of words, which sound alike but are spelt differently:

    e.g. pear: The pear is the first we have picked from our young tree.

        pair: The two crooks made an ugly pair of rogues.

taught	there	quite	tail	mail	fair
taut	their	quiet	tale	male	fare

scene	scent	advice	root
seen	sent	advise	route

Revision Exercise 12

We noticed in Book 2 that there are many *phrasal verbs* (e.g. turn down, send back, get over) in English. Where there is a simple single word as an alternative, it is better style to use it. What are the single verb alternatives to each of the following?

(a) e.g. to *put in* for a grant—to apply
to *put back* a book; to *put forward* an idea; to *put off* an interview; to *put together* a kit; to *put by* some money.

(b) e.g. to *set down* a heavy load—to deposit
to *set off* on a journey; to *set out* the arguments; to *set* something *right*; to *set up* a statue; to *set upon* a victim.

(c) e.g. to *get back* somewhere—to return
to *get down* from a high place; to *get off* a bicycle; to *get round* a person; to *get through* a test; to *get up* from a chair.

Books Recommended

An alphabetical author index of the books recommended in the Further Reading sections in this volume.

HOLM, ANNE	*I Am David*	Methuen; Penguin
HORAN, J. D. AND SANN, P.	*Pictorial History of the Wild West*	Spring Books
HUXLEY, SIR JULIAN	*The Story of Evolution*	Rathbone
INNES, HAMMOND	*The Land God Gave to Cain* ...	Collins; Fontana
IRWIN, KEITH GORDON	*Men of Chemistry*	Dobson
JEEVES, STANLEY	*Journey to the Lost World* ...	U.L.P.
JENKINS, ALAN C.	*Wild Life in Danger*	Methuen
JESSUP, RONALD	*Archaeology*	Macdonald
LARSEN, EGON	*Men Under the Sea*	Phoenix House
MAGUIRE, P.	*From Tree Dwellings to New Towns*	Longmans
MALLALIEU, J. P. W.	*Very Ordinary Sportsman* ...	Routledge
MANKOWITZ, WOLF	*A Kid for Two Farthings* ...	Deutsch; Heinemann
MANSFIELD & NEWSON (ed.)	*Contrast I: Naughton and O'Flaherty*	Pergamon
MARGENAU, H.	*The Scientist*	Time-Life
MATTHEWS, SIR STANLEY	*The Stanley Matthews Story* ...	Oldbourne
MAXWELL, GAVIN	*Ring of Bright Water*	Longmans; Pan
MEADE, MARGARET	*People and Places*	Blackie
MITCHELL, EWAN	*You and the Law*	Max Parrish
MORTIMER, JOHN	*Lunch Hour and Other Plays* ...	Methuen
	Three Plays	Elek Books
O'FLAHERTY, LIAM	*Short Stories*	Four Square
RIEDMAN, SARAH R.	*Men and Women Behind the Atom*	Abelard-Schuman
ROWLAND, JOHN	*The Radar Man*	Lutterworth
SCHAEFER, JACK	*Shane*	Deutsch; Penguin; Corgi; Heinemann
SMITH, EMMA	*Maidens' Trip*	Penguin
SPRING, HOWARD	*Heaven Lies About Us*	Collins
STEINBECK, JOHN	*Grapes Of Wrath* and *Of Mice and Men*	Heinemann; Penguin
	The Red Pony	Heinemann; Corgi
SUTCLIFF, ROSEMARY	*The Mark of the Horse Lord* ...	O.U.P.
SWINTON, WILLIAM ELGIN	*The Wonderful World of Prehistoric Animals*	Macdonald
TAYLOR, DUNCAN	*Bob in Local Government* ...	Chatto & Windus
TAYLOR, REGINALD	*The Boy from Hackston ,N.E.* ...	Hamish Hamilton
TOLKIEN, J. R.	*The Lord of the Rings*	Allen & Unwin
TOWNSEND, JOHN ROWE	*Gumble's Yard, Hell's Edge* and *Widdershins Crescent*	Hutchinson; Penguin
TREECE, HENRY	*The Dream Time*	Brockhampton
	The Dark Island, Vinland the Good	Bodley Head; Penguin
TWAIN, MARK	*Huckleberry Finn* and *Tom Sawyer*	Various
WEBSTER, JEAN	*Daddy-Long-Legs*	Hodder & Stoughton; Brockhampton; Dent
WELLS, H. G.	*The First Men in the Moon, The Time Machine* and *The War of the Worlds* ...	Collins, etc.
WHITE, T. H.	*The Elephant and the Kangaroo*	Cape
	Mistress Masham's Repose ...	Cape; Penguin
	The Sword in the Stone ...	Collins; Fontana
WYMER, NORMAN	*Medical Scientists and Doctors* ...	O.U.P.

Index

An alphabetical list of the method work (only) in this volume. The references are to page numbers.